Praise for

Chakras -- p. 8

"Cynthia Sue Larson shares the key to energy management and chakra consciousness. I, for one, will be integrating some of the meditations in *Aura Advantage* into my daily spiritual practice. Carefully researched and eminently readable, *Aura Advantage* will change your life and expand your heart."
—Brenda Knight, author of *Gem Magic*

"In *Aura Advantage*, Cynthia Larson helps the reader to recapture the simple, childlike joy that comes with regaining natural auric sight. This books leads the reader through the amazing adventure that comes with understanding and appreciating your incredible aura."
—Joyce Keller, author of *Calling All Angels* and *Seven Steps to Heaven: How to Communicate with Dearly Departed Loved Ones in Seven Easy Steps*

"*Aura Advantage* is a complete and practical guide for improving and strengthening the aura while subsequently enhancing the quality of life!"
—Celeste Teal, author of *Predicting Events with Astrology* and *Identifying Planetary Triggers*

"*Aura Advantage* offers the reader a truly fascinating book as well as a practical guide to working with their energy field. I highly recommend it for anyone who wants to experience intuitive knowing, greater vibrancy, and clearer purpose."
—Lynn A. Robinson, author of *Compass of the Soul* and *Divine Intuition*

Aura Advantage is the finest book yet written on the Aura and its ability to transform your life. Cynthia Larson has written the 'Bible' of aura books. It will be my personal reference book on this subject."

—Donald Schnell, author of *The Initiation*

Cynthia Sue Larson has a precious gift to share with you-an amazing ability to explain, expound, and to inspire others in her writing about extraordinary experiences in her life. Having the gift to enter sacred dimensions of experience that were labeled imaginal by Henri Corbin, a noted writer and Islamic scholar, she also clearly tells us about these journeys in a manner lucid enough to instruct others on how to reach them. In *Aura Advantage*, Ms. Larson explains all about aura—that shining presence each of you has surrounding you—and what your aura tells about yourself. By the time you finish this book, you too, will know what auras are, how to look for them, and be well on your way to seeing them."

—Fred Alan Wolf, Ph.D., National Book Award–winning author of *Taking the Quantum Leap, The Spiritual Universe, Mind into Matter, Matter into Feeling*, and many other books

AURA
ADVANTAGE

How the Colors in Your Aura Can Help You
Attain What You Desire and Attract Success

Cynthia Sue Larson

Adams Media
Avon, Massachusetts

Dedicated to the inner light in all of us

Copyright ©2004 Cynthia Sue Larson. All rights reserved.
This book, or parts thereof, may not be reproduced in any form
without permission from the publisher; exceptions are made for
brief excerpts used in published reviews.

Published by
Adams Media, an F+W Publications Company
57 Littlefield Street, Avon, MA 02322. U.S.A.
www.adamsmedia.com

ISBN: 1-58062-945-8

Printed in the United States of America.

J   I   H   G   F   E   D   C   B   A

Library of Congress Cataloging-in-Publication Data
Larson, Cynthia Sue.
Aura advantage / Cynthia Sue Larson.
p.   cm.
Includes bibliographical references.
ISBN 1-58062-945-8
1. Aura. 2. Kirlian photography. 3. Color--Psychic aspects.
I. Title.
BF1389.A8L37 2003
133.8'92--dc21

2003004465

This publication is designed to provide accurate and authoritative information with regard to the subject matter covered. It is sold with the understanding that the publisher is not engaged in rendering legal, accounting, or other professional advice. If legal advice or other expert assistance is required, the services of a competent professional person should be sought.
—From a *Declaration of Principles* jointly adopted by a Committee of the American Bar Association and a Committee of Publishers and Associations

Many of the designations used by manufacturers and sellers to distinguish their products are claimed as trademarks. Where those designations appear in this book and Adams Media was aware of a trademark claim, the designations have been printed with initial capital letters.

Caution: The techniques, ideas, and suggestions in this book are not intended as a substitute for medical advice. Any application of the techniques, ideas, and suggestions in this book is at the reader's sole discretion and risk.

This book is available at quantity discounts for bulk purchases.
For information, call 1-800-872-5627.

Contents

Acknowledgments vi
Introduction vii

Part I I
Chapter 1: What's an Aura? 1
Chapter 2: What Your Aura Does for You 29
Chapter 3: What's My Aura? . . . . ⸱ 53

Part 2 81
Chapter 4: See and Feel Your Aura 81
Chapter 5: Strengthen and Transform Your Aura 104
Chapter 6: Attract What You Most Desire 127
Chapter 7: Protect Yourself 149

Part 3 169
Chapter 8: Aura Photography and Imaging 169
Chapter 9: Aura Meditations for Everyday Life 187
Chapter 10: Color Assessment and Therapy 208

Endnotes 228
Index 242

Acknowledgments

I am eternally grateful to the vision of my literary agent, June Clark, who helped this book grow from a twinkle in my eye into reality. I am also deeply thankful to my editor, Danielle Chiotti, who worked with tireless enthusiasm to make this book the best it could be.

Most heartfelt thanks to Edgar Mitchell, Dean Radin, Marilyn Schlitz, and Robert Whalen of the Institute of Noetic Sciences for inviting me to participate in their visionary work in the field of consciousness research, which has forever changed the way I see the world.

Deepest appreciation to Guy Coggins and Susana Madden of Aura Imaging Systems, who have involved me in their aura photography research and camera development projects.

Thanks to my mentors Fred Alan Wolf and Alijandra, who have provided me with invaluable support and inspiration.

Last but not least, I thank my family and friends for their ongoing support, love, and encouragement.

Introduction

How many times have you noticed that a pregnant woman has a "special glow," or how a friend, having just fallen in love, is "beaming"? That's the aura radiating in a full and positive way! If you've ever noticed that some days feel better than others, or have felt someone staring at you behind your back, you've experienced your own aura in action.

Are you seeking true love? Do you dream of the perfect job, but don't know how to find it? Do you want to attract money, success, or new friends to your life? Would you like to know which choices are best for you, and prevent people from getting you to do things you'd rather not? You have the power to do all this and more when you learn how to recognize and enhance your aura.

Auras hold the secret to what kinds of energy we pull to ourselves. The key thoughts and emotions we convey through our auras send messages to the universe, and the universe responds in kind. When we are afraid, we attract fear; when we are loving, we attract love; when we feel successful, we attract success. The auric field can do all this and more because it provides us with an interactive membrane between our physical bodies and the energetic fields that support all material things.

My interest in human energy fields began when I was a child and saw angelic spirits in the form of brightly colored light forms gathering around me. My earliest memories were of swirls of light shining, shimmering, and flowing around people, and seeing colors instantly change as doors closed, people entered the room or spoke to one another. Noises and colors changed simultaneously, like a coordinated sound and light show, and I saw colors and shapes associated with sounds from outside the room I was in. If the garage door suddenly slammed shut, a jagged flash of brilliant orange would leap into my room, momentarily interrupting the swirling pinks, greens, and blues. I also occasionally saw small, dark energy forms scuttle around the floors at the edge of my peripheral vision, just out of the corner of my eye. I was an energy being living in overlapping fields of energy that I could feel and see all around me.

In addition to those auric visuals, I could sense along energy cords (the lines of energy that connect us to one another) to check on those I loved. I knew how my father was feeling long before he returned from his day of work at the office, because I could feel his mood before he ever arrived home. This ability to remotely sense my father's feelings had a very practical purpose, since I needed to know whether he'd be cheerful to see my toys strewn across the living room, or he'd have no patience for such a mess. These inborn perceptual abilities were so natural to me that I gave them no more conscious thought than blinking or breathing. When I was about five years old, I became aware that others apparently did not see these fields of energy, since they did not speak of them and seemed to ignore them completely.

As I grew up, my inborn ability to see and feel auras subsided as I learned to focus my eyes on people and things, and paid more attention to what I could see when my eyes were open that I couldn't see when they were shut. Even as my aura viewing gradually faded away, I never lost my intuitive ability to sense good or bad "vibes." This talent helped me discern "live" from "dead" projects, which people I most needed to meet, which people I needed to avoid, what choices were best for me, where lost things were hiding, and even helped me avoid being kidnapped.

Though we may have lost our childhood ability to see auras, we can regain our natural auric sight. Through our auras, we can discern much about our surrounding environment and ourselves. Our auric fields also provide us with energetic reserves of strength that serve as a protective barrier as we encounter hardships in our lives. Through meditation, you can learn to keep a vital life force with you at all times, bringing you inspiration, strength, and courage as you face challenging times in your life. As I began meditating regularly, I found courage and strength while facing some of the most difficult and challenging times of my life—the death of a dear friend, divorce from my childhood sweetheart, and a complete change in career. Throughout all these radical life changes, I found comfort and joy in the gifts my aura brought me. My aura helped me define my personal space, accurately assess my environment, maintain a healthy body, sense my life purpose, effectively communicate my feelings and ideas, make good choices, non-locally feel connected to others, find lost things, attract what I most desire, and protect myself from negative energies from other people and the environment. By reading this book and learning to see and feel your aura, you too can reap the benefits of a vibrant aura.

It's my deepest hope that by the time you finish reading this book, you'll know how to choose the path that shines, recognize the top warning signs of a weakened aura, and actively enhance your aura. You will have a clear idea of what your energy body looks and feels like, what purpose it serves, and how it can help you change your life for the better. Most of all, you'll remember to visualize yourself as an energy being!

Part I

Chapter 1
What's an Aura?

Auras are our energy bodies in visible, palpable form. They provide us with a great deal of intuitive information about peoples' general character. They also give us "gut feelings," or invaluable and life-saving information in a timely fashion. These "gut feelings" make all the difference when we learn to trust our intuition and benefit from feeling what's really happening, rather than merely responding to what seems to be happening on the surface. Seemingly dangerous situations can be quite safe, and seemingly safe situations can be life-threatening.

Because of my "gut feelings" or heightened aura awareness, I have felt at ease with Masai warriors seated in the car beside me (their long spears sticking out through the open window), with headhunters in Indonesia, and even with Arabs resting semi-automatic rifles over bandoliers of ammunition strapped across their chests. Danger does not always broadcast itself with obvious outward appearances, but instead gives itself away in good or bad "vibes." One of the many advantages of having heightened aura awareness is that you will become better able to find yourself in the right place at the right time.

A woman friend of American clairvoyant Edgar Cayce once told him about a shocking incident she had witnessed. "One day in a large city I entered a department store to do some shopping. I was on the sixth floor and rang for the elevator. While I was waiting for it I noticed some bright red sweaters, and thought I would like to look at them. However, I had signaled for the elevator, and when it came I stepped forward to enter it. It was almost filled with people, but suddenly I was repelled. The interior of the car, although well lit, seemed dark to me. Something was wrong. Before I could analyze my action, I said, 'Go ahead,' to the operator, and stepped back. I went over to look at the sweaters, and then I realized what had made me uneasy. The people in the elevator had no auras. While I was examining the sweaters, which had attracted me by their bright red hues—the color of vigor and energy—the elevator cable snapped, the car fell to the basement, and all the occupants were killed."[1]

On a trip with my family to Tijuana, Mexico, when I was eight years old, I once felt extreme menace from a stranger. I was surprised to feel all the hairs on my body stand up simultaneously as I browsed through the marketplace. I felt an ominous presence nearby and sensed I was being watched. Someone was staring at me. As I turned around, I saw a man in his late twenties sizing me up from about fifteen feet away. I felt cold darkness around him, and felt that he intended to take me away from my family. I moved so fast to get away from him that I knocked sombreros, maracas, and moccasins over in my haste to reunite with the rest of my family. I met up with my sister first, who glared at my rampant disregard for neatness, good manners, and propriety. As I led her to our parents, I looked back to see the shadowy man stand for a moment before turning and walking away.

The Only Thing You'll Never Leave Behind

Your aura is the source of your inner beauty and inner strength. It is the true energetic essence that comprises your non-local body, connects you to all possible past and future selves, and links you to everyone and everything you know and love. Pregnant women and people in love are often said to "glow," because their auras are combined with their loved one's and are therefore brighter than most other peoples'. Any time two or more people are brought together in love, the auric effect is extraordinary. The energy of people in love attracts more good situations, people, and things to them, which further enhances the experience of being in love.

Auras are indicators of health, vitality, what we're preoccupied with, and even our personal destiny. When you feel and see auras, you know which choices are best for you, and can discern which things, people, and places resonate in harmony with who you are. You can avoid wasting your time and energy when you recognize your core energetic nature and personal style of relating to the world. You can feel better connected to everyone you love, and better protected from harm.

To those who can see it, the human energy body looks like a luminous ovoid surrounding the physical body, somewhat resembling a giant glowing egg. Each sound, breath, and heartbeat creates ripples and pulses of colorful energy around every living and non-living thing. As emotions change, so does the aura. Over time, habitual thoughts and feelings become a steady part of the auric field. Mothers could well caution their children, "Watch out that you don't keep that attitude too long—your aura could get stuck that way!"

Your aura is so much a part of you that you could say you're inseparable, for to lose your vitality and life force is to lose your life. More fun than your shadow, your aura is a real-time presentation of how you're feeling in general and at this very minute. It's usually the first thing people sense when they meet you. It gives them a kind of "vibe" or intuitive hunch about you, since it is the essence of who you truly are.

Many Children See Auras

You may recall having seen auras when you were a young child. Perhaps you could see the mood of your family members as waves and shapes of color that changed as they were angry, happy, or sad. Many children see auras around people and material objects, and can keep this ability if they are encouraged (or, rather, if they are not discouraged). While young children may not yet be able to describe the fullness of perception they experience with their beginner's minds, they can convey some of their auric perceptions through art. When children can nurture their artistic vision and inner "knowingness," they preserve their natural inborn talent to perceive the universe of energy as it truly is. Parents and teachers can provide support and help preserve these natural talents of children by being more aware of the effect of their words when they view children's art. A supportive mother might say to her artistic toddler, "I like the way you colored your sister red and the dog green," even if she doesn't see a red haze around the sister or a green fog around the dog. The child may not even realize he is drawing something that his mother does not see—but this kind of encouragement will help him keep his perceptions keen.

My first memories of being a baby were a blur of sights, sounds, smells, tastes, and feelings. When I was in a room, I saw and felt swirls of colors that ebbed and flowed around me like waves of light in an ocean of color. There was serenity in my solitude, which would change into a cacophony of color when my parents returned to my room. I could see these colors whether my eyes were open or shut, although they seemed brighter and clearer when my eyes were open. As my eyes developed the skill of focusing on objects, I gradually paid more attention to what I could see when my eyes were open so that I could not see so well with them shut. In this way, my natural ability to see auras gradually fell dormant as I grew up.

When I was an infant, all my senses seemed interconnected, most especially vision and hearing. This way of experiencing the world is known as "synesthesia," a Greek word that means "perceiving together." Whenever something made a sudden and surprising noise, such as a metal spoon falling off a table and hitting the floor, I would simultaneously witness a piercing flash of color that accompanied the sound. When my mother came home from shopping in a good mood, her colors would enter the house as she was still on the other side of the closed door, fumbling to open it. The auras around everything were vibrant. I perceived a sentience in all these glowing things—whether they were living or so-called "dead." Like colorful shadows that go wherever we will go, our auras are the one thing we can't ever leave behind, for they are our steady companions. Their ubiquitous presence in all things animate and inanimate has led many to wonder what the true nature of this wonderful energy is, and how it interrelates with the physical world.

Some researchers believe that all babies are born synesthesics, although relatively few adults (one in 25,000) are aware of having this perceptual ability.[2] Synesthesia is obviously common enough that several descriptive terms in both color and music share the same nomenclature: chromatic, color, intensity, pitch, tone, and volume. Several of the world's best musical composers have seen colors in music. Franz Liszt was known to say things like, "This is too black," "More pink here," and "I want it all azure." Ludwig van Beethoven referred to B minor as "the black key." Franz Schubert described E minor as being "unto a maiden robed in white and with a rose-red bow on her breast."[3]

The Aura After Death

I have seen two animals die upon being hit by moving vehicles, and on both occasions witnessed a most remarkable thing. When I saw a large poodle struck down by a motorcycle in front of a neighborhood park, the poodle's aura remained with its fallen body for almost a minute, while a huge puddle of blood pooled under its head. Suddenly, a glowing ball of light gently rose up from the inside of the poodle and hovered just above the scene of the accident. The motorcyclist seemed visibly shaken, but was able to stand up rather quickly and right his motorcycle. The shining light that had been so closely associated with the poodle hovered a few feet above it for several minutes, shining with a soft blue light. A crowd of people gathered at the scene of the accident. Eventually, the light moved away, heading south. Although the poodle's body still had a very faint aura around it, it was fading fast. I later learned that the poodle had lived nearby, in a house just to the south of the park where it had been hit.

The second time I witnessed an animal die, I saw a squirrel run over by a car as it dashed across the street. I parked my car so I could check on the squirrel, and saw a bright glowing light rise up out of the squirrel's body as its furry form spasmed a few times and fell still. The little shining light rose high up to tree level, and hovered on the side of the street from which the squirrel had been running. I felt very sad to see the squirrel die—yet I also sensed that whatever life force had been inside this squirrel's body was still very much "alive," and was now viewing the world from its familiar tree-height perch. I did not stay long to watch what happened to the little auric light in the tree; after ten minutes, it was still perched in the tree, apparently looking down at the scene below.

I had an opportunity to witness the aura at the time of death for a human being a few years ago. One sunny afternoon

I drove to a nearby park I'd never before seen, instead of my planned destination. Since I quickly found a parking spot at this park, right in front of a police station, I decided to read my book there. I got out of my car and as I strolled along a creek, I was annoyed to hear a woman raucously shouting, "We're HERE!" over and over again. I crossed the bridge over the creek to see what all the commotion was about. A woman dashed past me, asking if I'd seen any paramedics, and I replied, "No." She quickly explained that a woman had fallen off her park bench, and needed immediate medical attention. I rushed along the wooded path beside the creek to where she'd fallen, and saw only the slightest outline of aura around her body. Her fingers were gripping a dog's leash very tightly, and I felt how much this dog meant to the woman. I sensed her presence near me, and I promised her that I would make sure her dog was safe, as I removed the leash from her stiff fingers. Another woman on the scene then stopped administering mouth-to-mouth resuscitation, as the patient was turning blue.

When the paramedics arrived at the scene several minutes later, they demanded that I remove the woman's dog from the area, because he might attack them when he saw their attempts to resuscitate her. I pointed out that his dog tags had her name, address, and phone number on them. They took the tags away, and asked me to take the dog to the police station I'd parked next to. Throughout this entire situation, I felt the presence of the dead woman, and her energy stayed with me as I took her dog to the tender care of the animal control officer, who kept repeating in amazement as she stroked the animal and gazed into his eyes, "I wasn't even supposed to be working today, but now I know why I felt a need to be here."

Once I was certain the dog was in good hands, I drove past the woman's home, recalling the street address from the dog tag. I felt compelled to turn on my car radio, and heard Melissa

Etheridge's song "Come to My Window" begin playing. The lyrics, "I'll be home soon," repeated as I gazed up at the windows of the dead woman's house. Even though this woman's energy body was no longer with her physical body, she was having no trouble letting me know what she needed and how she felt. Such is the awesome power our energy bodies have to communicate across time and space. I later called the hospital where the woman had been taken, and confirmed what I already knew to be true. She had passed away, although her spirit continued to shine brightly on.

Human Energy Field: Auric Membrane and Auric Cord Strings

One way to visualize how your aura appears is to imagine colored filaments of light that encircle your physical body and radiate out from energy centers in your body known as chakras. Chakra means "wheel of spinning energy" in Sanskrit—these personal vortices of energy are aligned along our spine. The first chakra is situated at the base of the spine (root chakra), the second is located near the navel (sacral chakra), the third is found at the solar plexus (solar plexus chakra), the fourth is near the heart (heart chakra), the fifth is at the throat (throat chakra), the sixth spins at the center of your forehead (third eye chakra) and the seventh whirls around the top of your head (crown chakra). These chakras are the primary link between subtle energy fields and our physical bodies, and they work together to form the auric field that surrounds you.

You can expand and contract your aura to help you sense things in your immediate physical environment. Your auric field membrane forms an egg-like ovoid around you, which indicates by its size, color, and other characteristics your overall mental and physical health and emotional frame of mind. Any energy fields that touch or penetrate your auric field can give you an impression of the thoughts, feelings, and intentions that they contain.

Multidimensional auric cords connect you and your aura to everything and everyone you have vested energy in. These auric cords can be so small as to be nearly invisible, or so large that they look more like vines or cables than threads of auric energy. You are capable of sharing information across great distances with everyone and everything you have established auric cords with. With practice, you can increase your sensitivity to these cords so that you can tell when someone is thinking of you, and even how they are feeling. The auric cords that connect us to one another can be cut or severed if so desired by either you or the one you are connected to. Cutting of energy cords is frequently recommended for those in need of psychic protection, and can be done any time you do not wish to be non-locally linked with another. This is covered in more detail in Chapter 7.

A silver auric cord has been frequently witnessed by out-of-body experiencers (OBEers), who note that it connects the projected double (an auric entity containing a person's consciousness) to their resting body. The silver auric cord has been observed to connect to various places on the projected double, such as the chest, throat, and brow. Experienced astral travellers such as Robert Bruce reassure us that this silver cord is so strong that it cannot be damaged.[4]

Defining Your Personal Space

If you have ever colored things by what they felt like (instead of what others agreed they looked like), practiced yoga or martial arts, or received acupuncture or other energy body healing work, then you have sensed the human energy field. You have also sensed auras if you have "felt tension in the air" in a place where people have been arguing, or if you've picked up good vibes from someone you felt an affinity for. If you've ever felt crowded by people moving too close to you even though they weren't touching you, you've sensed auras. Your sense of personal space is closely related to the size and shape of your aura. You will tend to feel comfortable when people you like are inside your aura, and uneasy when strangers or people you don't particularly like enter your aura.

Next time you visit a mildly crowded place (like a restaurant, library, book store, or movie theater) where people are free to choose their own spots to sit or stand, pay attention to how far away you prefer to be situated from people you don't know. If your behavior is typical, you'll find you have placed yourself so you have more distance between yourself and others in front of you than behind you—and depending on your socialization (southern Europeans prefer more closeness than Americans and northern Europeans), you may be surprised at how you stay a certain consistent distance away. American psychologist Charles Tart notes with some amusement how, "One of the things that you frequently find at a cocktail party, shall we say, is a South European backing an American across a room. As the South European moves to the limit of his personal space, the American backs away, but the South European has not had his smaller personal space violated."[5]

Since we are all energetic beings, we notice non-physical intrusions into our personal space. These range from facing someone who is blatantly "in our face" to something as subtle as being stared at. Biologist Rupert Sheldrake includes a staring experiment in his book, *Seven Experiments That Could Change the World*, which shows how most of us can tell when someone is staring at us behind our back.[6] You can try a variation of this experiment for yourself with a friend, and see if your friend can tell the difference between the times you stare and times you don't. It helps for the observed person to be relaxed, so his or her high sensory perceptual acuity is enhanced. Even if you don't formally participate in such an experiment, you can practice catching people staring at you who are out of your visual range, and see how often you are right. You may even find your awareness of your personal space boundary increases and your perceptions become keener as you play this "Who's Staring at Me Now?" game on a regular basis.

The staring exercise demonstrates auric field interaction, because the auric fields of the observer and the observed interact with one another even when there is no physical contact of any kind. For this reason, we can sense when we are being stared at, just as clearly as we can sense when someone fans us with a breeze as he or she twirls around near us. It is not necessary for the person staring to be aware of seeing auras in order for this to work, since he or she is engaging the energy field of whomever or whatever she is staring at regardless of whether she is aware of what she is doing.

Exercise for Defining Your Personal Space: Who's Staring at Me Now?

Here's a game you can play by yourself any time you feel like it. It works best in a place where you can relax and engage in some other activity (such as eating, reading, or talking) at the same time. You don't need to tell anyone you are playing this game—unless you want to! You'll get a chance to further investigate the size and condition of your aura in Chapter 4, but this simple game will give you an excellent sense of the size of your aura.

Settle yourself into whatever activity you are doing—with your primary attention focused there—and relax as much as possible.

1. Notice whether you can sense how far your auric field extends. Imagine that your auric membrane is a big bubble that sends you sensual impressions, and notice what you can feel at its outer perimeter. Look

around your environment, and see what is located at that boundary edge. Pay attention to how you feel as your gaze falls on each and every thing around you.

2. As soon as you sense someone might be staring at you who is out of your visual range, stay calm and relaxed and turn around to check to see if you're right. You need only maintain eye contact for a very brief moment. Notice if they were within the auric membrane range you established.

3. Keep a mental or written record of how many times you felt that someone was staring at you, and how many times that actually turned out to be true . . . and how often you also correctly knew where they were physically located.

4. When you try this more than once, notice how you can enhance your accuracy by consciously extending your aura (or sense of personal space) out to where other people are. If you find people aren't staring at you enough for this game to be rewarding, you can make yourself more tempting to stare at by wearing brighter colors or a hat, or changing your hair style. ◎

We have been so conditioned to expect auras to be merely personal equivalents of the earth's aurora borealis that we've forgotten that *feeling* our energy body is one of the most basic and natural things we could do. Awareness of the health and condition of your energy body can help you know yourself faster and more completely than anything else. Studies have shown that the "stared at" phenomenon is quite real, as evidenced by changes in galvanic skin response by subjects being stared at by someone outside their field of vision. Without any subtle sensory clues, people's electrodermal activity levels have been found to be significantly different between randomly selected staring periods as compared with non-staring periods.[7]

Outer auric fields have been known to extend for miles. Some followers of great meditative and spiritual masters have been able to locate their guru by feeling and following the enlightened one's strong auric field of love. The auras of people who meditate look significantly different than auras of non-meditating people, as noted by reduction in clutter caused by extraneous mental and emotional "noise." While most people literally carry other peoples' energy around inside them, meditators' auras are clear of that din. As meditators learn to silence the chatter of their minds, their auras reflect this calmness and clarity. You may already have noticed that people who meditate are easier to be around, because they feel more steady, unflappable, and balanced than others. That same energy you intuitively sense can also be seen in the form of a brilliant, clear aura.

Many Layers of Expression

Many different layers exist within the human energy field. You've now gotten an idea of how far your aura extends by noticing how far away you can detect people staring at you. Within that vast expanse of personal auric space lie several differentiated auric layers. Just *how* many layers exist within the human auric field has been a matter of discussion for many years. Some systems of defining and describing the auric field have three layers, some have seven layers, and some have many more than that.

Within the seven-layer system, described by Jack Schwarz in his book, *Human Energy Systems,*[8] auric layers are usually associated with the chakras, so that the first layer of the aura closest to the body corresponds to the lowest chakra at the base of the spine and is concerned with physical safety, functioning, and sensation. The second layer and second chakra are associated with emotions and feelings. The third layer and chakra have to do with rational, analytical thinking. The fourth layer and chakra pertain to our heart, and reflect how we are giving and receiving love all around us. The fifth chakra and auric layer are associated with conveying our commitments via spoken words. The sixth layer and chakra are the energetic embodiment of the way we see ourselves connected to all that is. The seventh layer and chakra relate to our connections to our highest mind and divine spirit.

Exercise: Feeling the First Auric Layer

The innermost layer of your auric membrane hugs closest to your body. Sometimes called the etheric double, it is critical for your survival. You can feel the first layer of your aura in this exercise, which you can do by yourself in just a few minutes:

1. Briskly rub your hands together, palm to palm for a few seconds, and shake your hands out.
2. Imagine warmth and love energy rushing down your arms to your palms.
3. Hold the palms of your hands two hand lengths apart so that the palms face one another.
4. Slowly move your palms closer and closer together, until you can feel resistance (gentle pushing) between your palms.
5. You're now looking at the boundary of your first auric layer! This layer can be very close to the skin (a quarter inch), so you might notice the distance between your two palms is just half an inch.

You can try another variation of this exercise by closing your eyes and bringing your hands close to your face:

1. Rub your hands together briskly, palm to palm for a few seconds, and shake your hands out.
2. Imagine warmth and love energy rushing to your face and your palms.
3. Hold your palms away from your face as far as is comfortably possible for you, with the palms turned toward your face.
4. With your eyes closed, slowly move your palms closer and closer

together until you feel resistance (gentle pressure) in the gap between your palms and your face. Slowly move your hands through your first auric layer and touch your face gently. How close were your hands to your face when you felt your inner aura? ◉

When you practice these exercises at different times of the day and on days when you feel stronger or weaker, you may notice a difference in how close you can bring your hands to one another—or your hands to your face—before you can sense the innermost layer of your aura. You may notice that the size of your aura changes with your emotions and physical sense of well-being. For example, when you feel great, your aura will extend farther than at times when you feel sick, depressed, or afraid. You can also try variations of this exercise on other parts of your body, such as your shoulders, arms, and legs. The first auric layer extends around the entire perimeter of your body, so your entire body is waiting for you to explore your auric field!

If you notice that the palms of your hands push each other farther away than half an inch, you've begun to explore the exciting world of QiGong (pronounced "chee-kung") energy work! What you are now feeling is the sensation of your energy field pushing against itself. In much the same way that you can increase the physical strength of your arms by pushing them against one another in isometric exercises, you can also increase your auric strength by increasing the auric field strength between your palms.

Early History of the Aura

Over the past fifty centuries, humans have amassed a wealth of knowledge about the aura. The aura is so well known on every continent in the world today that most cultures and spiritual traditions have their own unique name for it.

International Words for *Aura*

Algonqian	*Manitou*
Chinese	*Qi* or *ch'i*
Christians	the *Holy Spirit* or *grace*
Greeks	*pneuma*
Hebrews	*ruah*
India	*prana*
Iroquois	*orenda*
Muslims	*baraka*
Ituri pygmies	*megbe*
Japanese	*ki*
The Lakota	*skah*
Malaysians	*kramat*
Polynesians	*mana*
Secular English-speaking westerners	*life force* or *vitality*
Sioux	*wakan*

The Chinese describe the body's essential life force as *Qi* or *ch'i* (pronounced "chee"), which circulates yin (feminine, receptive energy) and yang (masculine, active energy) along more than 700 points on the acupuncture meridian lines. In India, the energy source of all life is known as *prana*, and it has been documented in 5,000-year-old spiritual texts as circulating through a series of chakras that spin like vortices and travel along nadi energy paths. The Jewish Kabbalah documented these energies as "astral light" around 538 B.C. The Hebrew letter-symbol *aleph* represents the supreme (and primal) energy that is unknown to itself and active in all.[9] Numerous early paintings depict auras in the form of halos around saints and other religious and spiritual figures.

These very different cultures and traditions describe the life force energy of the aura (by whatever name) to be inextricably interconnected with our physical and emotional well-being.

They also indicate that there is an underlying order to our human energy fields in which layers of auric fields envelop us and contain information about how we are feeling and thinking. They describe the nature of our auric fields as being luminous and capable of sharing energy to either help or harm others, and indicate that such interaction can occur at a distance.

Practitioners of martial arts learn to master exercises that combine physical stances with breath work to increase Qi in the body, resulting in such feats as breaking boards of wood with a kick or punch. If you're wondering if this kind of Qi work is real or imaginary, you may be interested to know that recent studies have shown that it is very real, indeed. In 1996, a double-blind experiment was conducted with a pair of Japanese Toh-ate masters. Toh-ate is a form of Japanese martial arts, in which the sender applies Qi toward a receiver several meters away until the receiver steps back rapidly without any physical contact. When the Toh-ate masters participated in the 1996 experiment, they were physically separated between the first and fourth floors of a building, yet video recordings of the energy sender and energy receiver showed clear signs of simultaneous motion.[10]

Acupuncturists know that illness and disease will result where energy does not flow properly, so they place needles or use heat or pressure to balance the flow of Qi along the acupuncture energy meridian lines. Hatha yoga practitioners learn to build and balance their chakras and the flow of prana through physical postures, breathing, mental exercises, and diet. People who do Tai Chi and QiGong learn to build and circulate Qi according to a variety of movements, postures, and breathing. Much more than mere physical exercise, these eastern arts revitalize one's energy and mind at the same time that they strengthen the body.

You may be wondering, "If auras have been studied for so many years, why don't we learn about them in school?" We don't see auras included in standard classroom curricula because public acceptance of aura research has faced tremendous resistance. Researchers who have studied auras have often been willing to risk their lives and reputations as they present new ways of thinking that are typically non-quantifiable. Part of the resistance to accepting aura research has been due to a tendency among some scientists toward evangelical "scientism," which is the inaccurate conception of science as being a body of knowledge rather than a method of knowing. American physicist Percy Williams Bridgman summed up the primary problem when he wrote, "It is difficult to conceive anything more scientifically bigoted than to postulate that all possible experience conforms to the same type as that with which we are already familiar, and therefore to demand that explanation use only elements familiar to everyday experience."[11] Another part of the resistance has been due to popular preference for taking things apart and painstakingly analyzing each component, rather than studying living, whole organisms, ecosystems, and environments.

Despite the lack of mainstream acceptance, auric research has been slowly but surely asserting itself as a worthy and challenging field of study. Scholars throughout history have been intrigued by the human energy field, and through their observations and inquiries, we have learned a great deal over the last 2,500 years.

The Pythagoreans

The Pythagoreans became the first western scholars to describe the healing effects of vital energy in about 500 B.C., approximately the same time that Kabbalists were describing light around angels and Old Testament spiritual figures. This energy appeared to the Pythagoreans in the form of a body of light, which brought healing effects to those it touched.

Paracelsus

In the sixteenth century, Philippus Theophrastus, Bombast of Hohenheim—known more commonly as Paracelsus—gave the healing energy found in nature the name "mumia" and described this energy as consisting of both a vital force or energy and a vital matter that radiated around every person and could be used for healing. The son of a physician, Paracelsus left home at age fourteen to travel the world as a student, and eventually became widely recognized as a wonder healer. Some of his healing practices were truly ahead of their time.[12] When Paracelsus died in September 1541 at the age of forty-eight, he was living in the country, internationally recognized for his prowess as a healer, yet badgered by critics. Some people were alarmed that Paracelsus gave diseases strange names, that his prescriptions were poisonous, and that his theory of the nature of things was new (and therefore not to be trusted).

Johannes Baptist Van Helmont

Belgian mathematician Johannes Baptist Van Helmont's (1579–1644) claim to fame is for coining the word "gas" and being "the father of pneumatic chemistry." Van Helmont also proposed that there is a pure vital spirit that penetrates and supports every material thing—including our physical bodies. Van Helmont sought evidence to support his theories that animate and inanimate objects could be positively or negatively charged with this pure vital fluid, and that material bodies could therefore affect one another non-locally. He asserted that cures could be found in magnetic treatments, using mumia, or magnetic force. Van Helmont understood that there was a connection between cells from the same body, and he told the tale of how a newly fabricated nose dropped off the face of its recipient at the same moment its donor died.[13] Despite his excellent reputation as a scientist, Van Helmont was arrested for heresy and brought before the Inquisition in 1634 for interrogations regarding statements he made such as, "God in the production of miracles does for the most part walk hand in hand with Nature." The church proceedings against him were formally ended in 1642, just two years before his death at the age of sixty-five.

Gottfried Wilhelm Leibnitz
German mathematician Gottfried Wilhelm Leibnitz (1646–1716) hypothesized that the essential elements of the universe are centers of force that contain their own sources of motion, and that the basic microscopic units of the universe are psychic, not materialistic, moving in the direction of increasing clarity from confusion. Leibnitz believed that everyone and everything is interconnected energetically, so that information can be readily communicated across time and space.

Baron Karl Von Reichenbach
German industrialist and scientist Baron Karl Von Reichenbach devoted three decades of his life in the 1800s to designing and conducting experiments with what he named "odyl" or "od" energy. Von Reichenbach discovered paraffin, eupion, creosote, and pittacal, and published scientific papers on chemistry, mineralogy, geology, and meteorites. In his later years, Von Reichenbach became keen on the notion that certain people are more sensitive to seeing auras, and he conducted a number of experiments with hundreds of these so-called sensitives. Von Reichenbach's sensitives could see colors around people and objects, and sometimes influence objects without touching them. In one remarkable experiment, Von Reichenbach noted that his former housekeeper, Mrs. Ruf, was able to deflect a one-inch magnetic needle in an ordinary compass box from 40 degrees to a complete 360-degree revolution. Comparing the odic force to the electromagnetic field that Scottish mathematician and

physicist James Clerk Maxwell described in 1865, Von Reichenbach demonstrated several unique properties of the odic field: some odically polarized objects are not also magnetic (e.g., crystals); odic poles feel consistently either hot and unpleasant, or cold and pleasant to sensitive observers; and oppositely charged poles repel (rather than attract). Von Reichenbach also showed that similar to electromagnetic fields, odic fields can be conducted through wires (where velocity of transmission depends on the density of the material), and that objects can be charged with this energy. Further experiments in his castle near Vienna showed that odic fields flowed in response to air currents, much like a fluid, yet also could be focused through a lens like rays of light. Von Reichenbach's research into "od" heralded the beginning of the New Age movement's "Theory of Attraction" in manifestation, by which it is understood that what you focus your attention on will be attracted to you.[14]

Aura Research in the Twentieth Century

The next hundred years propelled aura research into mainstream awareness, as scientists explored exciting new areas of research into subtle energy fields. While the general public became increasingly aware of terms like Qi, chakras, and auras, some pioneering medical doctors and scientists led the way toward a clearer understanding of the structure and functions of these energy fields. Even though many researchers who have delved into exploring the human aura have been persecuted, ridiculed, and died without having gained the respect of their scientific peers, these pioneers have broadened our view of the reality of human energy fields. With each new body of work in human energy field research, these men and women devoted themselves to bringing us a better understanding of the aura.

Auric X-Rays

In 1908, in the early days of X-ray technology in hospitals, Dr. Walter Kilner (1847–1920) observed the aura of his medical patients in London's St. Thomas Hospital's X-ray Department through colored screens made of thin, flat glass cells containing dicyanide dyes in an alcohol solution. The dicyanin coal-tar dye made observers temporarily short-sighted (like infants), which helped them more easily see ultra-violet spectrum radiation of the human energy field. Kilner described how the inner aura followed body contours, while the outer aura was larger and ovoid in shape. Kilner's breakthrough discovery was that most of us *can* see auras when we change the focus of our eyes. Kilner's findings prompted the development of "auraspecs" and "kilnascrenes," which were patented and developed in the late 1920s by Harry Boddington, a noted British spiritualist. Prior to publishing his findings, Kilner viewed how the human aura varied considerably in appearance in more than sixty patients, yet people with infectious, psychological, and physical diseases consistently had areas of no aura or dark patches. Kilner noted that anger and intense behavior expanded the aura, while depression and poor health contracted it. Kilner's book was favorably reviewed in the February 1921 issue of *The Medical Times*, and in the March 1922 issue of *The Scientific American*.[15]

Energetically Interacting over Distances

In the late 1800s and early 1900s, French scholars Emile Boirac and Auguste Ambroise Liebeault were the first western scientists to report how people can energetically interact with one another at a distance, along the lines of Franz Anton Mesmer's theory of animal magnetism. "Mesmerism," as it was known, was the forerunner of modern-day hypnotism. Boirac and Liebeault noticed that these interactions at a distance can be either helpful or damaging.

The Theosophical Society

In 1875, Helena Petrovna Blavatsky and Henry Steel Olcott founded the Theosophical Society to further study human energy fields and thought forms, and to gain a better understanding of enlightenment. Based on a foundation of teachings from India, the Theosophical Society was instrumental in popularizing some of the otherwise esoteric information about auras and chakras. In her 1879 article, "What Are the Theosophists," Blavatsky wrote, "For to be one, one need not necessarily recognize the existence of any special God or a deity. One need but worship the spirit of living nature, and try to identify oneself with it."[16]

Radionics

Dr. George de la Warr of England and American Dr. Ruth Drown developed a system in the mid-1900s for helping people heal at a distance with instruments capable of detecting radiations from living tissues. Dubbed "radionics," this exciting new technique proved useful for recording formations of diseases (such as tumors), and even imaging an in-utero fetus using the patient's hair as an antenna. Dr. Drown treated her patients non-locally with blood crystal information she kept on file, utilizing a Kabbalistic numbering system based on the Tree of Life.[17] Dr. Drown was charged and convicted of fraud by the American Medical Association; however, she remained a vocal advocate of radionics until her death at age seventy-three. "No matter how small or diluted it may be, there's a resonance between the whole human body and each of its parts," Dr. Drown wrote shortly before she died in a California prison in 1965 while awaiting trial.[18]

Viewing Auras with Microscopes—The *Orgone*

In the mid-1900s, German-born psychologist Wilhelm Reich studied a universal energy he named "orgone." Reich observed that living organisms under microscopic observation were surrounded by orgone, and that plants and animals thrived in the presence of it. At first, Reich thought that orgone was specific to living organisms, but later he reconsidered it to be a kind of universal energy that is found in everything. By 1935, Reich's criticisms of Russian "red Fascism" made him unpopular with the Nazis in Germany, so he moved to America in 1938. Reich constructed orgone accumulators, which he claimed could help restore living organisms and entire ecosystems by restoring water to drought-stricken places. Unfortunately for Reich, Mildred Brady portrayed him as a dangerous schizophrenic in two articles she wrote for the *New Republic* and *Harper's*. It didn't help matters when reporters turned up Reich's view that sexual activity was a good thing for teenagers. In 1954, the Food and Drug Administration (FDA) sued Reich for mislabeling his orgone accumulator as a cancer cure, and Reich lashed back at the FDA in court, causing such a ruckus that he was convicted on a charge of contempt of court, and sentenced to two years in federal prison. Reich died in prison after serving only nine months of his sentence.[19]

The American Pioneer of Aura Reading

American intuitive and psychic Edgar Cayce popularized the concept of aura reading in his writings for the Association for Research and Enlightenment (ARE). Cayce displayed amazing psychic talent when he placed himself into self-induced trance, with hands folded over his stomach as he reclined on a couch. From this meditative, relaxed state, Cayce answered questions that visitors asked or merely thought of, without even putting into words. He also answered questions pertaining to faraway places and both the future and the past. Cayce has been called "the father of holistic medicine" for his visionary emphasis on the importance of the patient's diet, attitudes, and emotions in the treatment of illness—decades before western medicine began saying the very same things. Cayce died in 1945 at age sixty-seven, after having left behind a legacy of teachings and devoted students connected with the ARE.

Detecting Illness Early Through the Fields of Life

American neurologist, Harold Saxton Burr, a professor at Yale School of Medicine, was certain that all living things were created and sustained by energy fields. Burr's fascination with these "fields of life" led him to the discovery in the 1930s that the timing of women's ovulations could be determined by comparing daily electrical field measurements between one finger from a woman's left hand and another from her right. Burr hypothesized that diseases such as tumors would reveal themselves energetically prior to physically manifesting, and conducted experiments on mice in the 1940s in which large voltage charges were indeed detected before tumors physically appeared. Burr's vision of developing effective non-invasive cancer detection tests for humans began to be realized in 1998, as researchers reported successful clinical trials for finding breast cancer with skin electropotential measurements.[20]

Prayer and Plants

The Spindrift Institute was formed in 1981 by a small group of Christian Science practitioners to study effects of consciousness in the physical world. The father–son team of Bruce and John Klingbeil conducted a series of experiments on the effects of prayer on plant growth. They discovered that plant growth is most significantly improved when people prayed for the best of them.[21]

The Institute of Noetic Sciences

In 1972, the Institute of Noetic Sciences (IONS) was founded by astronaut Edgar Mitchell, the sixth man to walk on the moon. After getting off to a bumpy start when the initially promised seed money fell through, IONS followed the advice of biochemist Brendan O'Regan to focus on health issues such as the effectiveness of acupuncture, meditation, and biofeedback. Membership in IONS steadily grew from 2,000 in late 1980 to more than 10,000 by the mid-1980s, and it continues to climb today. Research funded by IONS has focused on measurable, repeatable, well-designed studies—rather than open-ended and unprovable or untestable experiments.[22] Research has been conducted at IONS to study non-local interactions between two or more participants. Researchers measure changes in brainwaves, heart rate, and skin conductance during experiments that suggest that even the subtlest changes in intention and attention have noticeable and measurable effects.

Detecting Energy Movements

In 1977, American neurophysiologist and energy field researcher Dr. Valerie Hunt published her recordings of the frequency of low millivoltage signals from the human body during rolfing massage treatments in a study at UCLA. Aura viewer Rev. Rosalyn Bruyere of the Healing Light Center provided comments of the energy movements she witnessed on the same tape recorder that also recorded the electronic data of frequencies picked up on the probes. Intriguingly, the frequencies measured occurred in the same sequence as visible light, with blue having the lowest observed frequency and red the highest. Dr. Hunt noted:

Chakras frequently carried the colors stated in the metaphysical literature, i.e., kundalini—red, hypogastric—orange, spleen—yellow, heart—green, throat—blue, third eye—violet, and crown—white. Activity in certain chakras seemed to trigger increased activity in another. The heart chakra was consistently the most active. Subjects had many emotional experiences, images, and memory recalls connected with the different body areas rolfed. These findings give credence to the belief that memory of experiences is stored in body tissue.[23]

Measuring the Human Energy Field

Americans Barbara Ann Brennan, Richard Dobrin, and John Pierrakos conducted a number of experiments to measure the human energy field in 1978. In one of their most exciting experiments, light measurements inside a dark, empty room were found to increase when people entered. In one case, the light level decreased when an exhausted person full of despair entered the room.[24]

Frequency Range of Energy Practitioners' Hands

In the 1990s, American and Japanese researchers published findings that energy practitioners produce measurable bio-magnetic pulses through their hands. American Dr. John Zimmerman used a SQUID (superconducting quantum interference device) to measure energy fields of the hands of energy practitioners at the Colorado School of Medicine in Denver. Most of the detectable signals for energy practitioners were measured in the frequency range of seven to eight hertz; the hands of non-practitioners were not found to produce such bio-magnetic pulses. In 1992, Japanese researcher Seto and his colleagues published findings from experiments conducted in Japan that corroborated Zimmerman's discovery that energy practitioners produced biomagnetic fields. These fields were measured to be in the range of eight to ten hertz, using a magnetometer with two 80,000-turn coils and a highly sensitive amplifier.[25]

Chances are good that you sensed the human energy field when you were very young. There are many ways to personally experience auras, which you can demonstrate to yourself if you have an open mind. It's helpful to examine both what the aura is and what the aura does for you, since sometimes you can best understand a form when you comprehend its function. In Chapter 2, you'll get a chance to discover ten things your aura does for you.

Chapter 1 Questions for Review and Reflection

1. Have you ever perceived the special glow of a pregnant woman, or someone in love? How does it feel different than people who aren't in love or pregnant?
2. What's your earliest recollection of seeing or feeling an aura?
3. Think about a time when your intuition or aura helped you recognize and avert disaster before it happened. How did you feel?
4. What do you wish that parents and teachers would do to nurture children's natural high sensory perception abilities (such as aura viewing)?
5. When and where were you most aware of your aura's outer perimeter and the auric fields of others?
6. What name or names—and from which cultures—do you prefer for vital energy and auras?
7. When you put your palms together, what does your first auric layer feel like to you?
8. Which aura sensing exercise worked better for you—noticing being stared at, or feeling the first auric layer?
9. If you could learn one new thing about auras, what would it be?
10. What kind of aura research would you like to see scientists pursue next?

Chapter 2

What Your Aura Does for You

When I was twelve years old, one of my most torturous classes was physical education. While I was an introverted straight-A student, most of the rest of the girls in my class were loosely organized into a gang, complete with a leader and band of girl-thugs. In the locker room they practiced extortion, and routinely stole lunch money, combination locks, and personal belongings from the most timid of the rest of us. I maintained a strong protective outer auric boundary whenever it was time for my PE classes, but one day as I began walking home after school, I was taken by surprise to meet the ringleader and three of her inner circle unexpectedly blocking my path. I called on every ounce of inner resolve as the ringleader approached, staring menacingly at me. A long, tense silence fell upon us as she sized me up, obviously itching for a fight. "Going somewhere?" she asked sarcastically, her voice dripping with disdain. I strengthened my energy field by calling silently for assistance from everyone who loves me, and pushed it toward her, feeling a great rush of energy surging upward inside me. "Leave her alone!," "Let her go!," two of the others suddenly exclaimed. "It's not worth it," the third pleaded with her leader, and I marveled that they could sense how my

Qi was steadily rising—I felt it now surpassed that of their leader's. Reluctantly, the leader stepped back away from me, allowing me to pass, as our eyes remained locked on each other.

In this experience, as in many others in my life, I've witnessed first-hand how the strength of my aura can make all the difference in how well my day turns out, and the same can be true for you. You can get a true sense or "read" of any situation by accurately assessing your environment—going beyond superficial observations to pick up the underlying "vibes." Far from being something you are "stuck with"—as you might feel about your height—there is a whole lot you can do to change your auric field. Since your aura is responsible for your physical, mental, emotional, and spiritual well-being, you can benefit greatly when you find out how something so mysterious and sublime is the secret to achieving every kind of prosperity in your life. Your aura helps you to:

1. Define your personal space.
2. Accurately assess your environment.
3. Maintain a healthy body.
4. Sense your life purpose.
5. Effectively communicate your feelings and ideas.
6. Attract what you most desire.
7. Protect yourself.
8. Make good choices.
9. Non-locally affect others.
10. Find lost things.

We'll take a closer look at what your aura can do for you in this chapter, with the exception of defining your personal space (described in Chapter 1), attracting what you most desire (covered in Chapter 6), and protecting yourself (discussed in Chapter 7).

Accurately Assess Your Environment

Since your aura is very sensitive to communicating information beyond your physical body, it can provide you with a very accurate assessment of your environment. To ensure you are clearly reading what is going on around you and not overlaying your own "stuff" and emotional baggage on a given situation, you'll need to learn how to clear your auric field quickly—even in times of great stress and/or danger. You will learn how to trust your own first impressions—even if they sometimes don't seem to make sense. Whether you receive visual images or memories of people or places you have known, these impressions are a gift of your energy body that are not confined to logical, rational reason but operate instead in the ebb and flow of currents of energies that connect all things. Simply by *thinking* about a person, place, or thing, you have made a connection to it, and when you relax and allow yourself to gather any and all (and I do mean *all!*) impressions, you will find you can develop your ability to glean intuitive information.

American psychologist Carolyn Miller documented in her book, *Creating Miracles*, how ordinary people who found themselves in extraordinary life-threatening situations managed to survive. Miller writes, "If you want miracles, you must forgive the people who seem to be hurting you and resist the temptation to see yourself as anyone's innocent victim."[1] The most important thing you can do is to change your *perception* of yourself in context with the world. As soon as you have accomplished this transition, the most amazing and miraculous things can happen. Attackers will turn away, rescuers will appear out of nowhere, and careening cars will land safely. All of these miracles are possible for us when we see ourselves as vital energy beings capable of loving and being loved.

You can most clearly receive information from the outside

world when your mind is free from being a disorganized jumble of assorted thoughts, all vying for your attention. Meditation is one of the best ways to clear your mind quickly and effectively in all kinds of stressful situations. The following meditation exercise is designed to be simple enough that you can remember it even when you're not reading this book. (That is good, since you'll more likely be in need of it when you're not reading this book!) Take a few minutes now to practice this meditation, so you can remember to put it into effect the next time you find yourself feeling stress in your environment.

Exercise for Accurately Assessing Your Environment: Clearing Tornado Meditation

1. **Ground**—Imagine a cord of light energy running from the base of your spine down into the center of the earth. Through this energetic cord, release all extraneous thought-forms from your field down to the earth. Whatever you are worried or upset about can safely be forgotten now. Be assured that everything you need to remember in the future, you will be reminded of. You can safely let it all go right now.

2. **Visualize Yourself Bathed in White Light**—Allow yourself to be surrounded and bathed in divine white light of love, temporarily washing out all your auric colors so you may look through a clear lens into the world. This white aura offers you a much more accurate perspective on what is actually going on right now.

3. **Swirl a Clearing Tornado**—If you can see or feel or otherwise sense remaining energies that don't belong in your space, imagine a great swirling tornado of cleansing energy. This storm removes remaining doubts, fears, insecurities, grudges, and angst. As it swirls around you, it leaves your energy and the white light energy intact and collects all extraneous energy, taking it away from you as it leaves.

4. **Vacuum Up any Crumbs**—If you still sense some remaining dark spots of unwanted negativity, imagine a giant vacuum cleaner plugged into the center of the earth, sucking up every last remaining crumb of

unwanted "stuff." You are now completely clear, and ready to accurately assess the situation you are in as what it is—not what you perceive it to be through false coloring. ◎

Maintain a Healthy Physical Body

There are two very different yet complementary auric components that help maintain good physical health. The first is the condition of our energy body, including our chakras, and the second is the quality and quantity of energy cords to others who love and support us. These energy cord bonds are very real, and you can easily see the advantages of these bonds of love and affection in close-knit communities, where family and friends help group members resist unhealthy behaviors and feel more relaxed and less stressed. A six-year study that began in 1955 of a close-knit Italian-American community in Roseto, Pennsylvania, found that the death rate from heart attack was half that of the U.S. average, and significantly lower than that of neighboring towns. Researchers concluded that the Roseto population was protected from heart disease by its strong social network, since other factors (such as diet, nationality, and age) were individually reviewed and factored out.[2]

The Roseto researchers foresaw that the very factors that afforded residents of Roseto protection from heart disease were vanishing as the small-town way of life gave way to more modern times. The days of three generations of family living together in one house were coming to an end; evening strolls, social clubs, and church festivals became a thing of the past when nuclear families moved into large single-family houses. When people sought to attain greater trappings of material success, they ended up feeling isolated and separated from loved ones. Ironically, as the vulnerability to heart attack began to decline in the United States due to improved diet and exercise, the Rosetans' heart attack rate continued to rise until it reached the national average.[3]

Recent studies have confirmed that social support helps keep people healthy. This includes *all* kinds of social support, including the support from bosses and coworkers, spouses, family, and friends.[4] While we may live in large houses that are separated from others around us and leave us feeling lonely, we can find ways to get involved in our communities and create the kind of energy bonds that help foster good health. We can volunteer our services at local charity centers, organize neighborhood events, or just take time each day to talk to our neighbors. The health benefits of good auric cord connections are cumulative, so every new connection you make counts!

Many people who work with auras and human energy fields today are involved in healing, because there is such a clear connection between the appearance, shape, and texture of our energy field and the physical health of our biological body. In their excellent books on this important subject, energy body healers such as Barbara Ann Brennan,[5] Caroline Myss,[6] and Donna Eden[7] provide a wealth of information on how one can recognize patterns of physical health ailments before they become intractable. Within the general area of bioenergetic healing, there are many different approaches and techniques. Medical intuitive Carol Ritberger[8] helps her clients identify and strengthen the chakras that tend to be weak for their color/personality type. Pranic healer Master Choa Kok Sui[9] teaches students to scan patients for areas of illness, infection, and disease and then apply treatments of pranic light energy. Color energy therapist Alijandra[10] utilizes many different healing modalities, including color rays, chakras, and multidimensional symbols. Reiki practitioners such as Diane Stein[11] are making universal energy attunements readily available to all, regardless of income.

Good physical health depends upon good auric health

because imbalances in energy fields almost always later manifest in physical form. We store our interpretation of everything that has happened in our lives in both our energy and physical bodies, and medical intuitives can show us how we can release negativity and energy blockages from our auras and notice immediate, dramatic improvement in how we feel. If negativity is allowed to become the dominant emotion in one's life, it can and will create physical disease, or "dis-ease." An emotional dis-ease such as depression is seen by medical intuitive Carolyn Myss to be ". . . a release of energy—or life-force, if you will—without consciousness. If energy is like money, depression is like opening your wallet and announcing, 'I don't care who takes my money or how it is spent.'"[12]

Physical problems often appear in the energy body in patterns. Areas of the body that look bright when healthy will appear to be occluded by dark or sticky clouds of energy when the body is under stress. Energy intuitives often help prevent serious physical ailments from worsening or even developing in the first place. These medical intuitives have the greatest success when the person being viewed is willing to listen to the assessment and make changes in their lives that are indicated by the problem energy areas.

I once assisted a woman who was initially diagnosed with squamous cell carcinoma (cancer) of her uterus with energy visualization exercises to help clear her energy field of the sludge I saw and felt all around her abdomen. I began by asking her to place her hands in the air several inches in front of her stomach, and to tell me what she felt and saw there. As she moved her hands back and forth through her auric field near her uterus, she remarked that she felt a "heavy thickness" there, which was harder for her to move her hands through. She did not at first see the darkness I could see in a cloud around her mid-section, but as she relaxed and we compared observations,

I could see her amazement that she could feel the energy imbalance associated with her cancer.

After taking some time to absorb this experience, I suggested that she learn how to do a simple "auric love blast" energy visualization, which would clear out the heavy, dark sludge in her energy field. She enthusiastically agreed, and I walked her through the exercise, which blasts out the dark energies we sometimes accumulate in our energy fields. She reported feeling lighter and clearer after the initial energy treatment, and smiled brightly for the first time I'd seen since she'd been diagnosed with cancer. I recommended that she continue to practice this exercise every time her mind began to worry about her cancer, starting by feeling how her energy felt, and then going through the auric love blast exercise. Worry is counter-productive to healing, I explained, and by keeping her energy field clean and clear, she'd greatly improve her chance of recovery.

After a couple of months of these self-assessments and visualizations, the woman saw her doctor, who informed her that he could find no sign of squamous cell carcinoma—and now diagnosed her with adeno cell carcinoma, a much milder and slower-growing form of cancer. A small surgery was performed to remove a section of her cervix in which doctors found cancerous cells at the margins of the piece they removed, right along the edge of their incision. Following this surgery, she and I continued the energy visualization treatments. Her doctor told her she might be free of cancer, but could only be sure if she had a vaginal hysterectomy. She chose to have the hysterectomy, just to be sure the cancer was gone. When the doctors finished this operation, they informed her that they had found no traces of cancer—there was no more trace of cancer at all! This was especially amazing, considering that cancerous cells had been found so close to the last minor surgery. I was very pleased to see how she had learned to sense her energy field and take effective steps to remedy energy imbalances, because these are skills that will continue to help her for the rest of her life.

Exercise for Maintaining a Healthy Physical Body: Auric Love Blast

You can cleanse your aura with a visualization exercise by imagining a blast of love so intense and powerful that it clears out energy blockages, sludge, and slime in your aura.

1. Begin by sitting comfortably in a place where you won't be interrupted for a few minutes, and close your eyes.
2. Imagine that you are connected with the source of all life and love, and that through this connection you will bring pure, 100 percent clean love down through your crown chakra into the center of your body near your heart. Picture this as something like a light bulb, but much more powerful. It is controlled by a switch that you will turn on when you are ready.
3. Breathe out all your worries and resentments, and breathe in pure love.
4. When you are ready, throw the imaginary switch, and watch the explosion of love as it blasts from inside you to clear out all energy blockages, replacing them with brilliant light. ◎

Exercise for Maintaining a Healthy Physical Body: Energy Cords

1. Visualize all the connections of love you feel, starting with an overall sense of how loved you are by everyone who has ever cared about you. Begin with your earliest childhood memories of every kindness you have received.

2. Slowly working your way forward in time, recall each tender moment you shared with others who genuinely cared for you and who you cared for. Savor your feelings of connectedness with each and every person, place, animal, and thing who loved you and whom you loved. These energy cords of attachment are like life-lines for you, from which you can draw strength. ◎

Sensing Your Life Purpose

If you've ever wondered if you are doing the work and living the kind of life you are meant to, you are not alone. A survey conducted by the nonprofit group The Conference Board in 1995, 2000, and 2002 based on a representative sample of 5,000 U.S. households asked Americans, "To what extent are you satisfied with your present job?" and found that overall satisfaction had slipped from 59 percent in 1995 to 51 percent in 2000 and 2002.[13]

People are seeking more satisfaction from their lives than ever before, and are realizing in increasing numbers that true satisfaction is best found within and with spirit. A recent survey conducted post–September 11, 2001, by ACT-1, a national employment agency, found that more than 55 percent of working Americans consider spirituality to be "very significant" or "important" on the job, while an additional 16 percent surveyed stated that they felt spirituality plays at least a small role in the workplace. Respondents with the highest levels of education were most likely to value spirituality in the workplace, and more than one-third said this role has increased in the last year.[14]

So how can you get the spiritual guidance you desire? Fortunately, it's fairly easy to access the deep inner wisdom that is meant specifically for you. When your aura is clean and clear and your crown chakra is open, you can easily receive intuitive guidance from your higher self. This guidance may come to you in the form of dreams, visions, or coincidences that open your eyes to new possibilities and ways of seeing the world. Foremost amongst the inspiration you receive will be a sense of your true mission in life—what it is that you are uniquely suited to doing. If all you feel at first is a sense of calm and inner quiet, don't worry. This can be the best place to start.

You can use many methods to access your inner knowingness of your life purpose, as long as you are open to receiving this information through your crown chakra. You can sit quietly at home or outdoors in a park, receive information in your dreams, or even walk a labyrinth. The main thing you'll need to do is keep your crown chakra open, and trust that the information you most need is coming to you right now.

Exercise for Sensing Your Life Purpose: Opening the Crown Chakra to Inspiration

The crown chakra is the key to accessing your higher spiritual self. Through it, you can discover your life purpose and learn what you need to do to feel most fulfilled. The crown chakra is the energy center that is associated with the pineal gland and the pituitary. The coronal or crown chakra has been described in Indian books as a "thousand-petaled" lotus flower, since it has 960 radiations from its primary center—far more than any other chakra! The crown chakra has an additional center of twelve more undulations with the 960-petaled primary energy center that also sets it apart from all other chakras with their one primary "wheel" or lotus blossom with rotating petals apiece. This chakra begins like all the others—and at first is the same size a depression in the etheric energy body—but as the person begins to shape his or her knowledge of the divine and all other chakras have been awakened, this chakra becomes truly like a crown, from which brilliant light shines forth around the head. Due to the brightness of this chakra, some aura viewers find it to be the easiest to see at first.[15]

1. Ground yourself by visualizing all your concerns leaving your body from your root chakra at the base of your spine and traveling to the center of the earth.

2. Meditate on your heart chakra, feeling warmth and love in your heart. Feel your love for life and what you are living for.

3. Meditate on your crown chakra, visualizing yourself connected to divine inspiration. Imagine that brilliant white light is shining down on you from above, illuminating you and gracing you with unconditional, infinite love.

4. Receive intuitive guidance by simply being open to new ideas. Wait . . . and listen.

5. When you finish your meditation, close with the intent that you will continue to remain open to receiving new inspiration. ⦿

Effectively Communicate Your Feelings and Ideas

Whether you are aware of it or not, you are constantly broadcasting your thoughts and feelings across your energy field. Anyone who has the ability to see these thought-forms can tell at a glance how you're feeling and sometimes even *what* you are thinking about. Close friends are able to know without a word what is on one another's minds, and sometimes this information travels across great distances without any need for a telephone call. Charismatic communicators know how to charge their words with lots of energy, so their ideas actually do have a life of their own. Our auras make it possible for us to communicate in between our words, conveying information most clearly when ideas are fully formed and carried with sufficient emotional charge. Each idea or thought is a packet of information that is carried from sender to receiver on a charge of energy from the sender's emotions.

Our auras are our energetic homes that unite spirit with corporeal reality, which we decorate and array with the colors and shapes of our recurring thoughts and feelings. Whether intentionally or unintentionally, every strongly felt emotion and clearly visualized idea can become a more or less permanent feature of our energy body, even when we are not consciously aware of our beliefs. If we wish to make changes in our personality, we can start in small steps, one emotional experience at a time. Meditators know this, and realize that every day they meditate brings them one step closer to being a peaceful person.

Aura researchers have described how the thoughts we think produce two effects: (1) the vibration of energy that radiates out into the universe, and (2) a "floating form" or symbol.[16] These images sometimes appear as portrayals of entire scenes, like mini-movies.[17] Thought-forms communicate what one is contemplating, so others who are sensitive to viewing such information can pick it up quite clearly. I once had a conversation with a woman following a meeting and as I was talking with her, felt an overwhelming sense that it was her birthday. She had not done or said anything to indicate this, yet I felt unable to think about anything else until I blurted out, "Happy Birthday!" to her, which I did. Her eyes got wide and she looked astonished as she asked me, "How did you know it was my birthday? I haven't told anyone!" I stammered that I felt I had to wish her a happy birthday, because that was all I could think about, even though nobody had told me it was her birthday. I had picked up her unspoken thought so clearly that she might as well have been wearing a T-shirt that said, "Today's my birthday!" This is also how psychics receive a great deal of information during a reading—by picking up these "floating form" images in peoples' auras.

Sometimes, unspoken thoughts and feelings can manifest in amazing ways through anyone nearby who is receptive to them. A husband and wife who lived with three cats asked for help from animal communicator Carol Gurney, because their two female cats were viciously attacking their male cat. When Carol came to talk to the cats, all she heard from the female cats was, "We're going to kill him. We want to kill him." Carol's reaction to this was simply, "When I hear things like that, I know there's something else going on." And indeed there was! Carol discovered that the wife was away from home so often that her husband spent a lot of time with new friends, which the wife reacted to with unspoken anger. When the wife followed Carol's suggestion to tell her husband how she felt, she was amazed with the results. The female cats stopped attacking the male cat as soon as the emotionally charged air was cleared![18]

Regardless of what emotion holds these thought-forms in place (or releases them to wander or target something else in the universe), they broadcast key elements of their thoughts into the psychic level of the aura that say, "This is who I am, this is what I am fascinated with." Psychics and intuitives describe seeing such thought-forms when they read peoples' auras. Your life experiences are directly affected by these predominant thought-forms. Fearful thought patterns bring on fearful experiences, and ideas of deep value to your spirit and heart bring on spiritual and loving experiences. Those who make their livings by their wits on the street also have an unerring knack for discriminating between the weak and the strong. To the degree that you are able to meditate or pray with greater feelings of joy and love, you can revise your auric body's frequency to bring you more enjoyable life experiences. You can think of this as "lighting your way," for you bring those things to you that light you up. You will know what you love most by how good it makes you feel.

Our auras are extraordinary communication tools that give us tremendous range of expression. Your aura can help you be as charismatic or unobtrusive as you wish, and as clear or mystifying as you prefer. For those occasions when you'd prefer to be invisible, you can collapse your aura and bring it in as close to the edge of your physical body as possible. You can enhance this effect of invisibility by broadcasting thought-forms that are focused on distracting situations, people, or things. These misdirecting thoughts give people something else of interest to focus their attention on, so they'll be less likely to notice you. When you prefer to stand out from the crowd, you can expand your aura and charge your ideas with energy so they take on a life of their own. When you wish to keep a conversation clear and on-track, you can visualize light surrounding the areas of discussion to "light them up." If you wish to be mysterious, intriguing, or unclear, illuminate fascinating questions about yourself or your ideas that have no easy answers.

Effectively Communicating Your Feelings and Ideas with Your Aura

Desired Effect:
Increase your charisma
What to Do:
Expand your aura, ensure connection via auric cords to everyone present, and charge thought-forms with energy so they have a life of their own

Desired Effect:
Keep conversation focused
What to Do:
"Light up" ideas in your mind's eye where you would like to focus the discussion

Desired Effect:
Hide yourself
What to Do:
Compact your aura as close to your body as possible and/or broadcast misdirecting or misleading ideas in your aura

Desired Effect:
Be mysterious
What to Do:
"Light up" fascinating questions about yourself or your ideas that have no easy answers

1. Next time you have a discussion with someone you talk with fairly often in person or on the telephone, "light up" an area of discussion in your mind's eye, as if it had a spotlight on it.

2. Pay attention to where your thoughts go. If you find your attention wandering (new thought-forms dancing through), clear out the extraneous thought-forms with a mental vacuum cleaner and keep only the essential thought-forms in your mind's eye.

3. What difference (if any) do you notice now in the way the conversation is going? Did it go more or less smoothly? Did it stay on topic? If it feels easier to communicate, notice any particular details that are significantly different. ◎

Make Good Choices

The art of making good choices consists of selecting the path that shines most brightly. Equally important to seeking the bright path is the skill of avoiding dark paths—like the well-lit elevator full of people that seemed so dark to Edgar Cayce's friend before its lethal descent (see Chapter 1). You may be wondering how it can be possible to sense which choice is best, since this seems to imply that in some way we are looking into the future, or perhaps seeing something that is physically out of view. Indeed, you are accessing information that may seem remote from you in time and space, but is actually much closer than you think. There is strong historical support for the practice of remote viewing among many ancient societies (such as in the Sutras of Patanjali[19]) from 400 B.C., as well as experimental and scientific support from Princeton[20] and Stanford[21] universities, and even some theoretical support from new models of space and time.[22]

Whether you are choosing which road to take, which book to read, or which show to watch, there will usually be one that shines most brightly for you. This is perhaps the most useful technique for anyone who seeks a roadmap to success. When you use it regularly, you can skip over the "dead" ends and possibilities in life, and find your way to the very brightest possible future. I used this technique while working at Citibank as a project manager when I was consistently assigned more projects to work on in any given day than I could handle. I was so successful at correctly assessing which of my assigned projects were "live" and which were "dead" that my managers commented that I appeared to be doing the work of five or six people. It was relatively easy to give someone this impression, since I wasn't wasting time on dead-end projects. I worked exclusively on projects that glowed with an inner light, showing me their strong Qi, which indicated that they had a bright future. I presumed everyone was doing this, because it is such a simple thing to do, and felt as natural as breathing to me. This adaptive edge prevented me from spinning my wheels on activities destined to go nowhere, and gave my work the appearance of ultimate efficiency.

Swedish inventor, scientist, and philosopher Emanuel Swedenborg described how at times when he was in the presence of truth, he felt a certain "cheering light," "joyful confirmatory brightness," and "a kind of mysterious radiation—I know not whence it proceeds—that darts through some sacred temple in the brain."[23] You can experience similar flashes of illumination when you learn to see auras and then hear or think about good ideas—much like the stereotypical cartoon image of a light bulb appearing over a character's head. The lights you will see may look a lot like flashes from miniature cameras that shine brightly for a moment in a burst of light, before they vanish. It is much easier to make better choices when you choose the path that shines or flashes brightly, because one choice will usually have more Qi than all the others. In this way, by viewing the auric field of various alternatives, you can make better decisions in your personal and business lives. Whether you are making a hiring decision, a choice of which movie to see, or choosing the best color to paint your home, you'll find this technique to be immensely helpful.

Exercise for Making Good Choices: Choosing the Path That Shines

1. Think about a choice you need to make today that involves two things for you to decide between. You may already have a pretty strong inclination toward choosing one alternative over the other—or you might not.

2. Ground yourself by visualizing a cord of energy running down from the base of your spine (root chakra) to the center of the earth.

3. Energize yourself by raising your vibration up with loving, grateful feelings, so you attract positive people, situations, and things to you rather than negative.

4. Put your hands out, open in front of you, and while thinking of one of the two options you are deciding between, imagine that you are holding it in your left hand.

5. Imagine that you are holding the second alternative in your right hand.

6. Looking at your hands, close them slowly, visualizing that the choice each one is holding is now inside each hand's grasp.

7. Shut your eyes as you continue to hold your two hands shut in front of you.

8. Ask yourself which hand is shining more brightly . . . and give yourself a few minutes to notice a difference. Notice if one hand feels heavier, tingly, or begins to open.

9. Choose the alternative from the brighter hand, or the hand that felt tingly or heavy, or opened up. ◎

Non-Locally Affect Others

The model of energy cords that most closely matches what I observe when I view auras is that of the Hunas of the Pacific

Islands. The Hunas describe the appearance and significance of *aka* lines, or auric cords of energy, between auric fields as being much like a nervous system, with these auric cords being connected subconsciously from our auras to everything we perceive with our senses or think about with our minds.[24] We can therefore know what is happening across remote distances, and influence events remotely. Just as drops of dew attach to a spider web, we are attached to these energy lines. Even as we relax and meditate (or just zone out in front of the television), every one of our strongly felt thoughts vibrates out along the *aka* energy lines until it finds similarly tuned receptors. In this way, we can be either the source of great love and healing for others, or much pain and misery.

Medical studies have recently been published in reputable, refereed journals describing how non-local healing occurs when people pray for advanced AIDS case patients[25] and coronary care unit patients.[26] Patients who were prayed for had fewer medical problems than those who were not, even though the patients and their doctors did not know which patients were being prayed for. These experiments were rigorous, repeatable, and reliable, and their impact on Western medicine and thinking has been and will continue to be profound.

Perhaps one of the most exciting things about these studies is that they show we are moving away from a time when stories of spontaneous remissions of cancerous tumors and other supposedly incurable diseases were discounted as being mere "anecdotal stories." A new era of medicine, which embraces the reality of non-local healing, is opening up. Dr. Larry Dossey states, "The two main lines of evidence for non-local mind are (1) the everyday experiences of millions of people and (2) scientific findings."[27]

Through auric cords, mystics and shamans collect information non-locally by transporting their consciousness energetically to whatever or whomever, whenever they wish. These energetic cords act as a web of life that non-locally connects everyone and everything, with all the criss-crossing energy cords looking very much like a spider web. Your prayers and feelings of affection can reach loved ones every time your thoughts reach out to them across these auric cords. While your aura is sensitive to everything in its immediate environment—and you can easily tell when someone in the same room with you is staring at you behind your back—you can also develop sensitivity to your non-local connections along auric cords of energy. As you practice feeling others contacting you non-locally, and as you reach out to others along auric cords, you will gradually become more conscious of this process.

You can better understand how auric cord sensing works when you do the following exercise for non-locally affecting others.

**Exercise for Non-Locally Affecting Others:
Touching Others on the Web of Life**

1. Choose someone you care about or think of fondly. Picture him or her clearly in your mind's eye, recalling many happy details, such as the sound of his voice when he laughs, or an expression on his face when he is happy.

2. Imagine you are reaching out to this person with an auric cord to bring the love you feel to him; touch him gently with your hand, or embrace him in an imaginary hug.

3. Note what you see and feel at the time of contact—write it down with date and time, and all other details you felt about what he was doing, thinking, or feeling.

4. Next time you see or talk to this person, ask him if he was thinking of you at some time—and when that was. Ask what he was doing, thinking, and feeling at the time you wrote down your impressions. How closely does it match what you observed? ◎

Find Lost Things

Just as love can reach through auric fields to help soothe the most savage of beasts, it can also help people reunite with their lost pets or personal belongings. People have found all kinds of precious belongings (such as wedding rings, earrings, keys, and letters) many years later in highly unusual places and times. Pets who have been separated from their owners have traveled great distances to be reunited once again—sometimes arriving in new places they have seldom been before.

In his book *Dogs That Know When Their Owners Are Coming Home,* English biologist Rupert Sheldrake describes how a dog named Pepsi, a Border Collie–terrier mix, consistently managed to find her way to one of six different destinations around her home city of Leicester, England. Sheldrake conducted experiments on two separate occasions, releasing Pepsi somewhere in the city where she had not previously been. On both occasions, Pepsi quickly made her way to the nearest place she had once visited (long ago) by car. Pepsi could not have located these destinations by scent, because the wind had been steadily blowing from the opposite direction. She had not seen the streets she'd traveled on, since she'd been kept down low in the car before being released. To the surprise of the researchers, she managed to make her way to whichever friend or relative's house happened to be closest to where she'd been released. Sheldrake speculates that all animals feel a pull of attraction toward familiar places through "morphic fields," which connect the animal and those places. By sensing auras and auric energy cords, animals feel the kind of connection they have to all places nearby— whether positively (attractive) or negatively (repulsive).[28]

How can such things be possible? There is one astonishingly profound yet simple answer: We are all connected through energy cords between our auric field membranes in an energetic web of life. You are connected to everything and everyone you love in this energetic web of life, so in a very real sense, nothing can really ever be completely lost to you. Even dearly departed family members and friends can manage to convey information to us after they've passed away. Auric cords are "sticky" energy lines that adhere to anything we subconsciously think of or sense, uniting us all and providing pathways by which consciousness may travel freely. As Max Freedom Long describes it in *The Secret Science Behind Miracles*, "It is like touching flypaper with a finger, and when the finger is pulled away, a long fine thread of the adhesive substance is drawn out."[29]

Exercise for Finding Lost Things

Have you lost something recently that you want to find? Whether you've misplaced a book, an important photograph, a favorite piece of jewelry, or a beloved pet—you can enhance your connection to it, helping the two of you reunite. You do this by strengthening your connection to what you have lost by focusing on the auric cords that connect you.

1. **Ground Yourself**—It might seem that the hardest thing to do when you've just lost something is to relax; however, it's the most important thing to do. Your anxiety can *and does* create conflict in the physical world. By calming your mind and your heart, you will allow for harmony to manifest itself in the outside world. We ground our electrical appliances to prevent them from sparking and starting fires . . . and we need to do the same thing for our energetic bodies. You can ground yourself by visualizing a long cord running down from you, down below your feet, far into the core of the earth. Imagine that all the worries that trouble you are falling down, down, down that cord . . . never to return.

2. **Choose Your Subconscious Method**—Access your subconscious mind by deciding whether you'd rather (1) pray, (2) meditate, or (3) be hypnotized. Choose whichever method you already feel most comfortable with, and access your subconscious connections to everything in

the universe—including what you have lost.

3. **Reach Out to What Is Lost**—Visualize yourself sending out a long arm to touch what it is that is temporarily lost. Gently touch it, and let your touch pierce through the auric shell surrounding it so you can touch your loved one or object directly with your hand.

4. **Connect**—With your hand stretched out far to touch your loved one or object, sense the surroundings. Do you see light or dark? Do you see colors or motion? How does it feel—cold or dark, wet or dry? Use all your senses (smell, sight, hearing, touch, taste) to collect clues to the whereabouts of your lost one or object. You might see a visual image of what you have lost, or receive a feeling, or even hear words that provide you with clues. In whatever form you receive intuitive information, accept what you sense and ask questions to receive further clarification. For example, if you ask, "Where are my keys?" and glimpse a visual image of a pocket in your mind's eye, you might then ask the follow-up question, "Which pocket?"

5. **Send Love Along the Energy Cord**—Send all your feelings of love along the thread of your long energy arm and the hand that is touching your loved one or object. Keep the energy line open, so you can continue to reassure your beloved lost one that you are waiting for it, and ready for it to return to you. ◎

Chapter 2 Questions for Review and Reflection

1. What is your favorite thing that your aura does for you?
2. How can your aura help you do a better job with your work?
3. How can your aura improve your home life?
4. What are the two main ways your aura helps you maintain good health?
5. Which of the things your aura does for you is the biggest surprise?
6. Which of the things your aura does for you comes most naturally to you?
7. Do you remember one time when you "chose the path that shined," and another time when you didn't? How did you feel about those decisions?
8. Have you been aware of times when you non-locally affected others, or they affected you? How did it feel?
9. What (or whom) have you lost track of for which you would like to use the "Finding Lost Things" exercise?
10. If you've seen a charismatic speaker give a talk, do you remember feeling how the thought-forms in the talk were energized, and how the speaker's energy felt?

Chapter 3

What's My Aura?

Your aura is filling the space around you with light and energy at this very moment. Never before has there been an aura in the world that looks exactly like yours does right now. As your moods and ideas change, new colors and designs of varying intensity and beauty appear around you. If you have a cold or illness, your aura hugs your body more closely than usual. If you feel sad or scared, your aura is smaller than usual. If you are feeling loving or loved, your aura is much bigger than usual. When you are dreaming or are "out of body," part of your aura stays close to your body, and another part of your aura—the "etheric double"—travels.

In this chapter, you'll get a chance to find out what condition your aura is in without even looking at it. By truthfully answering sixteen questions, you'll soon have a much better idea of your overall auric health.

The Healthy Aura Self-Assessment

You can assess your overall auric health and find where your energy leaks are located by observing the answers to questions on the healthy aura self-assessment test.

The healthiest auras (regardless of their color) can be described as clean, bright, and tight. People with healthy auras typically enjoy good physical and emotional health, good luck, and prosperity. People with dark, muddy, or ill-defined auras are at risk for a wide variety of health ailments, bad luck, and accidents. They also tend to attract unpleasant and less-than-enjoyable people and situations. To find out how you score, take the quiz below and give yourself one point for each "True" answer.

Healthy Aura Self-Assessment   T   F

1. I sometimes feel quite irritable and grouchy.   ❏ ❏
2. I've worried so much that I couldn't get to sleep.   ❏ ❏
3. I often can't remember what I was about to
   do next.   ❏ ❏
4. I've become so angry with someone I felt
   I'd explode.   ❏ ❏
5. I sometimes feel depressed for days at a time.   ❏ ❏
6. I envy those who have what I should have.   ❏ ❏
7. I often feel like I'm drifting away, high
   above everything.   ❏ ❏
8. I have alcoholic drinks every day.   ❏ ❏
9. I feel intimidated by people who are angry
   with me.   ❏ ❏
10. I often worry about things going wrong.   ❏ ❏
11. I take recreational drugs regularly.   ❏ ❏
12. I frequently fantasize about being rich
    and famous.   ❏ ❏
13. I've sometimes held a grudge for weeks,
    or longer.   ❏ ❏
14. I often complain about how badly things
    are going.   ❏ ❏
15. I smoke cigars or cigarettes regularly.   ❏ ❏
16. I often feel fatigued for no apparent reason.   ❏ ❏

Ranking

0–1 **Radiant:** an all-around radiant person to be around
2–4 **Average:** fairly bright, with typical amounts of dark areas
5–10 **Scattered:** bright and dark areas of aura are about equal
11–16 **Muddy:** aura has more rips, tears, holes, and/or dark areas than brightness

If you answered the questions above honestly, and were rated "Radiant" on this test, congratulations! You've developed a healthy lifestyle that supports excellent auric health in every facet of your life. You are the kind of person that other people love to be around, and most likely find yourself welcome wherever you go, feeling good about yourself and your life.

If your score was in the "Average" range, you're in good company. Most people aren't saints, and subsequently have several energetic weak spots. If you would like to change some of the behaviors that indicate problems in your aura, you now have a better idea of what changes can make the biggest improvements in your life. If you don't feel like making any changes at this time, that's fine, too. While your aura won't be shining at its maximum potential, it will be strong enough to maintain an average quality of life.

If your score put you in the "Scattered" range, you will definitely benefit from reviewing areas you can improve. Doing this review will greatly enhance your energy body, and therefore the quality of your life. If you feel overwhelmed by the idea of making so many changes at once, choose just one thing to work on first. Promise yourself that when you start seeing improvement with that one thing, you'll move on to looking at a second area for improvement. Keep track of your score on the healthy aura self-assessment test in a journal, so you can observe the steady improvement you make.

If your score put you in the "Muddy" range, your aura

colors are not appearing to be anywhere near as bright as they can be. You can make a big difference by even making one small change as indicated on the self-assessment, so choose one thing you can change today. Setting the intention that your aura will be brighter is the necessary first step for making this change, so congratulate yourself for being honest with yourself! You will likely find a lot of value to the practical suggestions of things you can do to strengthen your aura in Chapter 5.

The most important part of taking this healthy aura self-assessment test is that it allows you to examine parts of your life in which you may be experiencing a loss of a sense of personal power. There is great value in learning to constantly observe the state of your energy body—noticing where problems may be cropping up, so you can start taking steps to reclaim your essential life force. When you feel brave enough to ask, "Why am I losing energy?" you will be rewarded with seeing ways you can stop the energy leaks. At first you may feel a bit overwhelmed, like the Dutch boy in the age-old fable who stopped the leak in a dam with his finger. As your skills at sensing how and why you are vulnerable to energy drains increase, you will find it becomes much easier to quickly assess and resolve your auric energy leaks.

There are striking similarities between auric energy levels and self-esteem. We know from studies conducted on people with low self-esteem that they are more likely to suffer from all manner of psychological and physical disorders ranging from anorexia nervosa, to suicidal tendencies, teen pregnancies, and homicidal impulses.[1] When self-esteem improves, so does the quality of your energy body, and when your energy body becomes more radiant, clean, and defined, your self-esteem improves. There are obvious advantages to improving your self-esteem: You will be more likely to feel inspired to do creative new things, make new friends, be an involved member of your community, and complete your tasks.

Shining Bright in Dark Times

Remember that whatever the source of your energy leaks, you are the one who is best able to make changes that will bring about improved energy levels in your life. As tempting as it may seem to blame someone or something else for past injustices or handicaps in your life, you will gain the most energy from adopting a responsible role for maintaining your own energy body's health. "Giving away" your power by playing victim merely continues old patterns of unhealthy energetic connections.[2]

People who lose energy by feeling victimized often identify so strongly with their particular handicap that they can't seem to imagine letting go of it. In truth, every single one of us is probably burdened with some kind of physical, mental, or emotional handicap. Even so, many people don't allow their handicaps to become steady energy leaks. People such as Stephen Hawking, Christopher Reeve, and Lance Armstrong inspire us with their seemingly superhuman ability to rise above limitations. They keep their spirits and auric energy up in the face of what can appear to be insurmountable difficulties. These people are not only successful in life, they are our heroes. We look up to those who manage to shine as bright examples of success in spite of overwhelming odds. How do they do it? What is their secret?

Bicyclist Lance Armstrong demonstrates his stellar attitude in the face of cancer in his book, *It's Not About the Bike,* when he writes, "If there is a purpose to the suffering that is cancer, I think it must be this: It's meant to improve us." With five consecutive Tour de France wins, Lance has attained a level of cycling excellence matched by only one other athlete in history. While Lance's mother instilled in him the life-affirming philosophy, "Make an obstacle an opportunity, make a negative a positive,"[3] it was through his own dogged determination in following that advice that he managed to face cancer and keep on going. Armstrong's coach, Chris Carmichael, said, "Lance gives us all evidence that hope is alive and miracles do happen."[4]

Ever since actor Christopher Reeve was thrown headfirst from a horse and broke his neck in 1995, his doctors predicted that he would never breathe on his own or recover from being paralyzed from the shoulders down. Every morning, the actor who had once played the role of Superman would ". . . have to emerge from the dreams in which I'm completely healthy and able to do anything and adjust to the reality of paralysis."[5] Reeve found ways to channel his anger into laughter, maintain close relationships with family and friends, exercise his muscles regularly, and act as a spokesperson for paralyzed people. In September 2002, Reeve astonished his doctors by lifting one of his fingers, wiggling his toes on both feet, sitting in a chair for half an hour, breathing on his own for ninety minutes, and feeling hugs from his family. "To be able to feel just the lightest touch is really a gift," says Reeve.[6]

When physics student Stephen Hawking was diagnosed with ALS (amyotrophic lateral sclerosis) during his last year at Oxford, he had no idea how quickly the debilitating disease would progress. "Before my condition was diagnosed, I had been bored with life. There had not seemed to be anything worth doing. But shortly after I came out of the hospital, I dreamt that I was going to be executed. I suddenly realized that there were a lot of worthwhile things I could do if I were reprieved."[7] At age sixty, Hawking travels the world giving lectures on theoretical physics from his wheelchair, and is recognized by his peers as one of the greatest physicists of all time.

What Armstrong, Reeve, and Hawking have in common is a steady focus on the positive in their lives. This positive attitude energized their auras in new ways, as each of them increased their overall auric brightness during dark times. It would have been easy for them to slip into despair, blame others, or give up. Instead, these courageous men rose to the challenges of cancer, paralysis, and ALS by continuing their lives as positively as possible. They each found energetic auric cord support from family and friends, and set a wonderful example of the power of staying focused on what is going well *right now*, as they continually strove to achieve their personal best.

This winning combination of keeping one's personal aura bright while accepting energy cord support from others is the key to success in life, even when one's situation seems discouraging. One simple way to improve the brightness of your aura when you are facing difficult times is to take a look at the way you view yourself, and change your self-definition to more accurately reflect who you are. The following exercise is intended to help you transform your self-image and brighten your aura.

Exercise for Shining Bright in Dark Times: A New Self-Definition

1. Find a quiet place where you won't be disturbed for twenty to thirty minutes, and bring a pencil or pen and your journal or some paper.

2. Make a list of five to ten things you feel are often obstacles in your life. These can include physical ailments as well as anything that appears to interfere with your life being as enjoyable as you'd like it to be. Examples might be: nagging spouse, noisy neighbors, mean boss, arthritis, unemployed, overweight. The idea here is to really *vent* and get these things out of your system and onto the page.

3. Look at this list, and acknowledge that while these are your obstacles to overcome in life, they are not you. You are not defined by them. In fact, you are much, much more than them!

4. Now make a list of qualities you embody that do a better job of defining who you are. As you create this list, look for all your qualities—even ones you don't often show to the rest of the world. Examples for this list are: inspired, creative, meditative, passionate, empathetic, painter, writer, singer, inventor.

5. Look at these two lists and compare how you feel when you read each list.

6. If you like your new self-definition, post it somewhere that you can see every day. ⦿

Your True Colors

You are an energy being as well as a physical being, and the colors in your aura are influenced heavily by your thoughts, feelings, and beliefs. People who work as healers are often seen to have green auras, those who do a great deal of logical thinking often appear yellow, and people who are spiritual or meditate frequently have violet or purple in their auras. Saints and enlightened masters are often said to radiate completely white light, with occasional highlights of gold or violet.

Over the past hundred years, there has been some discussion among modern-day mystics such as the Theosophists and Edgar Cayce about white auras being preferable to colored auras. The main reason given for this is that white light does not interfere with one's perception of the world, whereas all other colors present a biased impression of reality.[8] The expression "seeing the world through rose-colored glasses" is an example of this, as a person who views the world through rose-colored glasses or a rose-colored aura will see everything in that rosy hue, whereas someone who has lots of darkness in their aura will tend to see the world as a dark and foreboding place. People who wish to aspire to seeing the world as it is will therefore aspire to a white aura.

Psychic and intuitive Edgar Cayce believed that the best auric color to aspire to is white, because white does not distort one's view of the world.[9] This goal of becoming more enlightened is a noble one, and something we can continually strive toward. Prayer and meditation can bring more white light into our energy bodies and lives, and the more we practice these prayers and meditations, the more enlightened we become. However, we are doing well to simply get a sense of which colors are surrounding us, and what thought-forms we habitually create.

We need people of every auric color in order to maintain diversity in ways of thinking and living. Our world needs people who study math and science, and we also need doctors and teachers and farmers. Everyone has his own special contribution to make, and shares it most fully by simply being who he is. Like Cyndi Lauper sings in her song "True Colors," there is beauty in expressing your own energetic essence just as it is. Your true colors are beautiful!

So what do our auras look like? Interestingly, if you are active in a field of work you truly enjoy, chances are good that your aura shares similar characteristics to others in your field. Aura viewer Mark Smith likes to play a game with his aura-viewing students in which they "pin the profession on the aura."[10] In this game, Smith's students typically have no trouble noticing the tell-tale aqua-green color of nurses, the dark blue or indigo color for doctors, the sky-blue color associated with engineers—often with a square or boxy shape. Very religious or spiritual people (regardless of faith) have higher frequency colors such as indigo and violet, often with gold or silver included as well. As you develop your skills for viewing auras, you can better understand what motivates certain individuals, based on characteristics you see in their auras. People have unique ways of pursuing the three primary motivators of power, achievement, and affiliation, and these differences can be seen in the aura.[11] This chapter includes descriptions of personality characteristics that are most commonly associated with each of the seven colors found in the rainbow.

Color Self-Assessment

A number of aura readers have associated colors with personality traits. While these experts sometimes have minor disagreements over which colors represent which characteristics, there is general consensus on many common personality traits that are typically associated with each hue of the rainbow. One color may predominate in a person's aura, or there may be quite a few different colors present. Chances are good that your favorite colors are also the major colors present in your aura. American author Linda Clark once asked Edgar Cayce what her primary aura color was. After gazing at her for a bit, Cayce surprised her by naming her favorite color.[12]

We often feel drawn to the very same colors we are radiating in our auras, and repelled by colors we sense indicate personality characteristics we don't like. Throughout my childhood, my artistic mother frequently voiced a very strong dislike for a color she called "puke green" (also called "gaslight green" by others). I was amazed that my normally easy-going mother had such strong negative feelings about a shade of color, since she hardly ever says an unkind word about anything. I later discovered that this yellowish shade of green is a reliable indicator of deceit, dishonesty, and evasion. No wonder my mother dislikes it so!

The following section of this chapter contains brief summaries of the seven primary colors in the visual spectrum. As you read through each description, ask yourself, "Does this fit me?" and you'll get an idea of which color or colors are predominant in your aura. You may also find you gain a better understanding of your friends, family, and colleagues by reading this section. Aura researcher Barbara Bowers believes that some relationships between certain color combinations (such as blue and yellow, or orange and green) are naturally much more harmonious than others.[13] As you read the following color personality descriptions, notice if any of them remind you of someone you know, or of yourself. You can get a fairly good idea of who you are and whom you like to be around by reading these aura color personality descriptions.

Muddy Colors

All of the colors in your aura can be clean and bright, or they can contain some dark discoloration or "muddiness." When colors are muddy, their natural inner beauty is obscured by some dark emotion like fear, greed, laziness, bossiness, or depression. Most people have occasional dark moods and areas of their personalities that make them feel unpleasant for others to be around. These muddy colors are a reflection of inner emotional stress, angst, or "issues" that a person is currently dealing with. Hopefully, you'll find that any muddy colors you might discover in your aura are temporary, as you explore new ways to brighten your perspective on life.

Red

Red almost always indicates physical vitality and passion. Red is a down-to-earth color that is often associated with hard work and practicality. Red people have a great deal of energy and enthusiasm for what they are interested in. Material comforts are usually very important to those with red featured prominently in their auras, although they don't worry much about money details. Not ones for procrastination, these people dive right into even very large tasks with gusto.

People who have lots of red in their auras tend to be vigorous, energetic, and forceful individuals. When they enter a room, you may notice the way they move as if they are at one with the earth. These people also always seem to be moving. Seldom do you see them sitting for hours at a time, unless they are sick. They may show little understanding for people who are less active than they are, since they sometimes have a hard time realizing that not everyone has as much energy as they do. These people have an easy self-confidence in every situation, almost always standing with both feet squarely on the ground. Chances are good that if you see someone who is constantly *doing* things (such as rearranging furniture, puttering, fixing things), they have a lot of red in their energy field. Reds are diligent workers who can keep going when everyone else tires out. They have the ability to revive projects that had seemed to be dead, and once they make up their minds to do something, their resolution is amazing.

Reds tend to be loners who do not relate well to their feelings or the feelings of others. While they do have many friends, they prefer to keep conversations focused on activities and things that are happening rather than on esoteric ideas or deep emotions. Reds do have intense emotions—they just prefer not to talk about them. These people are intensely loyal and honest straight-shooters who admire others who are equally trustworthy and hard-working. Occasionally hot-headed and impatient with others, Reds would rather focus on tasks than figure out complexities of interpersonal relationships. They can be very appreciative of others when they feel people are working with them, but can seem harsh or bullying when they feel they aren't getting their way. Reds need to recognize that to most other people, they can seem like a force of nature that wouldn't care who or what gets mowed down in their path. Reds can benefit from tempering their need to succeed by recognizing that others have feelings and needs, too.

Reds excel at jobs that require physical prowess and stamina. They often enjoy working as construction crew members, physical therapists, professional athletes, short-order chefs, firefighters, singers, and paramedics. Reds make excellent football and soccer players, wrestlers, dancers, and gymnasts.

Some famous personalities who have red energy in their auras include singer and actress Madonna, singer Bruce Springsteen, singer Tina Turner, actor Heath Ledger, actor Danny DeVito, actress and singer Cher, actor Sylvester Stallone, actor James Gandolfini, actress and singer Bette Midler, and tennis champion Serena Williams.

If you have a lot of red in your aura, you will tend to:

- Prefer to be doing something rather than sitting still
- Not give a lot of thought to money
- Feel strongly about what you believe in
- Work extremely hard at what you do
- Prefer intensity of experience to intellectual discussion
- Feel confident when you're working with your hands
- Be original and charismatic
- Roll up your sleeves and jump into action when something needs doing
- Consider yourself a "no-nonsense" kind of person
- Work with what you have, and not make excuses

Shades of Red

Dark red	Physical vitality
Rose red	Love for family
Bright, clear red	Faith, hope, and courage
Scarlet	Egotism
Medium orange-red	Healing
Pink	Universal love, youthfulness
Dark, muddy, or cloudy red	Nervous, angry, obstinate, brutal

Orange

Orange is the color of health, warmth, sociability, courage, and joy. It is warm, innovative, cheerful, and expressive. Orange people love to speak out and voice their unusual and unique opinions and views. Endlessly creative, orange people often blaze their own trails in life as they break down barriers along the way. Freedom is extremely important to these people, and they will go to great lengths to achieve autonomy and independence. Excitement and risk-taking are essential to Oranges, and they often refuse to "play it safe." More apt mottos for these individualists would be "carpe diem" (seize the day) and "live large"! Oranges are excellent listeners who have wonderful intuition about how people are feeling without being told. They are often sought after as counselors by peers and friends.

In romantic relationships, people with lots of orange have an easier time sharing feelings of raw passion than they do with remembering to express tender warmth and compassion on an on-going basis. These people are happiest in relationships in which they can express themselves dramatically; they feel much more alive this way. Oranges constantly test everyone and everything around them. Oranges love partners who keep things perpetually new, with exciting new activities to share and places to go. Oranges are also thrilled by exotic new ideas, and love to explore them as if they were an exciting expedition into unknown territories.

Oranges do best when working on their own, and chafe when given orders. They love their independence, and prefer to move on when things seem stuck. Oranges are often eager to move away from their parents at the earliest opportunity. With time, Oranges temper their impetuous disposition with wisdom earned from numerous brash actions and escapades. Their tales of growing up are packed with hilarious misadventures, daring stunts, and narrow escapes. More than any other color, Oranges are connoisseurs of the best things life has to offer. They are in their element when surrounded by fine furniture, art, food, music, and friends. Oranges are so good at moving on that they can benefit from spending time with old friends, things, and family members. More than any other color, Oranges need to learn to find stability right where they are, instead of continually searching for it outside of themselves.

Oranges are adept in a wide variety of occupations in which they can have fun being fearless in their own unique way. Oranges make excellent police officers, real-estate agents, animal trainers, jewelry designers, translators, racecar drivers, clothing designers, Arctic explorers, professional musicians, interior designers, stand-up comedians, and hair stylists.

Some famous personalities who have orange energy in their auras include comedian and actor Steve Martin, singer Celine Dion, actress and singer Barbra Streisand, actress Julia Roberts, singer Alicia Keyes, actress Kate Hudson, actor and comedian Bill Cosby, actor Mel Gibson, actor Nicolas Cage, and actor and comedian Adam Sandler.

If you have a lot of orange in your aura, you will tend to:

- Follow the beat of your own drum
- Be fearless in the face of new situations
- Have an unusual job or career
- Make things more fun wherever you go
- Have a knack for knowing how people are feeling
- Tie your self-esteem directly to the quality of your personal relationships
- Be extremely concerned about making a good impression
- Love making guests and visitors comfortable and feeling at home
- Keep your home and work environment tidy and organized
- Feel happiest when everything you own is of the highest quality

Shades of Orange

Golden orange	Wisdom and spiritual energy
Brownish orange	Lazy, arrogant, vain, freeloading

Yellow

Yellow is a color that indicates mental activity, learning, and intellect. People with lots of yellow in their auras understand the power of ideas and the importance of expression of intellect in their lives. Often bright and creative, people who have a great deal of yellow tend to be naturally open and filled with awe about what they can learn and experience in the world. These people see problems as providing exciting opportunities for finding new solutions, and they relish the chance to learn new things as they meet these challenges. Yellows love to help others by doing something useful, such as planning a trip to take together. These people excel at showing how something is to be done by setting a good example. They especially love to do things outdoors, in the sunshine. Yellows are true visionaries in the world, who often are leaders in their fields.

Yellows have a unique childlike sense of joy and wonder that they manage to sustain throughout their lives. Even as the hairs on their heads turn gray, Yellows still look like children at heart when they are laughing and having fun in life. Their sense of curiosity never ends, and they continue learning new things until the day they die. Their youthful exuberance can feel tiring at times to those around them, although many find such playful inquisitiveness refreshing and invigorating. More than any other color, Yellows seem a lot like little children on the inside, no matter how old they may be chronologically.

Yellows can seem naïve to others, because they naturally tend to believe that people are generally good. People with lots of yellow in their energy field can be overly critical and authoritarian at times, and are their own worst critics. They need to remember not to overanalyze everything with their extraordinary thinking abilities. These people will find true happiness in life when they do whatever brings them the most joy—since this helps prevent them from feeling like they lead a deprived life. Yellows bring a fresh new way of seeing the world, and they are fast and incisive about making decisions that are fair for everyone involved. They are the living embodiment of alertness, brightening the world for everyone they meet. Yellows are sometimes so fast and such great thinkers that they skip right over how they feel about things. Yellows can benefit from slowing down a bit and asking themselves, "How do I really feel right now?"

Yellows make exceptionally good park rangers, sales people, tour guides, geographers, landscape architects, archeologists, inventors, teachers, anthropologists, and coaches. They most especially enjoy jobs in which they can move around, be outdoors, and put their phenomenal intellectual and leadership powers to work.

Some famous personalities who have yellow energy in their auras include television talk show host Johnny Carson, comedian and actress Ellen DeGeneres, actor Danny Kaye, actress Reese Witherspoon, actor and comedian Mike Myers, comedian and actor Eddie Murphy, actress Goldie Hawn, singer and actress Janet Jackson, late night talk show host Jay Leno, actress Marisa Tomei, and actress Allison Mack.

If you have a lot of yellow in your aura, you will tend to:

- Love finding new solutions to problems
- Laugh and have fun almost every day
- Enjoy intellectual conversations
- Bring a playful approach to everything you do
- Think about the future more than most people seem to
- Pride yourself on your expertise and intellect
- Love to turn ideas into reality
- Become preoccupied with your thoughts
- Be competitive, but not with those who are less skilled or competent than you
- Love to acquire new skills and ideas

Shades of Yellow

Pale yellow   Spiritual development
Lemon yellow   Mental strength

| Orange yellow | Artistic |
| Muddy yellow | Overly critical, hasty, preoccupied, dogmatic |

Green

People who have green in their auras tend to be sensitive, compassionate, reliable, and calm. If the green is bright and with a bit more blue than yellow, then healing abilities are strongly indicated. Green is the color of intuition, and people with lots of green in their energy field are often fascinated by metaphysical topics. They are champions of underdogs and the environment, and feel great satisfaction from finding ways to make others happy.

People who have green in their auras are driven to be productive. They are capable of coming up with endless plans and ideas. Greens are ingenious thinkers who can leap from the beginning to the end of a problem effortlessly. People who have a lot of green in their energy fields are highly selective about whom they spend their time with and what they spend their money on. They are perfectionists who would rather wait for the right person, situation, or thing to come along rather than act impulsively.

People with green in their auras are fortunate to be able to balance their rational and intuitive thinking processes, and can easily identify patterns in a whole variety of situations where others would see only a confusion of raw data. Their intuitive skills allow them to be amazingly empathetic, and they can feel the emotions of others as clearly as if they were their own. Their subconscious/intuitive skills provide them with built-in tools for making energy cord connections to others, which are necessary for non-locally viewing energy fields of others and contributing to distant healing. Greens often get impatient with others who don't keep up with their speedy assessment of situations and problems, or have trouble matching their level of efficiency at getting things done. They can benefit from realizing that not everyone shares their unique and often extraordinary talents.

Good careers for Greens include gourmet cooking, speech therapy, dental hygiene, social work, psychology, nursing, public relations, marketing, writing, banking, massage therapy, publishing, and sales. Greens succeed at pretty much anything they put their minds to, but they will tend to be happiest in occupations in which they are responsible for finding hidden patterns.

Some famous personalities who have green energy in their auras include actor Kevin Spacey, actor Tom Hanks, actress Lisa Kudrow, actress Sarah Michelle Geller, actor Tobey Maguire, psychic John Edwards, singer Mariah Carey, actress Shirley MacLaine, television talk show host Oprah Winfrey, actress Drew Barrymore, and golf pro Tiger Woods.

If you have a lot of green in your aura, you will tend to:

- Love to be an observer in social gatherings
- Enjoy providing new ideas and information to groups
- Be extremely efficient at getting things done
- Easily find patterns and work backward from the answer
- Genuinely care about humanitarian and environmental causes and issues
- Be intrigued by metaphysical topics such as angels, auras, and spirits
- Be open and receptive to change
- Have so many talents that you may find it hard to know which to focus on
- Need to be liked so much that you sometimes attract needy or abusive people to you
- Continually seek to better understand what your life purpose is

Shades of Green

Emerald green	Healing
Aqua	Peace and healing love

| Greeny-yellow | Deceitful, dishonest, jealous |
| Muddy green | Miserliness, obsessive-compulsive, suicidal |

Blue

Blue is the color of calm and quietness, devotion, honesty, and commitment. People who have a great deal of blue in their energy fields experience a deep sense of tranquility and inner peace in their lives. You can see this quality of calm when you look into their eyes and feel how these people are the living embodiment of peacefulness. Blues have tremendous depth of feeling and empathy, and need to feel they belong. They love serving others so much that they sometimes suffer by spending too little attention on their needs, or by being taken for granted by family and friends.

People with a lot of blue in their auras have a marvelous intuitive grasp of emotions. They can convey tremendous feeling in one glance—whether it's an inquisitive look or a withering stare. Because they have such a clear sense of feelings, they prefer to make decisions that *feel* right, and sometimes have a difficult time explaining their rationale to others. Once their family and friends begin to appreciate the usefulness of their amazing gift of intuitive feelings, they can be recognized for their insightful contributions.

Blues thrive when they can devote their lives to a significant other or others. While Blues may enjoy periods of solitude to refresh themselves, they need a home in which they can actively play a supporting role of service to others. They love to talk about feelings, and help solve problems that require emotional intelligence. Blues are often masters of coming up with memorable original proverbs or sayings, which can be almost as calming as their physical presence.

Blues feel it is equally important to provide service to others in their work, which they take very seriously. They do best when they can put their attention into handling the feelings of many people, and not have to deal much with handling money. Blues prefer for someone else to work out the financial details. Blues tend to avoid conflict to a fault, and can benefit from learning it can be safe to express their feelings of resentment with loved ones. It is okay to say "No!"

Doctors often have a great deal of blue in their auras, as do engineers and scientists. Blues are good technicians, and make excellent repair people. They are also wonderful teachers, counselors, thespians, air traffic controllers, veterinarians, surgeons, and museum curators. Their innate sense of calm and desire to help people make them perfectly suited for many occupations in which such emotional reliability is required.

Some famous personalities who have blue energy in their auras include actress Andie MacDowell, actress Grace Kelly, actor and film-maker Ron Howard, actor Denzel Washington, actress Isabella Rossellini, actor James Van DerBeek, actor Tom Welling, NFL ex-quarterback Don McPherson, actress Kristin Kreuk, actress Penelope Cruz, and actress Katie Holmes.

If you have a lot of blue in your aura, you will tend to:

- Love spending hours reading a book or gardening
- Especially enjoy being with family and friends for the holidays
- Enjoy giving and receiving gifts
- Have trouble saying "No"
- Constantly look for ways you can be of service
- Enjoy sports that feature camaraderie and grace
- Strongly prefer consensus when group decisions are being made
- Laugh and cry very easily when overcome by emotion
- Be a natural nurturer and caretaker
- Have trouble knowing what you need and asking for it

Shades of Blue

Pale blue	Seeking greater maturity, spiritual
Medium blue	Hard-working
Royal blue	Honest, loyal, good judgment
Muddy blue	Melancholy, malicious, ruthless

Indigo

People who have indigo in their auras possess a deep inborn awareness of how and where they fit in the universe. These individuals thrive when allowed to pursue their specific interests to great depth, without spending time on areas of study that have been rigidly formulated by others. Graced with a memory of knowledge retained from before this lifetime, people with the color indigo know what they want and who they are. This knowledge is apparent in how selective these people are when they choose friends and activities. Deep thinkers, Indigos are able to quickly assess situations, easily seeing intricacies and connections that most others would overlook.

Indigos are individualists who do not seem to care whether or not they attract any followers, or whether or not they have an audience watching them. Indigos have an innate understanding of how the world would be if everyone were operating at their highest levels of being: unselfish, hard-working, supportive, respectful, modest, and compassionate. The inner structure that Indigos sense is one that they feel transcends shallow forms of justice. Since Indigos compare everything to these inner standards rather than external examples set by authoritarian figures, they may disregard admonishments to "conform or else." Indigos have no interest nor desire to conform, and can calmly look anyone directly in the eye and say so. Indigos believe that individuals can and will make the correct choices when they are given the chance to remember that they already know the best thing to do in any given situation.

Indigos thrive when given opportunities to learn things quickly and work independently. They can succeed at just about any task they set their minds to, as long as it continues to hold their interest. They prefer to do work that makes a real difference in the world, in which they can continue to develop proficiency. These people become craftsmen at any trade they remain in, since they never stop honing their skills and trying new things. They are naturally gifted artists who excel at keeping their work fresh and original. Indigos also have a gift for clearly seeing the intrinsic value of things that other people are only dimly aware of. These spiritual seekers grace everyone whose lives they touch with a deep sense of appreciation for the divine mysteries in this world. Occasionally, Indigos may become so convinced that their view of the world is the best one that they can seem obsessed or fanatical to those around them. Indigos need to remember that each person walks his own path, and needs to learn the lessons from making his own choices.

Interesting career options for Indigos include computer programming, art, astronomy, clinical laboratory science, choreography, film-making, law, and medical technology. Indigos set themselves apart from everyone else with their unique style and points of view, and will be happiest in jobs in which they are appreciated for their innate sense of high personal and social standards.

Some famous personalities who have indigo energy in their auras include actor Val Kilmer, actor Richard Gere, actress Sigourney Weaver, film-maker Spike Lee, singer/songwriter David Bowie, singer/songwriter Sinead O'Connor, painter Georgia O'Keefe, singer/songwriter Prince, singer/songwriter Bono, and actress Angelina Jolie.

If you have a lot of indigo in your aura, you will tend to:

- Ask people to do things differently than they've done before

- Know what you want and need
- Not feel governed by rules
- Be deeply committed to a few close friends
- Enjoy observing people and things around you
- Love having time to yourself to pursue your interests in depth
- Cherish favorite old clothes, books, friends, and toys
- Feel exhausted and/or overwhelmed in noisy crowds
- Feel already familiar with the "new" things you learn
- Be open-minded about different lifestyles and ways of living and being

Shades of Indigo

Indigo	Spiritual seeker
Muddy indigo	Anarchistic, disillusioned, rebellious, fanatical

Violet

Violet is a spiritual color of transmutation and divine intuition and guidance. People with a great deal of violet in their auras may seem to be aloof or cold on the surface, but are deeply passionate individuals on the inside. They prefer to make the most of every social encounter in the form of intense conversation that serves some obvious and significant purpose. These people have lofty ideals and love to share their vision of the future with those who truly care. People with lots of violet in their energy fields are natural leaders who intuitively know how best to achieve their goals with a combination of universal life force energy and practicality.

Violets are often visionary leaders whose drive to achieve is capable of bringing about vast social and political revolution. These people have a magical quality about them, although it is often a serious kind of magic-with-a-purpose. Violets feel a tremendous sense of responsibility for helping make their dreams a reality, so they are seldom jovial sorts. Violets do possess an excellent sense of humor and love to laugh, but don't much appreciate jokes that poke fun at their cause. These are people "on a mission," and have tremendous need to be effective catalysts for change. Because their visions are often at odds with the status quo, Violets' intuitive sensing of others' feelings about what they are doing often causes them to doubt themselves. This inner doubt is invisible to everyone around them, who see only a courageous individual with amazing visions for how the world can be a better place. Violets can benefit from realizing that if they are questioning their competence, they are probably much more competent than most.

When Violets are able to inspire others, they are some of the most amazing leaders this world has ever seen. They can almost appear to be super-human at times because of the way they single-mindedly pour all their time and energy into their dream. When Violets accept the fact that they have made a promise and a commitment to serve the greater good, they can truly come into their own.

Fulfilling career options for Violets include politics, ministry, public speaking, fund-raising, motivational coaching, journalism, teaching, medicine, and law. Violets excel at any kind of research, and in any job that requires them to light the way for others to follow.

Some famous personalities who have violet energy in their auras include French spiritual heroine Joan of Arc, poet and author Maya Angelou, consumer activist and political leader Ralph Nader, political leader Jesse Jackson, author Marianne Williamson, actress and film-maker Jodie Foster, U.S. President Jimmy Carter, actor Arnold Schwarzenegger, Reverend Dr. Martin Luther King, and environmentalist Julia Butterfly Hill.

If you have a lot of violet in your aura, you will tend to:

- Be a visionary who can imagine things that have previously never been described
- Feel driven to follow your vision even if it seems bigger than you can handle
- Feel bitter and angry if you don't heed the calling of your life task
- Be a natural researcher
- Be something of a loner much of the time
- Intuitively understand foreign and ancient ideas
- Love talking to people one-on-one about your vision
- See connections and messages in everything around you
- Be much more emotional and passionate than you show to the outside world
- Love to make a noticeable and positive difference in the world

Shades of Violet

Lavender	Humility and worship, artistic explorer
Orchid (pink shade of purple)	Spiritual
Purple	Practical and worldly
Violet	Great and unselfish leader
Red-purple	Passionate and strong-willed
Muddy purple, muddy violet	Overbearing, stingy

Chapter 3 Questions for Review and Reflection

1. What can you do to improve the health of your aura?

2. When you finished the "New Self-Definition" exercise, did you post your new self-definition where you can see it every day? How do you feel when you look at it?

3. Have you ever noticed the yellowish-green "gaslight green" color in someone's aura? How did you feel about what they were doing or saying at that time?

4. How do the descriptions of your favorite colors match your personality?

5. What color descriptions match the personalities of your parents?

6. Have you seen people demonstrate the personality characteristics of muddy colors? How have you felt when you were around muddy colors?

7. Have you had the same dominant color or colors all your life, or have you noticed a change over time?

8. What kinds of color personalities do you pick most often for friends? Do you notice how these friends bring what you need to your life?

9. Are your favorite movie stars and singers mostly grouped in one or two color personality types, or are they spread across the spectrum fairly evenly?

10. If you dream in color, do you notice what colors you tend to see most often in your dreams?

Part 2

Chapter 4

See and Feel Your Aura

Auras can be felt as well as seen. Learning to feel auras is an important first step in reading auras, and one that is fun and easy to learn. Several years ago, I traveled from California all the way to a museum in Royston, England, in northern Hertfordshire. I had read that Royston's mysterious cave full of carvings lies near a convergence of the Saint Michael and Saint Mary energy ley-lines—part of a grid of energy lines that criss-cross their way through England.[1] These energy lines are invisible to the human eye, yet are reputed to be felt by people on an unconscious level and to be important conduits of an energy grid that encircles the earth. The Royston Cave also intrigued me because it has many carvings from 1,000 years ago depicting saints and religious scenes, and it lies beneath the ancient Icknield Way, which was first used during the Iron Age about 2,000 years ago by an ancient tribe of Celts called the Iceni.

When my husband and I arrived at the museum, we found it closed and quiet. I felt we had come much too far to simply walk away, so I knocked on the museum door. Shadowy figures moved inside, and after several long moments, the door swung open to reveal the curator, a middle-aged English woman. She shook her head and said, "The museum is closed today."

Barely able to conceal my disappointment, I explained how I had come all the way from the United States to see the Royston Cave. The English woman sighed thoughtfully, and after a long pause, agreed that she would open the museum just for me, but that the cave was closed that day.

"Have you ever dowsed before?" the curator asked me, as we walked through the museum. I told her that I had not, and she replied, "Oh, dowsing is a simple matter that almost anyone can learn to do! Just hold these wire coat hangers, one in each hand, and show me where you feel the energy lines," she instructed, handing me a pair of hangers. When I took the hangers, I was astonished to feel them moving of their own accord, apparently indicating the presence of unseen energy fields. When I stepped forward toward an energy line (which I could not otherwise sense), the hangers would either swing wide open, or swing shut so they clanged against each other— and I was simply holding the coat hangers loosely without turning them! "You've found them! You've found the lines!" the curator beamed at me. I was astonished. "What you are sensing are the Michael and Mary energy lines that run right through this museum. You can see for yourself how they cross back and forth over each other, and continue right on through the walls of the museum and beyond. Where the lines converge, you will find there are usually important buildings, like museums or churches, because the energy is much stronger there."

I was so impressed with my newfound ability to dowse energy fields that I took wire coat hangers with me everywhere else I visited after we left Royston that day—including the ancient stone circle at Avebury Henge. At Avebury Henge, I found I could locate the precise spots where missing stones had once been situated. I discovered I could also use these coat hangers to dowse human energy fields—and saw how easy it is to discern how energetic a person is feeling by dowsing their field.

Before you read any further, I hope you will set this book down and do the following exercise, so you can see for yourself how easy it is to feel the perimeter of auric fields around people—using just two regular wire coat hangers! Demonstrate to yourself how these energy fields exist all around us, even when we aren't consciously aware of it.

Exercise: Dowsing with Coat Hangers

This exercise allows you to feel the perimeter of auric fields using coat hangers as dowsing rods, rather than viewing them with your eyes.

1. For this aura viewing technique, you will need two wire coat hangers, and a friend. It's lots of fun to demonstrate someone's energy field to them, so you should have an easy time finding a volunteer!

2. Start by holding one wire coat hanger in each hand as you stand comfortably (with no straps or other dangling things hanging from your shoulders). Hold the hangers loosely by the long, flat straight edge so that the curved hook parts point forward. Keep the hangers loose in your hands and pointing straight up from the ground so that they can swing freely to the left and right as you walk.

3. Step back about fifteen feet away from your friend.

4. Then, holding one hanger in each hand, begin slowly walking toward your friend, who should be standing still.

5. When the coat hangers begin to swing together (like doors closing) or swing apart (like doors opening), or when one or the other swings in either direction, you've encountered the human energy field! Slow down when this happens, then back up (straightening your hangers), and slowly walk forward again. Notice if the hangers respond at the same distance from your friend each time.

6. Now, try this again, after asking your friend to boost the energy field by remembering favorite friends, experiences, foods, books, and vacations. Any happy thought will do!

7. What difference did you notice in the size of the energy field?

Typically, auras expand with feelings of love, and contract inward toward the body with feelings of fear, anger, or sadness . . . or in times of illness, when the energy field seems to prefer to hug tightly to our bodies in protective fashion. ◎

The coat hanger exercise is one of the most impressive ones to share with other people, because you can feel the hangers pulling and responding to the energy fields around you. Once you get the hang of this, you can even demonstrate to a skeptic that you can discern whether they switch from positive to negative thoughts, or from negative to positive thoughts, by seeing how far out their auric field extends after they secretly select two different kinds of emotional states. And who knows? One day, you may see auras all around you!

Learning to See Auras

When I was in my late thirties, I dreamt that an angel told me, "You've wondered how it looks to see the world through an angel's eyes. Now you can!" My dream felt peaceful as I strolled past trees, flowers, animals, and people, seeing such brilliant colors around everything that I was nearly blinded by the light. The colors shimmered like rainbow-hued flames, burning without destroying what they touched. I blinked several times and stared at these colors. I saw how the auric fields around everything were constantly interacting, and was amazed to see my own auric field reach out to a tree's field. Like a shining bridge of light, a streak of rainbow colors leapt from me to the tree, and the tree met this beam of energy with a matching stream of light. Our auric fields combined via a beam of light as thick as my wrist, which expanded to surround us both, changing colors to combine elements of both our auras across the bridge. A blending of colors began where our auras merged, and within a few moments, both of our auras began to match as the colors mingled.

I awoke from this dream with my heart pounding, sat up and rubbed my eyes, and was greeted by a shocking sight. *Everything* around me was still alive and burning with flames of color! I was awed by this experience, and felt that my dream with the angel had been true, because I could still see those bright, exotic colors around me for another hour after I awoke. I promised myself that I would never forget my vision of a world of light.

To those who can see it, the human aura looks and feels like a glowing, egg-shaped light that surrounds the human body. It is most pronounced around the head and shoulders, but extends outward for several inches (and sometimes several feet) from our heads down to our toes. Even if you can't yet see the waves of energy that are burning brightly all around us, enveloping and connecting us to everything on earth and throughout this universe, you can certainly feel them. Good physical, mental, and emotional health appears in the form of large auras that are full of bright colors, clear tones, and active patterns. When you start viewing your aura, you will see how its size varies from hour to hour, and day to day. You'll notice how your life feels more vibrant on days when your aura is brighter and more challenging on days when your aura is dimmer. You'll get insights into any tendencies you might have toward depression, being accident-prone, or illness . . . or be able to see the locations of infection. Healthy auras are colorful and free of dark areas, tears, breaks, holes, asymmetries, and other similar problems.

Edgar Cayce wrote in *Auras: An Essay on the Meaning of Colors*, "Ever since I can remember I have seen colors in connection with people. I do not remember a time when the human beings I encountered did not register on my retina with blues and greens and reds gently pouring from their heads and shoulders. It was a long time before I realized that other people did not see these colors; it was a long time before I heard the word aura, and learned to apply it to this phenomenon that to me was commonplace. I do not ever think of people except in connection with their auras; I see them change in my friends and loved ones as time goes by—sickness, dejection, love, fulfillment—these are all reflected in the aura, and for me the aura is the weathervane of the soul. It shows which way the winds of destiny are blowing."[2]

Your aura is the energetic boundary around you that defines your personal space. Notice how good it feels to sit under a tree or on the shore next to a body of water. Natural places that are ecologically balanced are full of energy that can help to equalize your own energy systems. This is why it feels so good to be out in nature! We humans are part of the intricately interconnected system of energy waves, and can heal and be healed by the energy systems around us. You can prove this to yourself the next time you feel hemmed in by the manmade world. Take a break from your usual routine and go to a natural setting where you can spend a little quality, quiet time. Once you arrive at this place, ask yourself, "How do I feel?" Regardless of what you do or don't do, chances are very good that after you've spent twenty or thirty minutes in this natural setting, you'll be feeling energized and your aura will be shining more brightly.

The feelings that nature evokes—soothing, relaxing, energizing, and healing—can help lay the groundwork for how to feel and see auras. The earth has a harmonic resonance that has been measured to be approximately eight cycles per second, or eight hertz. It is no accident that humans also vibrate at this same resonant frequency of eight hertz when we are in states of deep relaxation, and that we can be healed simply by lying down on the grass and allowing ourselves to feel this healthy energy of the earth.

Since children typically spend so much time outside in nature, they are often naturally aware of energy fields, and love to play with their intuitive knowledge of auras in games of hide-and-seek, blind man's bluff, and Marco Polo (a kind of blind-man's bluff game in the water). Even experienced aura viewers like author Barbara Ann Brennan often start out with more of a feeling sense of these energy fields than a visual sense of them. When Barbara was a child growing up on a farm in Wisconsin, she spent hours at a time alone in the woods, sometimes sitting still until small animals came close to her, and other times walking blindfolded past trees that she could feel long before she could touch them with her hands. In her book *Hands of Light*, Brennan describes how she remembers special times in her childhood in the woods in which she entered an expanded state of consciousness, and could see and feel the energy fields around trees and small animals. She noticed how the energy fields that connect and surround everything look "somewhat like the light from a candle."[3] The auras we see and feel around people, plants, animals, and other material things are that part of the universal energy field that is associated with physical objects. When we develop our innate ability to perceive this energy, a whole new world of color and light opens up for us to explore.

While many adept aura viewers find their skills enhanced by rising kundalini (energy that opens chakras, from the Sanskrit word meaning "coiled," since this energy feels like an uncoiling of energy that comes up from the bottom of the spine), near-death experiences, meditation, sweat lodges (outdoor saunas designed for physical and spiritual cleansing), vision quests (spiritual solo outings in which one remains in a natural setting until visions come), or energy training, almost anyone who has a sincere desire to learn and takes the time to practice can learn to see and/or feel auras with one of the techniques described in this chapter. The ability to see human auras is a skill that often unfolds gradually, starting with the ability to see a faint bluish-white haze around the edges of the body, then up to seven layers of auric colors and views of the corresponding seven spinning chakras, sometimes as symbols and other information. Occasionally, aura viewers develop "internal vision," in which the inside of the body can be viewed as thoroughly and quickly as if it were being scanned with the most deluxe and accurate medical scanning devices. QiGong masters in ancient China are often taught several different methods of diagnostic scanning, such as passing a palms of one's hand alongside someone's body to detect problems.

Even medical doctors often see and feel energy fields, although they are sometimes reluctant to publicly admit their abilities. Neurologist and psychiatrist Shafica Karagulla coined the term "higher sense perception," or HSP, to describe the ability to see the human energy field. Karagulla documents her experiences with gifted intuitive doctors in her book, *Breakthrough to Creativity*. Karagulla was intrigued that doctors who had the ability to accurately diagnose patients with higher sense perception were so secretive about it, and that they seemed unaware of the fact that many other doctors and medical professionals were similarly gifted. These doctors described what they saw as being an "energy field" or a "moving web of frequency" that surrounded and penetrated the physical bodies of their patients. Some also described seeing "vortices of energy at certain points along the spine, connected with or influencing the endocrine system." They were seeing the chakras! Concerned about risking their professional reputations, these surgeons, university professors, heads of hospital departments and Mayo clinic physicians continued to use their gifts in secret.[4]

Hint: It is a lot easier to see auras when you look with an open mind and receptive attitude, willing to see what is *really* there with honesty, integrity, and love rather than what you hope or fear might be there. If you already cultivate your inner spiritual self through meditation and/or prayer, you can naturally develop this kind of clarity as you find yourself becoming more open to seeing auras. You will also have a much easier time seeing and feeling your aura at times when you are feeling relaxed or even—believe it or not—full of energy! Most of all, have fun doing the exercises in this chapter and realize that every minute you spend practicing the art of seeing and feeling the aura, you are developing your innate human ability to sense the energy body.

Listed below are three techniques for viewing auras in everyday things, and four techniques for viewing and feeling your own aura. Try all of them and use the ones that work best for you: you will likely find that certain techniques work better for you than others. Some people (even aura reading experts) don't actually see colors shimmering in auras, but instead get mental impressions or images of colors, symbols, or feelings as they focus their attention on various areas they observe. All of these different forms of sensing work just fine, and you can relax in the knowledge that you will begin to develop your abilities naturally in accordance with your life path and who you are. Just as you can learn to utilize the five fingers on your non-dominant hand, you can also develop high sense perception for touch, taste, sight, smell, and sound. We tend to use our five logical senses and five dominant hand fingers most of the time, but we can glean much more information when we learn to access our intuitive high sense perception (the sixth through tenth senses). These additional senses are the high sense perception versions of our primary five senses.

One great way to begin getting a sense of how energy fields shimmer and shine around everything is by looking at the auras around plants, animals, and rocks. It may seem a bit odd to you to start aura viewing by looking at things rather than people, but many people find it easier to first view auras of everyday objects and animals before looking at their own aura. For one thing, a houseplant or tree stays very still, and doesn't mind if you stare at it for a long time!

As you go through the following exercises in this chapter, please note that there is a table of helpful suggestions included at the end. If you encounter problems viewing auras and could use a helpful hint or two, check the troubleshooting guide.

Exercise: Viewing Plant Auras

1. Pick a time of day when you feel rested and alert, and will not be interrupted. If you like, put on some soothing music you like to relax to, and enjoy a favorite non-alcoholic beverage. Prepare a comfortable chair for you to sit on in a softly lit room, which has an off-white wall or background.

2. Select a healthy houseplant, preferably one with many green leaves (healthy plants have brighter, easier-to-see auras) and place it in front of the off-white background, in a place where you can sit near it and view it easily. You can also view a plant outdoors, if you wish—just be sure that you select a viewing location where you can gaze without interruption for several minutes on a day without much wind.

3. Sit down within three feet of the plant. Relax, breathe regularly and deeply, shut your eyes, and imagine yourself grounded to the center of the earth from the base of your spine.

4. Gently stroke or tap your forehead between your eyebrows and hairline. This area corresponds to the location of your sixth chakra, also known as the third eye. It is associated with the pituitary gland, and it will need to be healthy and open for you to see auras clearly. You can stimulate it by gently tracing a circle with a diameter of two inches softly and slowly on your forehead, feeling a tingling sensation as you intend for this chakra to be open, clear, healthy, and active. This sixth chakra is also the first recipient of psychic and intuitive information, so as you begin to see auras, you will likely become more psychically aware as well.

5. Open your eyes. Without focusing your eyes directly on the edges

of the leaves, look between them with your eyes focused as if on an imaginary leaf in that precise location.

6. Continue gazing at the spot you have selected until you begin to notice a shimmering aura extending out from the plant's leaves. You are seeing the plant's aura! Keep watching the aura, and notice what colors you see (if any) and where the aura seems to be strongest and brightest. If there is a break or tear or some other kind of damage to the plant, notice if you can see anything different around that area. Often, the aura will extend through the damaged area even when part of the plant is missing, demonstrating the famous "phantom limb" effect that was popularized with Kirlian photography (in which auras can be photographed as high voltage current is passed between two electrodes with the photographic subject— such as a leaf—sandwiched in between).

7. If you wish, you may draw the colors and shapes you observe in a journal. ◎

It's fun to view the auras of plants because they are conscious, living things that sit still so you can view them clearly. When plants have been hooked up to lie detector equipment, they've shown strong negative responses to being around someone who simply *thought* about burning a leaf,[5] and responded equally strongly when a visitor arrived who killed plants for a living.[6] Other researchers working with plants have found that they respond in a positive way to someone who feels love for them.[7] When I participated in recent plant studies conducted at the Institute of Noetic Sciences, I could see the auric field of the plant expand as it responded to IONS Senior Scientist Dean Radin, author of numerous scientific research papers investigating various psychic phenomena.[8] The plant reacted each time Radin stroked a tender new leaf, or brought some water for it when its soil was dry. At the same time as the plant's aura field increased, the ECG-like monitoring equipment displayed a prolonged spike.

You can see how your plants respond to your loving thoughts and gentle leaf massage by watching their auric fields, and find out what they like by noticing what expands their auras. Best of all, by being more loving with your plants, you'll probably feel happier about yourself, and note an improvement in your aura as well!

One of the fun things about learning to view auras is that the world will never quite look the same again, even if you only see a little bit of aura shining on a plant. You won't need any fancy equipment, and can enjoy your newfound skill anywhere there are plants. You can talk to your plants, and see how they respond to the love in your voice. The beautiful thing about auras is that they show us the possibility that mystics and spiritual teachers are right and everything really *is* conscious—and that consciousness shines forth like beams of light from everything and everyone around us.

Now that you've looked at a plant's aura, let's take a look at something completely inanimate, which nonetheless will shine with an aura uniquely its own.

Exercise: Viewing Object Auras

1. Select an object that has some meaning to you. You can use any object, of course, but objects that are cared for and loved will have stronger, easier-to-view auras. For example, a crystal or gemstone you really love would be an excellent viewing subject.

2. Place this object in a softly lit room with natural or indirect light, in front of an off-white background where you can sit about three feet away from it and view it easily.

3. Relax, breathe deeply and evenly, close your eyes, and imagine yourself being grounded to the center of the earth with an energy cord running down from the base of your spine.

4. Continuing your relaxed, even breaths, gently stroke or tap your forehead between your eyebrows and hairline to help stimulate your third eye chakra.

5. Sit comfortably, breathe deeply and evenly, and open your eyes. Without focusing your eyes directly on the object, look just to one side of it, or above it.

6. Continue gazing at the spot you have selected until you begin to notice a shimmering field of energy extending out from the object. You are looking at its aura! Notice what colors you see, and how the aura is distributed around the object. Are there places where the aura seems stronger?

7. If you want to see how an object's aura interacts with another object or plant, repeat this exercise with either two objects or an object and a plant. Notice what happens to the auras as you move them closer together; try positioning them differently and see what happens next. I love watching auric fields in action!

8. It's a great idea to record your observations while they are still fresh in your mind by drawing them in a notebook or journal. ◎

Hopefully, you were able to see an aura for the object you viewed, which goes to show that there is energy behind each and every physical thing. When you view this energy, you can see the way it responds to others in its environment, and how even a so-called inanimate object appears to be rather lively!

Exercise: Viewing Animal Auras

1. Choose an animal (preferably a pet that is resting or will sit still for you) for auric viewing. Wait and watch it until it settles down with you situated between three and ten feet away.

2. Relax, breathe deeply and calmly, rest your eyes, make yourself comfortable, and imagine yourself grounded to the center of the earth.

3. Gently stroke or tap your forehead between your eyebrows and hairline to stimulate your third eye chakra.

4. Open your eyes, and focus them at the same general location as the animal, but just a couple of inches away from it. Continue gazing just

an inch away from the animal until you see light shining forth. Notice what colors you see, if any, and where they are brightest.

5. If you happen to have two or more animals and they are resting together, you can observe their combined aura. Auras will often blend together, especially in groups that feel closely connected to one another. Notice if there is an especially bright place in the group aura, and if any bright auric links exist between animals with strong affection for one another.

6. If you like, sketch your animal aura picture in a journal or note-book. ◎

Now that you've taken a look at the auras in everyday plants, animals, and objects, you're ready to move on to the most important step—viewing and feeling your own aura! Once you learn to view your own aura, you will be able to discern ways to clean and brighten it to start enjoying better health, prosperity, and happiness. And who knows? Perhaps someone very special will notice a more radiant you, too!

Shining Bright with Inner Light

When you learn how to read auras, you will begin to recognize greatness in the people around you, even when they may seem ordinary or unremarkable otherwise. Using this skill, you can befriend those who are destined for greatness. You can find excellent friends, colleagues, employees, and even lovers by their energy fields. One such tale of auric discovery is Krishnamurti's. At the age of fourteen years, he was "found" by the Theosophical Society in 1909 when C. W. Leadbetter noticed "an aura of such brightness and glory as no one else in Adyar had" around the little boy while he was playing at the beach with his brother. Thanks in part to special training, education, and public exposure provided by Theosophists Leadbetter and Annie Besant, Krishnamurti became one of the world's great spiritual teachers. Some of those who considered him to be a great personal influence on their lives include Joseph Campbell, David Bohm, Henry Miller, Deepak Chopra, and Van Morrison. He was widely known in the western world as a beloved world teacher, and all of this was made possible because he was identified early on as having an extremely bright aura. Krishnamurti's bright aura may have saved his life. He had tuberculosis as a child, and owes his life to the excellent health care he received after being "discovered."[9] Krishnamurti's aura must have been truly amazing for it to have transcended the typical aura of someone suffering from tuberculosis.

Before we start the exercises for viewing the human aura, let's take a checkpoint. How are you feeling about your success so far with auric viewing? If you feel disappointed that you aren't yet seeing shining beams of color, please realize that it usually takes some time to develop full auric sight. Most people start by seeing a blurry blue haze around the perimeter of their viewing subject's skin.[10] With practice, your auric sight will improve. One day, when you least expect it, you may find yourself seeing auric fields everywhere! Just relax, and rest assured that the more you work on developing your aura viewing skills, the sooner you'll be seeing auras all around you.

Seeing Your Own Aura

We'll now try out four different techniques for viewing your *own* aura, so you can see which one feels best for you. Three of these techniques can be done entirely alone, and one requires help from a friend.

Exercise for Seeing Your Own Aura: Hands

1. Find a place where you can view your hands in natural or indirect light, with an off-white background. Paper or sheets of fabric do nicely, as do off-white-colored walls.

2. Relax, breathe deeply and calmly, rest your eyes, and imagine yourself grounded to the center of the earth.

3. Gently stroke or tap your forehead between your eyebrows and hairline to stimulate the third eye chakra.

4. Extend one hand as comfortably as possible at arm's length, and rest it in a comfortable position where it can stay for several minutes.

5. Gaze at an imaginary spot located halfway between your index finger and thumb, keeping your vision focused exactly where you imagine that spot to be. By not looking directly at your fingers and adjusting your focus, you improve your chances of seeing your aura.

6. Remember one of the happiest days of your life, and how good you felt at the very best moment of that day. Continue gazing at that imaginary spot between your index finger and thumb, until you start to see the aura around your fingers.

7. Once you see your aura, notice what colors it has, and how it is distributed around your thumb, palm, and fingers. Is it even, or is it stronger in one place than another? Draw a sketch of what you see in a journal or notebook, using colored pencils or crayons if you wish, and making note of how you were feeling at the time. ◎

How did you like this exercise? This hand-viewing exercise is a great one to repeat often because it's so simple to do, and you might find you can practice it when you are in a waiting room or any other time when you have a few extra minutes on your hands. I hope you took a few minutes to make a simple sketch of your aura, if you saw one this time. Keeping a record of what you observe is something that you'll grow to appreciate as you start developing your auric viewing abilities and noticing differences in your aura. It's fun to see how much easier aura viewing gets the more you do it!

Exercise for Seeing Your Own Aura: Mirror Image

1. Stand three to six feet away from a mirror. A full-length mirror works best here, but if you do not have one, a mirror that allows you to see most of your upper torso will do.

2. Relax, breathe deeply and calmly, rest your eyes, and imagine yourself grounded to the center of the earth.

3. Gently stroke or tap your forehead between your eyebrows and hairline to help ensure your third eye chakra is open.

4. While looking at the mirror, focus your vision just a couple of inches away from the perimeter of your face or shoulders, at the same focal length (staring at an imaginary dot just off to the side of you).

5. Eventually, you will see a ring of light shining around the edges of your body—what colors do you see? Which parts of you are shining more brightly?

6. Make your aura stronger for easier viewing by relaxing and remembering a favorite experience, person, or pet. As you feel love and joy, breathe out any resentments and worries. Your aura appears larger and brighter when you exhale, and contracts closer to your body with each inhalation. ◎

Now that you've tried a couple of exercises, compare the results. Do you find it easier to view your aura in the mirror, or by looking at your hands? Whatever you find easier is the one to keep practicing. Eventually, when you feel fully competent at a given technique, you may find you also have success with all the other techniques, too.

Exercise: Listen to and Feel Your Chakras

Your chakras are the power centers that keep your aura in vibrant, healthy condition. These seven primary energy vortices are positioned near the body's endocrine glands along the spinal cord, and have been called so many different names by different cultures that we'll keep it simple by referring to each chakra by number. Each chakra is associated with a particular layer of the auric field, and is also associated with a neighboring gland and organ nearby. The frequency of vibration of each chakra is slightly higher as they go up the body toward the head. In this exercise, you will be learning to hear the layers of your aura by listening to each of your chakras, or energy centers. Imagine that you can feel their vibrations. Everything in this universe vibrates, and these vibrations have audio, textural, and visual components. Mystics have associated certain colors and musical notes with each of the seven primary chakras in the human body. By taking a close look at the colors you carry closest to you, and by feeling your chakras, you can begin to appreciate and energize yourself in a whole new way.

1. **The First Chakra**—The first chakra is also known as the kundalini, base, or root chakra. It is located at the base of your spine, and is the center of energy for survival and sexuality. This is your grounding chakra that connects you to the earth, and it is associated with the adrenal glands. Your first chakra can give you sudden bursts of strength and energy when you need it, since it is responsible for your basic survival and sexual energy. With your "inner vision," focus your attention on this chakra and see if you can notice any color to it. This chakra is often associated with the color red, and the musical note middle "C" or the "Do" part of the "Do-Re-Mi" song from the musical *The Sound of Music*.

2. **The Second Chakra**—The second chakra is located just below your navel, is the center of your emotions and gender identity, and is associated with the gonads. This chakra is sometimes referred to as the Dan Tien in Chinese medicine, or the hara or sacral chakra. This is the place in which you may find yourself feeling what others are feeling, or inadvertently picking up other peoples' issues. It is easy to accidentally pick up "other peoples' stuff" in this area, but you can clear that out by meditating on restoring this chakra to its naturally balanced state. With eyes shut, notice what color this chakra below your navel appears to be and if you can hear its sound. The second chakra often appears orange, and resonates to the musical note "D" or the "Re" part of the "Do-Re-Mi" song.

3. **The Third Chakra**—Next, take a look at your solar plexus, between your navel and sternum—just below your lower ribs. The third chakra is associated with the pancreas, and is your center for relating to feelings of power communicated between you and your environment. This is the energy center in your body that aligns your physical body with your spirit and intellect, and is your center for self-esteem. The third chakra is a very powerful chakra that can control and manipulate incoming energy. If you are in difficult situations, you may notice discomfort in your stomach, and this tells you that you can benefit from strengthening your third chakra. What color do you see when you view it? What sound does it make? Typically, this chakra appears yellow and sounds like the musical note "E" or the "Mi" note in the "Do-Re-Mi" song.

4. **The Fourth Chakra**—Your fourth chakra is located near your heart, and is also referred to as the "heart chakra." The fourth chakra is associated with the thymus gland. This chakra connects your spirit to your physical body, and allows you to channel love energy both inside your body and out into the world. A compassionate sense of humor is a sign of a healthy fourth chakra—you can see this in people who laugh at their own foibles with good-natured fun. A healthy fourth chakra allows one to keep a healthy perspective even in the most troubling situations. Feel the area surrounding your heart, and see if you can get a vision of color. Listen to hear a sound. The fourth chakra is usually seen as being green, and often heard as the musical note "F" or "Fa."

5. **The Fifth Chakra**—Examine your fifth, or throat chakra next. Your fifth chakra corresponds to the thyroid gland, and is the center for expressive communication and making and keeping commitments. This chakra is the center for receiving clairaudient information (hearing voices), which allows people to hear psychic truths from seemingly mundane sources. What do you see, feel, and hear? The fifth chakra is your expressive center of communication, and is often seen as being sapphire or sky blue, and heard as the musical note "G" or "Sol."

6. **The Sixth Chakra**—Move your focus of attention to your forehead or third eye chakra. This sixth chakra is associated with the pituitary

gland, and is responsible for providing tremendous amounts of psychic information in a naturally clairvoyant manner. A healthy sixth chakra can ensure that you are on the right path in your life, and are constantly finding support and valuable information every day—sometimes in the most unusual and offbeat places. Notice what sound, vibration, or color you can sense here. The sixth chakra is related to your higher mental and intuitive abilities, and is frequently seen as being the color indigo, and heard as the musical note "A" or "La," which is generally agreed upon by musicians to correspond to 440 hertz. This is the note played on the oboe when an orchestra tunes up, and it's known as middle A on the keyboard.

7. **The Seventh Chakra**—Focus your attention on the area slightly above the very top of your head—at the place you would wear a hat, this is the seventh, or crown chakra. This chakra is associated with the pineal gland, and it is the chakra that connects your energy body to spirit, and where you receive information about your life purpose and spiritual path. This seventh chakra provides you with the highest level of spiritual knowledge, and a deep understanding of who and what you truly are. Notice what frequency you sense here. This is the chakra that connects your energy body to divine spirit—it is where you gain spiritual insights to your own spiritual life path. Do you hear a sound, or feel a vibration? What colors (if any) do you see? The color violet is often associated with this seventh chakra, as is the musical note "B" or "Ti" or "Si." Write and draw what you notice in the aura journal at the end of this chapter.

8. **The Hand Chakras**—Take a look at your hands. These chakras are secondary (not part of the line of chakras along your spinal column), but are very important for the way you do your work and take and give things to the world. What sound or colors do you see as you look at your hands?

9. **The Foot Chakras**—Examine your foot chakras. Like the hand chakras, these are secondary chakras, yet are very vital to your health and well-being. Your foot chakras help you connect to the earth and maintain and demonstrate a sense of self and presence. They also help you feel grounded. What colors and sounds do you see and hear when you look at your feet? ◎

You may or may not have much initial success with viewing colors and hearing sounds in your aura—a lot depends on the way you receive this kind of intuitive information. *But don't give up!* Like all intuitive perceptual abilities, you can develop your skill at this with time and practice, so try it again later if it didn't work for you this time.

Aura Viewing Troubleshooting Guide

Do you need help with some of the aura viewing techniques mentioned in this chapter? It's normal to have questions about what you experience when you first start looking at auras. Remember—aura viewing is something that can take time and practice to really develop as a working skill, so please have patience! When you practice a little bit each day (or week), you will notice gradual and steady improvement.

The following table contains tips to help get you up and running with the joy of successful aura viewing, by addressing the most common questions that come up when people learn how to view auras. This list of common problems also shows specific suggestions designed to resolve each problem.

Aura Viewing Troubleshooting Guide

Problem:

No matter how hard I try, I can't see auras at all.

Suggestion:

Stop trying so hard, and relax! Massage your third eye (forehead), play soothing music. Keep lights dim, viewing area clear of distractions, and your focus just aside of your viewing subject.

Problem:

I can't tell if what I think I see is actually an aura, or something else.

Suggestion:

It is normal to wonder at first what it is you are looking at, until you become accustomed to seeing auras.

Problem:

I can only see auras for one second, then they disappear.

Suggestion:

Stay relaxed with your eyes focused just off to one side of your subject. When the aura starts to become visible, do *not* look directly at the aura or change your focus.

Problem:

I can't see any colors in auras—just a blur.

Suggestion:

Auras look at first like whitish-blue blurry areas of light just around the perimeter of what you are looking at, and eventually (with practice) begin to show more definition of shape and variety of color.

Problem:

I feel frustrated when the aura flickers or shrinks back toward the subject.

Suggestion:

Keep practicing aura viewing and being relaxed while viewing auras, and this shrinking problem will go away. Keep practicing, stay calm, and hold your focus steady.

Chapter 4 Questions for Review and Reflection

1. Which aura viewing/sensing technique was most effective for you?
2. When you dowsed with wire hangers, did you feel the push and pull of energy around your subject?
3. How close did you get to your subject before you felt their energy field when you dowsed with wire hangers?
4. What kind of aura was the most fun for you to view and/or dowse (plant, animal, object, human)?
5. Which inanimate object that you viewed had the liveliest aura?
6. What aura viewing conditions helped you see auras most clearly (outdoors, indoors, music on or off)?
7. Which of the techniques for sensing/seeing your own aura worked best for you (hands, mirror image, listening, and feeling chakras)?
8. What kind of aura interactions, if any, did you notice (between animals, between plant and object, between fingers of your hands)?
9. What did you observe when you viewed the aura of a broken or torn leaf?
10. What differences (if any) did you notice in viewing your own aura while you were in different moods/energetic states?

Chapter 5
Strengthen and Transform Your Aura

A strong, centered aura can bring many magical experiences into your life. I had one such experience a few years ago. When my friend who was working with the Navajo tribe invited me to come see some sacred petroglyphs carved in ancient rock walls near Albuquerque, New Mexico, I eagerly agreed. My friend showed me how to place both of my hands in hand print carvings to most fully feel the energy from them. The energy of this sacred place was strong, and she explained how it was important to always have another person along when feeling the energy of these petroglyphs, since there was risk of literally being blown away by the energy of such a sacred space. Standing near the walls, I could indeed feel the power of the place.

When I touched the two hand print petroglyphs carved onto a vertical face of stone, I felt nothing different. Thoughts from an earlier discussion wandered through my mind, and I heard an airplane fly overhead. I then thought, "I must *let go* of all these distractions." The instant I let go, the wind picked up and I felt subtle energy surging around me. I saw a purplish circle of energy in front of me, and felt an unmistakable sense of calm. I savored these sensations for several minutes, then moved away to give my friend some private time with the petroglyphs.

As I rested quietly on a rock, I offered some mineral spring water I had brought from California to the rocks, some to the sun-parched soil, and some to small leafy plants growing at my feet . . . and then I drank a swig. As I did this, I silently thanked spirit for bringing me here, and felt my love for life and spirit and all that is. I then asked spirit, "Am I truly welcome on American Indian land? Am I an uninvited outsider, or a welcome part of all this beauty?" I exhaled my doubt, and breathed in love and compassion. Just then, two shining eyes appeared in the brush in front of me, and a five-foot-long diamondback rattlesnake smoothly approached me. The snake looked directly at me as it closed the distance between us with each swish of its sinewy body. My friend had a great fear of snakes, but I sensed that this snake was approaching me with purpose and curiosity about my auric field of love. As the giant rattler came within six feet of me, I broke the silence and calmly asked my friend, "Excuse me, but do you know what kind of snake this is?" As I spoke these words, the rattlesnake stopped.

My friend took one slow step back from the petroglyphs and said, "That is a dangerous snake. A *very* dangerous snake. You should pick up your things and slowly move away." We moved about twenty feet away, and the rattlesnake turned from us and began winding away toward some shady rocks. I felt the snake's message to me was, "We are with you. We are strong. We treat you with respect . . . as you treat us."

When you learn to enhance your aura, you'll get speedy answers to your questions, and achieve safety even in dangerous situations. You may even find that your life will become much more magical, enchanted, and divine.

Top Ten Ways to Enhance Your Aura

By following these simple ten steps to good auric health, you can significantly improve your chances of attracting what you *really* love to your life! The first five steps are part of a daily auric energy practice, and the last five are an ongoing, long-term energy practice, which are part of the life of anyone who wishes to become healthier.

1. **Ground**—Clear out all unessential energy from your aura by visualizing a grounding cord from the base of your spine to the center of the earth. Let go of all your worries and fears about the future and frustrations with the past. When you have let go of all that, you can feel what is real, *right now*.

2. **Assess Your Energy Centers**—Once you've grounded, chances are good that your first chakra is open and all negative energy is swirling away. Look at your next chakra up, the second chakra, and feel how your body feels there. If you are tense, allow those tensions to drop down to the root chakra and drop away. Continue up all seven chakras, feeling how your body feels and letting go of tensions as you find them.

3. **Meditate**—Whether you practice a traditional style of meditation or simply take regular breaks from the pressures of your daily routine, all such relaxation provides you with much needed stress relief that gives your aura a chance to recharge itself.

4. **Energize**—Visualize your energy field growing and expanding with love. Remember all the people, places, and things you have loved the most and who love you the most, and bask in the radiant light of that love!

5. **Seal Your Aura**—Since you don't want to lose your new-found sense of energy body balance and power, you can now benefit from visualizing that your energy is your own and not to be taken by others. While sitting down, cross your ankles and gently press your fingertips together, reinforcing your visualization that your energy is your own.

6. **Rest**—Get enough sleep every day. A general rule of thumb is that if you awaken naturally of your own accord

(without need of alarm clock or someone else awakening you) and feel refreshed and well rested, you've gotten enough sleep.

7. **Eat a Balanced, Nutritious Diet**—Eat plenty of fresh fruits, vegetables, and grains.

8. **Naturalize Yourself**—Spend time (as much as possible) outdoors in natural settings. Breathe fresh air; feel the earth beneath your feet; wriggle your toes joyously in grass, sand, and water! Children who often play outdoors usually have very bright auras, and their playful attitude helps keep them young and healthy. The earth has tremendous restorative energy that she shares generously.

9. **Exercise Your Physical Body**—Do whatever regular exercises you feel comfortable with that help you maintain and develop your strength, flexibility, and cardiovascular systems.

10. **Watch and Minimize Your Drug Consumption**—Minimize drugs (alcohol, stimulants, psychedelics), with exception of those recommended by your physician.

These ten steps are easy to remember in sequence, because the first letter in each of them taken together spells out a reminder message, "GAMES RENEW." Remember to be playful as you "work" to enhance your aura! You can gain the most advantage from these ten steps when you make them an integral part of your life. You'll likely find that these steps are familiar, which shouldn't be very surprising. After all, what's good for your physical body is also good for your energy body!

Below, we'll take a closer look at each one of these steps, so you can get a better idea of how to most fully incorporate the ideas that work best for you in your life.

Ground

Grounding is mentioned so often that some people feel inclined to skip over it, figuring that it's such a basic thing that it probably takes care of itself. It *is* a basic thing, and that is pre-cisely why it's so important that you remember periodically to make sure you are grounded! You are an energy being, and without ensuring that your extra energy is grounded, you run the risk of inadvertently creating chaos around you.

To ground yourself, simply visualize a sturdy energy cord running down from the base of your spine to the center of the earth. Imagine how this cord carries every single worry, doubt, fear, grudge, anxiety, and resentment that you have been holding onto. Know that when you let go of all these feelings, you will not lose anything. When you need to be reminded of something, you will feel inspired to remember it. You can release all this energy to the earth for recycling, and feel your-self relieved of what has probably been a pretty heavy burden for some time. Just let it all go, and feel how much cleaner and lighter you feel.

Grounding is something you can do for your family, your coworkers, and your friends. Every social situation improves when the group energy has been properly grounded—espe-cially if emotions are running high. I've attended some meetings that ignored this principle and some that have adhered to it, and found that groups that requested all participants to ground themselves before beginning were more productive and suf-fered fewer of the "Murphy's Law" types of glitches. Electrical and mechanical equipment is especially sensitive to human energy fields, and much unnecessary difficulty can be averted when everyone takes a few minutes at the beginning of any group meeting to get grounded. Since there are numerous exer-cises that involve grounding your own energy mentioned throughout this book, in the following exercise we'll practice grounding the energy of a group of people.

Exercise for Grounding: Grounding a Group

1. The next time you find yourself in a group of people, make a decision about how you wish to involve the group in the grounding process. You can do the grounding for a group without telling anyone present what you are doing—or you can announce to the group your intention to do a group grounding, and request their participation. You can also make a group announcement of your intent to do the grounding, and then do it all yourself. The process is pretty much the same no matter which choice you make, although the outcome may vary depending on how open people in the group are to the idea of a group grounding exercise.

2. If you choose to involve the group consciously in the grounding, make an announcement of your intention, and walk them through the process out loud. If you choose to simply announce the grounding, then do that before you begin.

3. Visualize each person's aura in the group and their energy centers all lined up from each person's crown to their root chakra. Imagine that every person is connected via energy cords to source/spirit/oneness at the crown chakra, and to earth via an energy cord from the root chakra to the center of the earth.

4. Visualize that all group members are energetically connected to one another through a central "group" energy point, which is also connected to the divine source above and the earth below.

5. Feel all the worries and resentments from the group drop away down to the center of the earth, and feel the group's energy being restored and refreshed from the divine source above and the earth below. ◎

Assess Your Energy Centers

When you review your energy centers every day, you become intimately familiar with which of your energy centers tend to become blocked, shut down, or uncentered. You are your own best energy monitor, and as you become familiar with how you feel stress in your body and chakras, you will be well on your way to learning to identify the source of the pain/stress blockage and looking at what is causing the problem. Your situation (no matter how difficult or bad it might seem) is not the *cause* of your pain and disease in your body and chakras—your *perception* of what is happening is what is increasing or reducing the pain you feel. By taking time each day to assess how you are feeling, chakra by chakra, you can learn to identify your own areas that most need assistance. If you have difficulty sensing your chakras, just pay attention to how your body is feeling, and where the tension and discomfort tends to lodge.

Your chakras are the gateway between your body and the sources of your auric energy (both feminine earth energy and masculine spirit energy). Keeping them in good working order will provide you with an immediate and noticeable difference in the quality of your life. Each chakra has a unique and identifiable harmonic frequency of oscillation. The root chakra has 4 spokes to its wheel (viewed by some as looking something like petals on a lotus flower), the spleen chakra has 6 divisions, the navel chakra has 10, the heart chakra has 12, the throat chakra has 16, the brow chakra has 96, and the crown chakra has 972.[1] As you can see, the chakras increase their ability to handle higher frequencies as they go up from root to crown. These frequencies range from about 350 to 600 cycles per second (cps) all the way up to 200,000 cps.[2] The chakras help us handle this tremendous range of frequencies quite effectively. Each of our chakras has its own set of strengths, and you will feel best when all your chakras are up and running smoothly. People sometimes deal with emotional upsets and traumas by shutting down their chakras, in an attempt to shut out any further stress. Unfortunately, this approach to healing only serves to lock the trauma into the energy and physical body, which is something most of us don't wish to do! You can use a dowsing tool, such as a pendulum, to help you discern which of your chakras is most in need of some tender loving care. By first detecting how open each chakra is, and then feeling whatever emotions or feelings arise as you concentrate on each chakra, you can greatly assist your chakras in being the healthiest they can be. This will in turn help you be the healthiest you can be—physically, intellectually, emotionally, and spiritually.

Exercise to Assess Your Energy Centers: Dowsing Chakras with a Pendulum

1. Find some kind of small, heavy object (like a key, pendant, or ring) that you can attach to a ribbon, string, or chain in such a way that it is free to dangle about five to ten inches down. This will be your dowsing pendant for this exercise.

2. Hold this dowsing pendant gently but firmly by the end of the chain so that the object is free to move in circles and back and forth like the pendulum of a clock.

3. Find a comfortable place where you can lie down for 20–30 minutes uninterrupted, and ground that place, yourself, and your dowsing pendulum. Visualize an energy cord running down from your root chakra to the center of the earth that carries away all doubts, worries, fears, concerns, anxieties, and negative energies.

4. Visualize a cleansing blast of white divine energy in this location, to clear out all negativity that may have been lurking nearby.

5. Sitting down in a comfortable position and holding the pendant suspended by the end of its string or chain, ask the dowsing pendant what it will do to show you a "yes" answer to your questions. Make note of this. Ask what it will do to show you "no" and "maybe," and note these. Now you are familiar with your dowsing pendulum, and are ready to dowse your chakras!

6. Lie down on your back, with your head slightly elevated so you can see, and hold your dowsing pendulum a few inches above your root chakra at the base of your spine. Start by holding the dowsing pendulum completely still, and expect that the pendulum will twirl in a circular pattern, which will indicate how far open the chakra is. A healthy chakra is typically about three and a half inches in diameter. If you get no movement at all,

or very little movement, consider what you can do to help the situation for that particular chakra, which will then help improve your life.

7. Continue up through all chakras (spleen, navel, heart, throat, brow, and crown), checking to see how open each chakra is and what issues (if any) need to be reviewed and addressed. ◉

Meditate

If you already have a favorite kind of meditation, all you need to do is make sure you spend some time each day practicing it. While some benefits from meditation are felt immediately, such as feeling peaceful and energized, many accumulate over time. You'll get the most benefit when you make meditation a regular part of your life. Chapter 9 explores a variety of aura meditations you can use in your everyday life.

There is no "right" way to meditate, but there are ways to meditate that work best for you. You may be surprised to find out that any time you are doing a simple task, such as washing the dishes or folding laundry, you could also be meditating! If you take these moments to relax and let go of your worries and racing thoughts, then you are indeed meditating. You can also meditate while jogging, biking, walking, taking a bath, gardening, listening to music, and even driving (although caution must be advised any time you are operating heavy machinery). To make one of your favorite activities a meditation, simply choose a way to focus your attention, such as letting go of all thoughts as they arise, paying attention to your breathing, observing the patterns of your thoughts and feelings as a detached observer, feeling energy flowing through your body, or focusing on a mantra (one special word or idea). You can figure out what kinds of meditation will work best for you by combining a favorite activity with a kind of mental focus. When you combine these two separate elements, you'll have your very own customized meditation technique that's exactly right for you!

Exercise in Meditation: Finding Your Center

1. When you have twenty minutes of uninterrupted space and time, make yourself comfortable and relax. Breathe deeply in, and deeply out.

2. Starting with your feet, feel the sensation of how each foot is currently resting.

3. Slowly going up your body, feel the sensations in your ankles, calves, knees, and thighs. Do you feel tension, fatigue, or numbness? What are the sensations inside your body at each point?

4. Take at least a minute for each part of your body, as you slowly move upward, asking each part of your body how it feels.

5. When you reach the very top of your head, and ask it how it is feeling, allow your whole body to relax even further as you listen for the answer.

6. Close your eyes (if you haven't already), and allow yourself to feel how your whole body feels at once. As you continue breathing deeply in and out, you may find yourself swaying gently. This is completely normal! This kind of motion often accompanies strong inner energy flow.

7. With eyes shut, visualize where the center of your body is, and how it feels right now. Continue breathing deeply and slowly. ◎

Energize

Have you ever started your day feeling tired, worried, or just plain out of sorts? Some days seem to get off to a bumpier start than others, no matter what you do to avoid it. By learning to energize yourself any time you need a boost, you'll more rarely feel as if your day is out of your control.

On "down" days, we tend to question what we're doing and whether it's worth all the effort we put into it. We begin to doubt our personal relationships, work, and even time and energy spent on fun projects and hobbies. We may begin to feel like Humphrey Bogart in *Casablanca* when he asked, "Don't you sometimes wonder if it's worth all this? I mean what you're fighting for?"[3] If we don't check our energy fields and energize ourselves, down days may expand to consume weeks, months, and even years of our lives. In most cases, the cause of this malaise is low energy in our auras, which is something we can remedy. When we energize ourselves, self-doubt tends to disappear and all the areas of our life shine more brightly as we feel inspired again.

Every time we allow ourselves to feel how loved and loving we are, we energize our auras. Love and compassion are the real fuel of this universe, and they are freely available to us all! By simply spending a few minutes every day feeling this bounteous supply of love, you will find yourself feeling energized and better able to handle everything that comes your way. Everyday rituals as simple as looking at photos of loved ones or remembering the happiest times in your life will keep you feeling refreshed and recharged.

Exercise for Energizing: Energize Yourself with Love

1. Find a quiet place where you will not be interrupted for at least twenty minutes, and make yourself comfortable. You may sit or lie down for this exercise.

2. Imagine that you are totally, completely loved and adored for being exactly who you are. Everything you have done in your life, including the so-called "bad" things, have been steps along your path. You have learned and grown from every experience, and are a gift to the world just by *being* who you are.

3. Savor this feeling of being adored. Feel yourself being cradled with love, and allow yourself to enjoy and accept more love than anyone or anything has ever shown you all at once. If this energy was a touch you could feel, what would it feel like? If this was something you could see, what would it look like? If this was a smell, what would it smell like? Would it have a taste? Savor each and every one of these feelings, and bask in this feeling of love. ◉

Seal Your Aura

Your aura provides you with a certain degree of energetic protection from outside forces, and benefits if sealed off from uninvited intrusion. Open auras are like open-door invitations for any kind of energy to intrude in your space—and this should be avoided. Empathetic people who are natural healers often have unsealed auras, so they may feel undue stress and strain almost any time they are out in crowded public places. Symptoms may include headaches, cramps, depression, and nausea. By leaving your aura wide open, you can pick up all kinds of energetic and physical ailments from people around you. Sealing your aura before leaving home is a good way to avoid this problem.

Your energy body is ideally neither completely open to the outside world nor completely closed. Instead, it is open to beneficial interactions and closed to harmful ones. Any completely closed or completely open living system will be short-lived, since it needs to exchange energy with the outside world in healthy ways. As most near-death experiencers tell us about what they learn "on the other side," we live our lives for love. A little boy who was hit by a car and then met two people in "very white" robes explains, "What I learned there is that the most important thing is loving while you are alive."[4] We need to be open to give and receive love, yet we also need some degree of protection around our auric membrane, which acts like an energetic screen.

So what is the best way to set your energetic screen? All you need to do is consciously intend that you will only be contacted by energies that meet some basic criteria. For example, you can choose to only be contacted by energies of love, peace, or healing. Visualizing auric helpers to act as "bouncers" can also help keep your energy body and the energy in your surroundings clean and clear. Auric helpers can be angels, animal guides, or plants. Whatever you feel most comfortable acting on your behalf as an energy sentry will be just right for you.

Exercise: Sealing Your Aura

1. Visualize the outer perimeter of your aura. If you have trouble doing this, simply imagine how close you'd allow a wall to be situated on either side of you.

2. Imagine that the exterior surface of your aura is made of a substance that only allows beneficial things (based on love) to penetrate, and reflects all other energetic would-be intruders back to their sources. You can think of this surface treatment as being a kind of filter or screen, although you may prefer to visualize it as Teflon or a mirror.

3. Do a quick "chakra check" to confirm that none of your chakras are too wide open, and finish the aura sealing by visualizing yourself bathed in divine white light.

4. If you wish to request additional auric protection from angels, animal, or plant or mineral guides, thank them for assisting you in keeping your energy space clean and clear. ◎

Rest

Most Americans don't get enough sleep. Many of us are chronically sleep-deprived, and sometimes proud of it. "Sleep in America" Gallup polls conducted in 1991 and 1995 reported insomnia and other sleep-related disorders to have increased 15 percent in those four years—with 49 percent of all respondents reporting some kind of sleep deficiency.[5] By 2002, this number had risen to 58 percent of adults surveyed reporting difficulty sleeping "a few nights a week."[6] Another price we pay for skipping on sleep is that we don't fully restore our energy body. Vitamins and meditation can help compensate somewhat for the damage we do by skipping sleep, but they can never fully restore our aura to its full vibrant self.

When you are sleep-deprived, you are a danger to yourself and others because you are running your energy and your physical body down. Most people require an average of eight hours of sleep every twenty-four hours, some require less or more, and some notice that their sleep requirements change with other factors. You require good sleep in order to gain maximum benefit from your dreams, since people who are sleep-deprived seldom recall their dreams. Dreams give you the chance to review situations of importance to your subconscious mind, and provide you with intuitive insights and answers to questions such as, "What is the ideal kind of work for me to be doing?" that you ask yourself right before you go to sleep. If you have been sleep-deprived for some time, and then catch up on your sleep, you'll probably notice you dream a lot more as your body catches up on the dream time it needs.

If you find yourself awakening in the middle of the night, practice one of your meditations for clearing your mind and energizing yourself. Keep a dream journal by your bed and jot down notes and record ideas. When you awaken with a mental list of concerns, write them down and put them where you'll see them the next morning, and then practice clearing your mind and letting all that noise go. Whatever the concerns and ideas are, they can wait for a few more hours. Our subconscious minds can be full of excess nervous energy, and sometimes all that unguided energy feels a need to burst out somehow. Sleep is often the one time our subconscious feels it can get the attention of our conscious mind. You can soothe this restlessness by listening to your subconscious.

Exercise for Rest: Sleep Therapy

The next time you have a few days to yourself with no set schedule, try this easy form of sleep therapy to pamper yourself and re-energize your body. This simple change in sleeping patterns will yield spa-quality results without the expense of visiting a spa! Rather than going to sleep when you think you should, take naps whenever you feel a need for naps, and go to bed when you feel like it. Wake up naturally when you feel like waking up, without concern for what time of day it is or whether you're "supposed" to be asleep or awake. You will be astonished to find just how much better it feels to actually do this exercise. In just a few short days, you will feel a significant improvement in your energy level and your outlook on life! ◎

Exercise for Rest: Intending to Feel Well-Rested

In these busy times, you may find that you simply don't have enough time to get as much sleep as you feel is ideal for you. While there is no replacement for sleep, you can help the situation by boosting your energy field. If you find yourself going to sleep much later than usual, take a few minutes before drifting off to sleep to boost your energy field by assuring yourself that you will get the rest you need. You'll wake up feeling as though you've had a full night's rest, and with a brighter outlook for your day. ◎

Eat a Well-Balanced, Nutritious Diet

One of the fastest ways you can improve the health of your energy body is by making healthy changes to your diet. The food that is best for you is food that energizes you without negative side effects. Just as your energy body depends on a steady supply of positive energy, your physical body requires good positive sources of nutrition to function properly. Fresh and lightly cooked foods contain the most nutrients, give your aura the biggest boost, and are also often the tastiest. While greasy or sweet foods may taste good as you eat them, they often upset your energetic balance soon after consumption, and also have a negative effect on your energy field. Headaches are a common complaint among people who have food sensitivities to foods such as cheese, wheat, chocolate, wine, coffee, pickles, mushrooms, yogurt, sweets, and sourdough bread. Not drinking enough water can also lead to headaches, due to the fact that constipation often results from dehydration.[7] Good energy health and good physical health go together hand in hand!

If you find you need to eat meat in order to feel healthy, but worry about consuming other animals, you may be glad to know that *all* fresh foods appear to show signs of consciousness. The implications of this simple fact are that we need to be aware, respectful, and grateful for all the food we consume. Even store-bought, unfertilized eggs register great stress when they are cracked open before being eaten. American polygraph instructor Cleve Backster was startled to make this discovery one day when he cracked open an egg for his dog, and was amazed to see that these eggs produced galvanometer readings of 160 to 170 beats per minute (appropriate for a three- to four-day-old chicken embryo), even though they were completely free of a physical circulatory system. Cleve Backster also contributed to a better understanding of how plants react to what people think (such as detecting the secret identity of a plant killer). He demonstrated how when one plant is injured, the others around it immediately feel the shock of the traumatic event, as recorded by galvanometric instrumentation connected to the leaves of the plants. Backster also found that plants respond to human thoughts and feelings from a great distance, once they have become bonded with those individuals.[8]

Indian biologist Sir Jagadis Chandra Bose deepened the mystery of what is conscious and what is not when he found in 1899 that his metallic radio-wave receiver lost sensitivity during steady use, but returned to normal after rest. He was intrigued to see that warmed metals showed fatigue curves, which were indistinguishable from similar fatigue charts for animal muscles. Bose's interpretation of this and many similar studies of recovery from stress for other metals led him to conclude, "How can we draw a line of demarcation and say, here the physical ends, and there the physiological begins? Such barriers do not exist."[9]

When we acknowledge this evidence of the consciousness of all things and all food, we are well advised to follow the example set by indigenous peoples the world over who bless the spirit of that which has offered up its existence in order to sustain ours. You will likely feel better nourished when you ask your body what it hungers for, and thank the food that you eat. Such mealtime prayers do three things: (1) they improve the flavor, consistency, and nutritive quality of the food, (2) they prepare the diner to be relaxed and most receptive to the goodness of the food, and (3) they welcome the food to you who are about to encompass it.

Exercise in Eating: Welcoming Your Food

Say a prayer of gratitude to your food the next time you prepare and/or eat a meal. Create your own prayer of gratitude, or you can use this one:

"Thank you, food, for bringing your sustenance to me.

May love bless us both as I welcome you in my life." ◎

Naturalize Yourself

In this modern world it's hard to escape the mechanization of human-shaped environments and experience the natural world that was here long before we were. The natural balance of the earth's ecosystem enhances the energy fields of everything nearby. Therefore, truly wild places are a rare and special treasure on this earth. Whereas the energy of man-made spaces such as parks can be clean and bright, it rarely matches the full-spectrum frequency range of the energy in naturally wild areas. Natural spaces are coherent; the energies within them stick together and belong together as a unified, united whole.

You absorb the benefit of nature's energies when you spend time in natural surroundings. Whether you just take a few minutes to sit on a bench under a tree, or are able to spend a few days or weeks hiking and camping, every minute spent in healthy ecosystems boosts your energy body considerably! Healthy environmental ecosystems exude strong positive energies, which can be miraculously healing, as some people have been astonished and grateful to discover. When psychologist Warren Grossman returned home from a vacation in Brazil where a parasite had laid eggs in his liver, he was shocked to hear doctors tell him that death was inevitable—and in his weakened condition he would surely die within a week or so. Grossman was barely able to think rationally, but in one of his more cogent moments during his year-long illness, he decided to spend his time lying down on the earth outdoors. It was in this moment that Grossman realized "the Earth was very much alive," as he gazed at the gold energy flowing along the trunks of nearby trees. Grossman credits his miraculous recovery to the healing time he spent each day, receiving healing energy directly from the earth.[10]

Every natural thing can provide you with a sense of love and connection. If you don't have access to natural areas, lovingly tending to a rock, a plant, or an animal can be just as deeply satisfying. Grief counselors often bring pet dogs to provide pet therapy to families who have recently suffered a death, and many gardeners know that they feel best when gently tending to rows of herbs or flowers. Even a small desk-top rock garden or sand garden can provide soothing mental, emotional, and intellectual release for you if you allow the energies of the natural minerals to merge with your own. If you love plants, but can't spend much time outdoors, consider getting a miniature tree (bonsai) to care for and commune with all year long. The energy fields of natural beings are designed to support and sustain one another, and when you know this and welcome such natural interchanges into your life, you will feel a great deal more vitality.

All the earth's energy can be shared by us as long as natural areas remain here on earth. These areas are healing centers for anyone and everyone who is open to the experience of being healed by the earth. If you think you're too busy to make time for nature, consider just going on a daily walk at lunchtime or after dinner and getting some fresh air. And if you have a bit more time, give yourself a real treat and take a nap on the grass!

Exercise in Naturalizing Yourself: Hugging the Earth

On a day when the earth is not too cold, wet, hot, or dry for your comfort, bring a blanket and spread it out on the ground. Settle yourself down comfortably on the blanket however you wish. Feel all your gratitude for the gifts the earth has bestowed upon you. When you are feeling full of love for the earth, lie down on the blanket however you feel most comfortable and give her a big hug! Feel how your energy surges with hers, and if you wish, stay for a while. Take a nap on the blanket if you wish, and see what energies you continue to perceive. ◎

Exercise Your Physical Body

Regular exercise is one of the best things you can do for your energy body. Keeping yourself physically fit helps keep your inner energy flowing properly, and minimizes risk of internal energy blockages. Our energy bodies and physical bodies are so closely interconnected that many energy techniques focus on very physical meditations, such as breathing. Body movement can also clear out energy blockages. When you do certain exercises, such as moving your arms in figure-eight patterns around your body, you gain benefits from crossing energies from each hemisphere of the brain to the opposite side of your body. Donna Eden describes this "Celtic weave" as an energy exercise that many healers can hear on their clients who do it. They report that it sounds like "a musical hum or resonance," and that it greatly strengthens the aura.[11] Exercise can improve flexibility, muscle strength, and the cardiovascular system while it stimulates flow of your vital energy.

Moshe Feldenkrais created a new form of body/mind therapy that utilizes gentle movements in the body to help realign the body as the person receiving the treatment becomes more aware of how their body moves. The Feldenkrais system of helping people recognize and change the way they move is based on a fundamental principle that changing the habitual way we move our muscles will open us up to new ways of thinking and feeling.[12] The easiest way to change your habits is to change the way you use your muscles. When you do new things and move in new ways, you open new doors to knowing yourself and becoming the best you can be.

I received regular weekly Feldenkrais treatments from a skilled practitioner for a period of several months, and was astonished during this time in my life (late thirties) to regain mobility in my back and neck that I hadn't even realized I'd lost. I left each session feeling about one inch taller than when I'd come in. I wasn't just imagining that I was an inch taller, either. My practitioner pointed it out, and I had to adjust my car's rear-view mirror to accomodate my new height! Most of all, I regained a sense of balance and body self-awareness from these Feldenkrais treatments, which stayed with me long after the treatments came to an end. As my posture improved, I felt more energized.

Another benefit of exercise for auric health is that it helps establish slow, stable breathing patterns. Our physical bodies thrive when they get enough oxygen, since they are composed of 59 percent oxygen, and require more oxygen each day than any other nutrient. As you breathe more deeply, you will not be as oxygen-deprived. Typical humans consume 550 liters of pure oxygen each day, and people who are exercising use more than that. When you exercise, you develop better breathing habits in three ways: your resting rate of breathing decreases, your respiration rate during exercise increases, and you increase the volume of air exchanged with each breath. These breathing-related benefits from exercise continue to help you better oxygenate your blood at all times.

Use good judgment in developing your exercise regimen, and gradually increase the duration and intensity of your workout. Select whatever exercise program works best for you, whether it's walking around your neighborhood or going to the gym. If you are not able to do even these activities, then look into doing some kind of very gentle movements, like Feldenkrais. Exercises that consciously include breathwork, such as yoga, tai chi, karate, and Feldenkrais will give you the strongest improvement in your aura, but all forms of exercise can include energy work (and therefore be a variation of QiGong!) Whatever form of exercise you choose can be enhanced by adding a practice of conscious breathing to it, as you can see for yourself when you try the following exercise.

Exercise for Physical Exercise: Get More Qi in Your Physical Exercise

1. If you already have a regular exercise program, prepare to pay more attention to subtle energies as you practice it. If you don't already have a regular exercise program, select something you can do (such as walking) and get ready to add some Qi to it!

2. As you begin your exercise, moving very slowly, breathe in and visualize vital energy flowing inside you, replenishing your energy reserves and giving you greater stamina, strength, and vitality. As you breathe out, feel your aura expand and shine more brightly.

3. Keep moving, feeling each breath deeply filling your lungs with air and your body with Qi. After several minutes and repeats of this, proceed with your exercise workout as usual. ◎

Watch and Minimize Your Drug Consumption

Drugs of all types can wreak havoc with your energy body. This includes substances that people often don't think of as drugs, such as coffee, caffeinated beverages, and food that contains lots of refined sugars. Cigarettes and alcohol are notorious for damaging auras, and they are well known for causing serious damage to the physical body as well. While the physical effects of drug use or abuse may take months or years to manifest in the form of disease, the damage to the human energy field is dramatic and immediate. The best thing you can do for your aura is to completely eliminate all manner of drugs from your life, to ensure that you are not continually damaging your energy body. If you find you can't or won't stop consuming some kind of drug, then at least do your best to minimize the amount you are taking. The exception to this general guideline is medicine that has been prescribed by your physician. Naturally, if your personal care providers recommend that you take drugs for better health and the medicine feels like it is doing a good job for you, then you are well advised to follow their recommendation.

There has been a great deal of interest and debate in recent years about the negative effect of medications that are improperly prescribed or have side effects. Antidepressants, estrogen, and antihyperactivity drugs are being prescribed at record levels, and in many cases are not truly necessary. In some cases, depending on the person and his or her sensitivity to a given medication, these medications can even be damaging to peoples' auras. You need to be aware of your body's needs when evaluating effectiveness of your medications, and thoroughly research a particular medication before taking it. The field of pharmaceuticals is ever changing, as doctors discover safer and more effective medicines, and it is important for you to be aware of the options available to you. Sometimes, herbal and dietary remedies are available that are better for your aura and also have fewer side effects than chemical medications. Consult your physician about the best treatment for your needs.

All addictions—whether to caffeine, nicotine, or more serious drugs—will interfere with your goal of improving the health of your aura. In order to truly improve your auric health, you must honestly assess your life and ask yourself if you are willing to change habits that do not serve to improve your energy level. If the answer is "no," recognize that by choosing to continue with your addiction you are limiting yourself.

Remain alert for future opportunities to release yourself from your addictions and take control of your life.

Here's a checklist of common aura-damaging substances:

- Sugar
- Caffeine
- Nicotine
- Alcohol

- Opiates
- Sedatives
- Stimulants
- Hallucinogens

Exercise for Watching Your Drug Consumption: Self-Assessment
Which substances listed above are common to your life that could be adversely affecting your energy body? Can you recognize how these substances may be reducing your energy? Are you willing to consider minimizing your consumption of them? Why or why not? ◎

Chapter 5 Questions for Review and Reflection

1. What is the memory phrase to remind you of the top ten ways to enhance your aura?
2. Think of one thing you can do today to enhance your aura.
3. What can you do to improve your auric health if you find yourself feeling drained or suddenly ill while in a public place?
4. What are the three ways you can use to ground a group of people, and which do you most prefer?
5. How can you use a pendulum to dowse your chakras?
6. What nutrient does your body consume and require most?
7. How can you get enough rest even when there aren't enough hours for you to sleep?
8. How can you be healed by the earth?
9. Think of a habit you have broken. How did you do it?
10. Which addictions have no effect on auric health?

Chapter 6

Attract What You Most Desire

ike a car, your aura will help you be at the right place at the right time when it's in good working condition. No longer will you find yourself attracting things, people, and situations that you don't thoroughly enjoy. Is there something you long for with all your heart, but feel is out of your reach? Whether you seek a satisfying career, a happy home life, friends, health, money, or love—chances are good that your heart's desire is much closer than you realize. When your aura is large, energized, and well connected, you'll naturally attract to you all that you expect to receive. Your aura is the only "good luck" charm you'll ever need, and by learning about your aura's inner workings, you can help it function even better than it ever has before.

There is a great gift in learning from our mistakes, and in noticing patterns in our life that we want to stop repeating. A man once told me, "I seem to keep finding myself in the same relationship, even though I meet, date, and marry a different woman each time. Each time I fall in love, I feel certain that I've found the love of my life. After a while, however, I discover that once again, I've married someone who is going to hurt me. I don't understand how this can keep happening to me. How can

I break this cycle and find someone I'll be truly happy with? I don't want to keep marrying the same woman!"

Someone who keeps attracting people who cause him harm is attracting exactly the kind of relationships that his subconscious mind most needs. He may have felt he was overly controlled by a domineering mother and abandoned by an alcoholic father, and his subconscious mind accepts those parameters as "normal home life," and tends to seek out women who provide him with those familiar qualities. As long as his conscious mind is unaware of this "hidden agenda" deep in his subconscious mind, psychologists will tell him that he is probably doomed to "keep marrying the same woman."[1] Fortunately, once your conscious mind becomes aware of the pattern you are repeating, you can begin a process of inner change.

This chapter will first review the three ways your energy body operates to attract what you most desire, and then present the six basic skills that will help you attract life situations that are most enjoyable for you. When we better understand the way our auric membrane and strings interact in the world, we begin to see how we are a defining part and co-creator of the web of life.

Expectation: What You Expect Is What You Get

The things we fixate on in our thoughts and charge with great emotional energy will likely come into being. Because we tend to most strongly attract people, things, and situations to us along unconscious auric cords, it helps to energize and release our desires in order to see them fulfilled. Buddhist teachings emphasize the importance of such detachment, since clutching tightly to a fantasy of what we wish to have keeps our hands full of fantasy instead of dream-come-true reality. It is in the release of our vision of our dreams that our dreams can attain a life of their own and return to us, fully formed in reality. When we give our dreams sufficient degrees of freedom to come true as they prefer, and don't look too closely, even the most amazing wishes can come true. We therefore have the ability to make changes in the physical world without lifting a finger.[2]

We continually draw to us that which we are most emotionally charged about. The key to attracting what we desire is to defuse our emotional attachments to troublesome things while visualizing truly enjoyable things, and feeling relaxed and confident about their arrival in our lives. You yourself *are* energy that is directed by the focus of what you are looking for. For example, when your day is going badly and you stay focused on that frame of mind, your day seems to just keep getting worse. Positive thinking is an important step in attracting what you desire. Visualize desired results rather than emphasizing your mistakes—see the cup as half full rather than half empty. By making these small changes, you will begin to attract more positive energy into your life.

This idea that "what you expect is what you get" has even been observed in scientific experiments by physicists who wanted to understand the nature of the smallest building blocks of matter. They were startled to discover that electrons behave like particles *or* waves, depending on what the physicists were expecting to see. Electrons showed a deep knowledge of what their final pattern was supposed to look like when they passed through double slits in single file, creating a perfect diffraction pattern of *waves*. Whenever the physicists placed particle detectors at the two slits (so they could find out which slit each electron was choosing), the electrons switched to behaving like *particles*.[3] What this means to you is that the tiniest parts of you (1) cooperate with past and future parts of you to be where they're expected to be, and (2) know when they are expected to be particles or waves. When you realize just how conscious you are in every particle of your being, you can see how important it is to expect what you most desire. Even at your most funda-mental level of physical being, what you expect is what you get!

This "what you expect is what you get" concept applies to much more than just the things we desire. It's equally true that when we expect unpleasant things to happen, they do. In his excellent book *Be Careful What You Pray For*, Dr. Larry Dossey points out, ". . . negative prayers are woven into the fabric of everyday life. We launch them not as formal curses, but simply through the process of thinking negatively of another person."[4] You can even inadvertently jinx yourself! Our thoughts and feel-ings are much more powerful creative forces in our lives than most of us realize, and they affect us both positively and negatively.

Your Auric Membrane: Master of Perception and Life Itself

If you've ever been concerned that you can't attract what you most desire because you weren't born with the right DNA or the best brains, you'll be glad to know that those things don't matter much. What *does* matter is your aura. Your auric membrane is the place where your thoughts and feelings interact with the out-side world to attract what you most desire. Why does it matter so much what you think and feel? Your learned perceptions are more important than your instincts, because your perceptions can override your instincts. Perceptions direct gene activity and cell behavior, and are instrumental in establishing the character of your life. Your cells follow the collective voice of your instincts and learned perceptions, which together form the sub-conscious mind.[5] American biologist Bruce Lipton is living proof of the model of "perception rewrites genes," because he suc-cessfully managed his own manic-depression utilizing percep-tual adjustments to override bouts of depression. Since Lipton knew that perception controls biology, he recognized that instead of listening to depressive ideas, he could do something else, such as going downtown to see a movie. Changing his behavior effectively helped him replace negative thoughts and feelings with the joy of getting out and about and becoming absorbed in interesting activities.

The idea that our cell membranes, not our DNA, act as the brains of each cell seems true when we consider what parts of the cell the cell can't live without. Cells die when their membranes are removed, since they require the control mechanism of the membrane to behave as both barrier and organic information processor. If the nucleus and its genetic DNA material are removed from a cell, however, that cell might well survive for two or more months![6]

In much the same way that cell membranes provide cells with a first line of interaction, communication, and defense, our auras give us the first hints of what environment we find ourselves in, and how best we can respond. Our auras connect us to everything outside us from divine inspiration (received through the crown chakra) all the way down to a sense that it's time to fight or flee (received at the root chakra). These intuitions and hunches are what we rely upon for survival in times of great danger, and what give us insights into how best to handle any given situation. The energy field membranes that surround and sustain us are what hold us together, give us our sense of individuality, and connect us to other energy field membranes through string-like energy cords of love.

Just as cells can survive with missing or damaged DNA in their nuclei, but not without their cell membranes, so too can humans survive with damaged brains but not without their energy field membranes. Many people once classified as "brain dead" have continued to live for some time after that diagnosis was officially made by a physician. A number of medical doctors have felt that a diagnosis of "brain dead" as a reason to remove life support is disturbing, because these patients don't look dead. They have spontaneously beating hearts, healthy skin color, body warmth, digestion, and metabolism. These doctors believe that despite the widespread acceptance of terminating lives of brain-dead individuals, this practice is incoherent in theory and confused in practice.[7] Some "brain dead" patients have even nourished and given birth to healthy children.[8] More than thirty cases of surviving "brain dead" patients have been reported, with half surviving more than two months, and some surviving up to fourteen years.[9] In one case, a "brain dead" patient put his arm around an assisting nurse as doctors prepared to remove his heart for a transplant donation, and there have been some cases in which brain dead patients have recovered consciousness.[10]

These facts make it clear that something other than your brain and your DNA define who you are. When you consider that your aura is your true essence, you begin to see how it doesn't matter what brain or DNA you have—because you can attract what you most desire with a healthy aura. Through your aura, you receive and process information from your environment. When you feel fearful, you experience a frightening world that seems like it's collapsing in around you. When you feel loving, you experience an expansive, loving world. You can therefore bring more joyful loving experiences into your life by being more joyful and loving. When you change your perceptions of the world for the better, you will change your life for the better.

Your Auric Energy Cords: Life-lines of Love

Once you know that at your most fundamental level of being, what you expect is what you get—and that your perception of the universe creates your reality through your aura—you have a nearly complete picture of how your energy body operates to bring you together with what you most desire. We've seen how unconscious connections to undesirable results can produce problems; now it's time to see how conscious connections to desirable outcomes can best be achieved. You can think of your auric cord connections as being life-lines of love to everyone and everything you care about. If you visualize your primary energy field as being an egg-shaped membrane around your body, your auric cords appear to be strings or threads of energy that extend from your auric field membrane to others' auric membranes. When someone tells you they've "bonded" with a new friend, they are describing this very real sensation of auric cord connection. Similarly, the phrase "Close-knit communities" indicates a multitude of auric cord connections. Just as the fabric of our universe may contain both extended and curled-up dimensions,[11] so too do our auric fields have both a strong local presence and an almost invisible collection of thin strings connecting us to other points of consciousness.

These life-lines of love bring what you most desire to you in two ways. They provide you with energetic support from those who send you their love through these auric strings, and they also connect you to other worlds of possibility, or parallel realities.[12] If you consider yourself as being a "You-niverse," as Fred Alan Wolf calls it, you realize that any time you tell a story that includes you, you'll see that the universe depends on you in order for it to exist the way it does.[13] The better you care about others and are connected to everything and everyone you love through auric cords, the better you will attract to you what you most desire.

Even the tiniest life forms, such as bacteria, show signs of having auric cords. Lactose-intolerant *e. coli* bacteria that were fed only lactose managed to successfully make an evolutionary leap and mutate into lactose-munching bacteria.[14] You can make similarly speedy transformations in your life when you connect through auric cords to your best possible future self. Since all new information must come to us from the future,[15] we can access it any time we need it through our auric cords.

Through your auric cords, your intentions, feelings, and thoughts will affect everyone and everything you care about, just as a nurse's feelings affects the health of her charges.[16] Your mind is not *inside* your brain, but rather something that exists independently of your physical body. We know this because people whose brains have ceased to function can still be aware of what is going on around them,[17] some children vividly recall things that happened while they were still fetuses in their mothers' wombs,[18] and our bodies sometimes strongly react to emotional stimuli significantly *before* any sign of the stimuli has even begun to appear.[19] You can even help randomly selected seeds sprout faster by sending them love ("holy thought") and wishing for the best for them from a distance.[20]

Six Steps to Attract What You Most Desire

Attracting what you most desire has always been within your grasp. You simply need to feel relaxed and energized while focusing your attention on how grateful and confident you are that what you desire is on its way to you right now! While this is simple to explain, it can sometimes be challenging to implement. Listed below are six common problem areas that most often frustrate people who are learning the art of manifesting what they desire. If you find yourself doing any of these things, you may be preventing yourself from attracting what you most desire:

1. Energize fantasies instead of dreams.
2. Get in your own way.
3. Ignore your chakras.
4. Expect trouble.
5. Focus on problems.
6. Lapse into a state of complacency and inaction.

If some or all of the items on this list apply to you, there's no need to worry! By looking on the positive side of each item on the list, you can learn six valuable skills to help you manifest what you desire.

1. Energize dreams instead of fantasies.
2. Get out of your own way.
3. Listen to your chakras.
4. Expect what you most desire.
5. Appreciate every moment.
6. Do something nice for someone.

Energize Dreams Instead of Fantasies

You entertain two very different kinds of visions of your future: fantasies and dreams. Fantasies are imaginative daydreams that may feel exciting and stimulating to think about, but would not be enjoyable to live through in real life. Dreams are your visions of what you would actually like your life to be like, which include something good for all concerned. Whichever visions you energize will be the ones that come true, so you need to be responsible about which thoughts you invest the most emotional energy in. Mexican shamans explain that our dreams become real when we "camay" them, which means to breathe unity into them.[21] When our dreams are in accordance with what is best for all, they are empowered with tremendous integrity. Whereas fantasies-come-true can feel like waking nightmares, dreams-come-true feel like heaven on earth. A perfectly enjoyable fantasy of telling your boss off or dating your married friend would not feel enjoyable if it actually came true, if it was selfishly inspired with only your interests in mind. One easy way to tell the difference between fantasies and dreams is that fantasies typically involve you playing a controlling role in the world, while dreams allow others to have freedom of choice.

When we seek to satisfy a desire for greed or power, like King Midas who wished that everything he touched would turn to gold, we discover such a reality feels empty and meaningless.

Most of us come to a point at least once in our lives when we question the dreams we've pursued, and wonder what dreams can bring us greater satisfaction. You don't need to be having a full-blown mid-life crisis in order to notice that you've taken a job you don't enjoy, dated a person who is not quite right for you, or are attempting to otherwise live the life of someone you are not. If you sense any such feelings of deep dissatisfaction in your life, you can request to receive a dream that will provide you with guidance for what you are meant to be, do, and experience. When *Thinking Allowed* host and co-producer Jeffrey Mishlove was a graduate student taking criminology classes at U.C. Berkeley in 1972, he was feeling "very uncomfortable studying only negative forms of deviance." His deep dissatisfaction led him to instruct himself that he would have a dream that would solve his career dilemma. When he subsequently dreamt of visiting a friends' house while his friends were away, and finding a magazine in the middle of their living room floor, he knew this was a dream he had to listen to. Upon awakening, Mishlove rushed to his friends' house, let himself into their apartment, and read the magazine that he found sitting in the middle of their living room floor, just as he had seen in his dream. That magazine was *Focus*, a publication for listener-sponsored television and radio in San Francisco, and it gave Mishlove the idea to start a radio interview show on public radio with leaders of the human potential movement.[22]

The following exercise can help you determine if what you desire is a dream or a fantasy. If it's a dream, then proceed to energize it to come into reality. If it's a fantasy, you can enjoy it as a thought you keep to yourself.

Exercise for Energizing Dreams Instead of Fantasies

1. Make space and time for yourself to do a private visualization/meditation exercise.

2. Imagine that what you desire has already come true. Feel it with all your senses. See it, hear it, smell it, touch it, taste it.

3. Ask yourself if this desire is in alignment with the best possible future for all others. Does it allow others freedom? How will it work to change our lives?

4. Remind yourself that you already know whether or not you wish for this desire to manifest in reality. You already know if it is a fantasy you will keep to yourself, or a dream to be energized and brought into existence that you desire with your whole being. ◎

Get Out of Your Own Way

Oftentimes, it is easy for us to be consumed by our vices. Try as we might to live up to our highest potential, we often get stuck somehow. Sometimes, reaching a point of extreme frustration with ourselves can motivate us to make some much-needed changes. It takes a great deal of honesty and self-awareness to recognize oneself as the source of some of our problems. Without realizing it, you may be getting in your own way!

There are lots of ways you can get in your own way, as you may recall from the healthy aura self-assessment test in Chapter 3. Every judgmental and negative thought you keep around you is an active force that seeks similar companions. In other words, misery loves company. The energies of your thoughts act like they have a life of their own, seeking to attract all similarly tuned energies to support that concept of reality, and actively repelling all differently tuned energies.

When you notice that your self-talk seems negative and is making you feel bad about yourself, flip the derogatory self-talk to positive statements instead. By doing this, you can create personalized affirmations out of each and every negative thought.[23]

If you hear yourself thinking, "You never do anything right," for example, simply flip that comment around to the more positive, "You always do your very best in every situation."

Sometimes, it's not the thought that is the harbinger of trouble, but the *feeling* behind the thought. Consider the thought, "It's too late to go back now." If this thought is charged with *feelings* of inferiority or failure, then the message of the thought will be negative, causing you to dwell on the mistakes of the past rather than looking toward the future. Imagine for a moment how this same thought, "It's too late to go back now," could be a cry of joyful relief.

Keeping a clean aura is mastering the art of living cleanly in the present moment, free from worries, doubts, and fears about the future—and shame, resentment, and anger about the past.

When we clean out the extraneous thought-forms in our minds, we benefit from having a cleaner energy field. Those cleaner energy fields will then naturally attract the kind of synchronicities and new acquaintances that we most enjoy entertaining, and we'll feel enthusiastic about life and its inevitable changes.

Exercise for Getting Out of Your Own Way: Letting Go of Wants

1. **Ground**—Release all extraneous fears and annoyances. Visualize an energetic grounding cord running from your root chakra down to the center of the earth, carrying away all your worries and concerns.
2. **Let Go**—Let go of all wants and desires. You may still feel your joy for what it is you are grateful to be bringing into your life—as long as you focus on the cup being half full, rather than half empty. The letting go is actually the letting go of your attachments to wants—it's a letting go of desire, and an acceptance of what is and what will be.
3. **Energize**—Feel a blast of energy and meditate on how grateful you are for the good things that have come to you and will come to you. ◎

Exercise for Getting Out of Your Own Way: Reversing Negative Self-Talk

1. Think about something you were responsible for that didn't go quite as well as you would have liked.

2. As you review each detail of what happened and what went wrong, listen to your thoughts and observe any negative self-talk.

3. When you notice something you're thinking about yourself that is less than positive, write it down. Look at that negative statement, and imagine how you might be able to flip it around into a positive affirmation.

4. When you've chosen an affirmation to make from the negative self-talk statement, write it down and put it somewhere you can view frequently. You've created your very own personal affirmation!

5. If you notice more than one negative self-talk statement, repeat steps three and four for each one. ◎

Exercise for Getting Out of Your Own Way: Identifying and Nullifying Rogue Thought-Forms

Rogue thought-forms can cause a lot of trouble. These thought-forms manifest in fear-based negativity toward the future and are filled with resentment about the past. One of the best ways to get out of your own way is to learn to recognize when you may be harboring these thought-forms. If you say "Yes" to either one or both of the following questions, you've found rogue thought-forms that you should remove from your energy body:

1. Does this thought inspire me to unduly worry about the future?

2. Does this thought inspire me to feel angry about the past?

Just like the old proverb, "One bad apple spoils the whole bunch," so too can one rogue thought-form. Once you have identified your rogue thought-forms, you can deal with them by discrediting them. If you feel unworthy of good things, *do good deeds*. If you feel lazy, *do some hard work*. If you feel scared, *do something brave*. ◎

Listen to Your Chakras

Training your energy body (which is largely subconscious) to work in conjunction with your conscious ego and your higher self takes time. Likewise, when you master the art of desiring something with your whole being, you can then relax and expect it to come to you. In order to attain what you desire, no part of you can be at odds with that desire. We sometimes fall victim to our subconscious urges, seemingly in spite of ourselves. Only by uniting ego, subconscious, and higher self do we best succeed in attracting what we most desire.

In order to unify these three aspects of yourself (subconscious, ego, and higher self) and achieve what you most desire, you must align every single one of your energy centers—from your root chakra to your crown chakra—so that you will be united in your desire for an expected outcome that is longed for by every part of yourself. Both meditation and prayer can assist you in aligning your chakras toward a common goal.

If you are not yet aware of what each of your chakras desires, then this is a good opportunity to do a chakra check to find out. First ask each chakra, "What do you most desire?" Do not attempt to force each chakra to do your conscious mind's bidding. Instead, listen to what your chakras need. You will find great wisdom and surprising insights from asking your chakras what they desire, and if you listen, you will find that your chakras will guide you to the path that is best for your overall happiness.

Exercise for Listening to Your Chakras

This exercise is very empowering, for in listening to your chakras, you demonstrate how you care about their questions, desires, and feelings. Such a simple act of compassion on your part will be met with grateful and enthusiastic support from your chakras, so be prepared to feel more energetic, enthusiastic, and motivated. Find a place and some time when you will feel safe and not be interrupted. Begin a dialogue with each one of your chakras by speaking to them of your conscious desire, and asking them what they most desire. Come to the discussion prepared to hear anything, however outrageous, with an open mind—and be sure to take notes. Listen *very carefully*, for things that you hear your chakras say that might seem incoherent, meaningless, or insignificant are most likely very important. Remember, you are the facilitator of this conversation, and your attention and intention allow for unification of all your energy centers, as you listen to them one at a time. ◉

When your chakras show you feelings that have been trapped or locked inside them due to traumatic events, you may find it useful to have a trusted friend or professional psychological counselor present to act as witness, keep you grounded, and stabilize your energy body. Chakra work can be the most intense way to experience personal issues, and it is very serious, essential, and deep work. If you ever encounter deep issues in your chakras that you do not feel capable of facing on your own, by all means call on a trusted friend or professional counselor to provide you with energetic support through this process. If you can't tell when to call for assistance, use the "Band-Aid" test as a rule of thumb. If you feel your energy wounds are deeper than can adequately be treated with an energy "Band-Aid," then you need an energetic support person to help you. If you already have a trusted friend to talk to, or a psychological counselor, let him or her know that you'd like him or her to witness a conversation between you and your chakras.

Expect What You Most Desire

The art of attracting what you desire begins with the removal of all doubts that would otherwise hinder your ability to witness miraculous manifestations of your dreams-come-true. These doubts may be much more subtle than rogue thought-forms, and instead may appear as your mind's way of thinking about probabilities, and pointing out that the odds may not be in your favor. When you allow yourself the possibility that your wishes can come true by *expecting* them to regardless of what the odds might be, you allow those confident thought-forms to travel freely. Unhindered by limitations of probability, they will connect with all that is resonant and harmonious with them, and return wonderful things to you, no matter how unlikely that may seem. This required expectation of success is not connected to any particular religion or form of spirituality, but rather can be imagined as the antithesis of skepticism.

Even if you don't have any religious or spiritual faith, you can benefit from believing that what you most desire is coming to you. A wonderful word to express this feeling of confidence that what you desire "comes true, being hoped for," is *tunátyava*, from the Hopi people of northeastern Arizona.[24] With such a supreme sense of gratitude and confidence in your energy field, you will naturally attract exactly what you are expecting.

The first step of expecting what you most desire is easy when you remove your inner skeptic, the voice that says, "It'll never work," in an annoying whine inside your head. This inner skeptic may have survived your elimination of rogue thought-forms because it claims to merely be stating the facts, which it then points out are against you. An excellent way to disable your inner skeptic is to recall the Chinese proverb, "The person who says it cannot be done should not interrupt the person doing it." If the skeptical voice inside your head is not serving any practical purpose, you'll do well to ignore it. If your inner voice has nothing constructive to say, recognize that it has no value for you and let it go. You can then move on to the important task of expecting success! Research studies have shown that feelings of success have been proven to facilitate learning, while feelings of failure inhibit learning, so we can be assured of greater success when we aren't sabotaging ourselves with needless doubts.[25]

Exercise for Expecting What You Most Desire: Expect Success

1. Visualize what you most desire to attract to you as clearly and simply as possible. As you imagine this idea, consider that it is "a done deal," and everything in your life right now is leading directly to this future.

2. Pay attention to your body and chakras. If any energy feelings arise in your chakra energy centers, ask what is wrong and listen for a reply from your chakra to determine the source of the concern. If you encounter self-beliefs in your chakras that cause feelings of discomfort as you do this visualization exercise, consider how valid each concern is in your life today. The pain you feel is most likely due to old issues that have been stored in your chakras and can now be cleared out. Listen to the concern, and respond with your assessment of how this present moment in time is very different from the time that the issues became stuck in your chakras.

3. When all of your chakras and your entire body feel good about what you are visualizing, hold that simple thought of what you most desire for a couple of minutes. Feel grateful that your dream is coming true, and allow your whole body to savor the sense of deep loving appreciation for the universe's generosity. Hold this feeling as long as you can, until it begins to fade.

4. Repeat steps one through three at least once a day for as long as your desire is on your mind. ◎

Pay attention to how you feel immediately after doing this exercise. Be alert for your inner skeptic and rogue thought-forms! Your continued vigilance will keep rogue thought-forms from causing trouble, as you keep your mind free from useless negativity. Continue to monitor your chakras, and if you find discomfort in any of them, choose a place to rest and converse with your energy centers. You can even talk out loud to them, as long as you are alone or don't mind other people overhearing you.

When you do these follow-ups on how your chakras feel after a visualization, notice if there is any particular chakra that frequently has energy blockages. By asking that chakra, "What's wrong?" you can find out what worries and fears may have been stored there. You can then breathe love into your chakra, and reassure it that it can let go of these worries and fears.

After clearing out that chakra, you can then reassess all your chakras and listen to any further issues, addressing each concern by responding to it with reassurance and love. One by one, you will sense your chakras gaining confidence in your vision of what you most desire, and feel your inner resistances slipping away.

After performing this exercise, you may eventually achieve total chakra alignment. Your senses will be keener. You may feel an energy "buzz" emanating from you. Colors look brighter, smells are more striking, and you will be aware of every sensation in your body. You may find that minor aches and pains vanish, leaving you feeling more alert and energized.

Appreciate Every Moment

It is important to appreciate the energy of every moment. My young daughter phrased this idea perfectly when I drove her to school one day and she told me, "These are the good old days." Life is good when it feels good *right now*. Regardless of what is happening, these can be the good old days for you, if only you allow yourself to appreciate that possibility. You can begin by appreciating the fact that you are alive, and that you care enough about yourself to explore your aura, open your mind, and learn new things.

Whenever your thoughts turn to how you'd love to attract what you most desire to your life, remember to appreciate everyday signs that your dream is already starting to come true, and continue working to make that happen. If you are dreaming of a new job, dress and act the part of already having it. If you are dreaming of meeting the ideal romantic partner, know that he or she is simply waiting for the perfect moment to walk into your life. If you are dreaming of financial prosperity, feel glad for every penny you have and allow yourself to feel rich with what you already possess.

As you take steps toward achieving your dream, appreciate your efforts to take positive steps on your behalf. Pat yourself on the back at every opportunity. Whenever you complete a task, praise yourself for doing it as well as you possibly could.

If you still have trouble believing that your dreams are coming true this very moment, you may need to go back to doing the exercises for getting out of your own way, listening to your chakras, and expecting success again. If you don't feel like you deserve recognition and praise because you haven't yet done anything toward making your dream come true, just appreciate the little things in your life that you love the most. Your goal is to achieve an emotional state of resonance that attracts success, because your emotions are the keys that unlock the doors to memories from the past as well as dreams of possible futures.

Exercise for Appreciating Every Moment: Ten Things I Love

1. Write on a piece of paper or in your journal a list of ten things you love. These can be external things such as, "I love this sunny day," or they can be your inner feelings such as "I love the way I feel good about myself today." They can be silly, "I love my belly button," or serious, "I love my friends and family." They can be general, "I love life!" or specific, "I love the way the mailman delivered my mail to my door today." Whatever makes you feel love and affection, write it down!

2. If you wrote down ten things and don't want to stop, please keep going! Write down as many things as you want for as long as you want to keep writing.

3. Review your list, and allow yourself time to appreciate all this wonderful prosperous abundance around you. ◎

The ability to appreciate what's going well in your life is a powerful force. It can pull you back up on your feet when external situations seem difficult. It can help you recognize how you are already moving toward fulfilling your dreams. It can give you strength to continue on, and courage to face challenges. When you do this "Ten Things I Love" exercise every day for a week, you'll find you have a much more positive attitude. You'll also likely find your list of things to appreciate keeps getting longer every day.

In addition to all the benefits mentioned above, doing this daily list of "Ten Things I Love" will help keep you in an energized, relaxed state, which best facilitates attracting what you most desire. You'll be more naturally confident of yourself, and will be more likely to smile and laugh when you already know how many good things there are in your life right now.

Do Something Nice for Someone

"When I do good, I feel good. When I do bad, I feel bad. That's my religion." —Abraham Lincoln

One of the best ways to ensure you receive good things in your life is to do good things. Every time you offer help to someone who needs help without expecting anything in return, you allow your subconscious to feel more worthy of receiving help. This just might be the easiest way to boost your aura, because it gives you a chance to "think with your heart." Since your heart is at the center of all your chakras, practicing acts of compassion helps to ensure that you are energetically connected (via auric energy cords) to others, and you can bask in their appreciation of your unexpected kindness.

Comedian George Carlin jokes, "If it's true that we're here to help others, then what exactly are the others here for?" As funny as that sounds, the truth is that we all depend on one another in this world. Recent scientific studies show that acts of kindness result in significant mental and physical health benefits for those who do them. People who do good deeds benefit from an endorphin rush, or "helper's high," which is followed by a longer-lasting period of improved emotional and physical well-being. Those who have personal contact when they volunteer are more likely to experience the helper's high than those who never meet those they help.[26]

Your aura also benefits from doing good deeds. Notice how beautiful your aura looks and how vibrant it feels when you perform an act of kindness. Let someone go ahead of you in line, smile at strangers, thank someone for something nice he or she did, or give an unexpected gift.

The more good things you do for others, the better your overall attitude and disposition will tend to be. You can think of this as performing a kind of emotional alchemy on yourself. The Dalai Lama explains this beautifully: "All the virtuous states of mind—compassion, tolerance, forgiveness, caring, and so on—these mental qualities are genuine Dharma, or genuine spiritual qualities, because all of these internal mental qualities cannot coexist with ill feelings or negative states of mind."[27] It's just not easy (or perhaps even possible) to maintain negative feelings and self-image when you know with your whole being that you are taking actions that make the world a better place in which to live. When you brighten someone's day, you become more radiant!

Exercise to Do Something Nice for Someone: Think with Your Heart

1. Find a quiet place where you can be undisturbed for a few minutes, and close your eyes.
2. Feel your heart chakra's radiance and warmth, placing one or both hands over your heart.
3. Make an effort to think with your heart, and imagine what you can

do for someone today. Let your heart guide you, and find something nice you can do for someone else today.

4. Go do something nice for someone! ◎

Chapter 6 Questions for Review and Reflection

1. Do you remember a time when you felt aware of things beyond your physical body?
2. Have you ever sensed someone intruding in your personal space? How did that feel?
3. Have you noticed times in your life when your presence affected what was happening around you? Can you imagine what would have happened if you weren't there?
4. What good things are you expecting for your future?
5. What rogue thought-forms have you identified in your mind?
6. Considering that new information comes from the future . . . what advice would your future self give you today?
7. What's the problem with attempting to force your chakras into alignment (rather than listening to them)?
8. What helps you feel more competent handling your inner skeptic?
9. What's the problem with "trying" to attract what you most desire?
10. What nice things can you do for someone today?

Chapter 7
Protect Yourself

Being in touch with your energy body means trusting your instincts. American psychologist Carolyn Miller tells of a time when a teenage boy named Brett was waiting to board an airplane with his mother and brother, when Brett's mother suddenly "went ballistic." She had a premonition of disaster, and began shouting at airline attendants to transfer their luggage to another flight, because she was not going to board this plane. Brett said his mother was normally "a rather reserved, polite person, but suddenly she was screaming at these people, and carrying on like a maniac." When their luggage had been moved to another plane, Brett and his mother and brother heard the news that the plane had indeed crashed shortly after take-off. Brett said, "There were only a few fatalities, but some of the people who died had been using our seats."[1]

Brett's mother had been a frequent flier who was not afraid of airplane travel. She had simply picked up strong intuitive feelings that on this particular trip, it would be best to take a different flight. She could sense a feeling of danger associated with this one particular flight to such a tremendous degree that she was willing to risk behaving like a maniac and embarrassing her sons. How did she receive such a powerful premonition?

Thanks to having had experiences like Brett's, half of all Americans believe in extrasensory perception (ESP).[2] Many of us know that our auras can be the key to alerting us to danger in our everyday lives. They can do this both via auric energy cords, which connect us to the future, other possible realities, and distant places; and through our auric membrane, which senses our immediate surroundings.

In order to protect ourselves, we must learn to master the skills that enable us to react during an attack, and to help maintain ongoing protection. Just as you can protect your physical body by being alert, there are five techniques with which you can aurically protect yourself by keeping your energy body alert.

Develop Your Intuition and ESP

Intuition expert Laura Day defines intuition as "a nonlinear, nonempirical process of gaining and interpreting information in response to questions."[3] If you've ever known something you had no rational way of knowing, your intuition was hard at work. The benefit of developing your intuition for protection is that your heightened awareness will serve to keep you safe in unfamiliar environments and with new acquaintances. Every person receives intuitive information in a way that is uniquely his or her own. This information may come in the form of daydreams, signs, coincidences, or extra-sensory perception.

The so-called "extra" senses in ESP actually consist of enhanced sensitivity to our five existing physical senses. This means that for each one of the five senses of sight, hearing, touch, taste, and smell there exists a high sense perception (HSP) for that sense. In this way, people can be clairvoyant (clear seeing), clairaudient (clear hearing), clairsentient (clear feeling), clairolorant (clear smelling), and clairgoutant (clear tasting). These high sensory perceptions act as communication tools that provide you with conscious awareness of people, places, and things that might be some distance away from you. The auric energy cords that link you to others are constantly carrying information to you, although you are probably not consciously aware of most of it. Developing these senses can prove invaluable to helping you follow your inner knowingness, or intuition. You'll become more certain that when something "smells fishy," "feels all wrong," or "looks suspicious," you've received clues that you may need to choose a different path. As your intuitive skills develop, you will more clearly see things that are not physically there, hear things that other people can't hear, and even feel, taste, and smell things that are uniquely for your benefit.

Your Physical and Auric Senses

Physical Sense	Auric Sense
Seeing	Clairvoyance
Hearing	Clairaudience
Feeling	Clairsentience
Smelling	Clairolorance
Tasting	Clairgoutance

As you develop your ability to see and feel auras, you are practicing your high sensory perception. You will naturally become better able to sense trouble coming long before it arrives, because its energetic presence will broadcast itself to you. There is no need to strain yourself in an attempt to become more intuitive, since every aura meditation and exercise you do will further enhance your intuitive skills. All of these intuitive abilities provide information received through your chakras and aura, which you have been opening and utilizing as you completed various aura viewing exercises in Chapter 4.

When you receive intuitive guidance, you are essentially reading the aura of a person, place, event, or thing. You can do this in one of two ways: (1) You can see the aura of someone or something where you are physically located, or (2) You can connect via an auric energy cord to someone or something else, transporting your five physical senses through space and time through this multidimensional string to pick up whatever sensations you can receive. Most intuitives access this kind of information through their subconscious, which requires the person to be in a relaxed, energized state of mind. You may find yourself more open to receiving intuitive insights as you daydream, drift off to sleep, or meditate. When you regularly practice meditation and/or prayer, you will become much more intuitive. You'll know things you didn't even know you knew. With the intention of protecting yourself and those you love from danger, you can receive warnings very much like the one Brett's mother received at the airport.

You are already highly intuitive. You were born with the ability to sense the energy fields of information around us, and have simply been blocking a great many insights and hunches as mental static. By paying more attention to how your body feels and what direction your mind wanders, you can begin to reap the benefits of intuitive awareness. Intuition begins when we ask a question, continues as we receive ideas in the form of physical signs and all manner of internal senses, and ends with an analysis of the clues we received. Right now, at this very moment, you are receiving intuitive information about everything you consciously and subconsciously have thought about. Most of the intuitive information you receive arrives so subtly that you hardly notice it at all. In this way, you may get a feeling that it's a good idea to go the post office today. Since that idea seems easily doable, you might decide to go there. When you arrive at the post office, you may then be amazed to find an old friend you haven't seen in many years standing in line as you arrive. While your intuition may have known in advance why you would enjoy going to the post office (because your friend is there), this information was not completely made conscious in your mind.

Fortunately, when we receive intuitive information of a protective nature, the feelings we receive are usually not so subtle. I once had a clairvoyant and clairaudient impression that a car would crash into a parked car on the corner of the street near where I lived. As my boyfriend parked his car in the doomed spot, I saw the image of a car crash and heard the sound of crunching metal. These clairvoyant and clairaudient impressions were so powerful that I demanded that he move his car immediately. He could see how serious I was about this, so he started up the car again and parked farther away in a less convenient location. I asked him to promise me that he would avoid the corner spot for several days . . . until the expected crash occurred. Once a car had been hit in that spot a few days later, I felt calm again and sensed no further danger there.

Recent research indicates that we are aware *at a cellular level* of everything happening in our immediate vicinity as well as with anyone or anything we have regular relations. Even when our cells are removed from our bodies, they continue to respond along with the rest of our body to external stimuli. American polygraph instructor Cleve Backster conducted a series of fascinating experiments to determine how mouth cells scraped from human donors would respond when the human subjects encountered spontaneous emotional stimuli. Backster found that the mouth cells reacted vigorously in their electroded culture tube at the same time as their donors viewed erotic photographs[4] or disturbing movie scenes.[5] When you allow for the possibility that you really can "feel it in your bones," and that every one of the cells in your body is actively aware of everyone and everything connected to you as well as events unfolding in your immediate vicinity, you will feel much more alive. Trust this inner knowingness, and cultivate it by asking questions and waiting for answers in the form of signs or intuitive insights. You can develop intuition for any kind of questions you might have, and as you develop your intuitive abilities you'll find your ability to accurately predict and avoid danger will naturally improve. It's preferable to develop your intuition by asking questions that are not fear-based, and that are randomized somehow so there is no way you can logically deduce which question you are answering. Like Johnny Carson playing the role of "Carnac the Magnificent," you can glean many important details about what you wish to know.

Many divination methods rely upon intuition and the accurate reading of energy field information. For example, transatuamancy involves interpretation of chance remarks overheard in crowds, stichomancy is the practice of opening a book to a random page and passage, and tasseomancy is the art of interpreting patterns of leaves left at the bottom of a cup of tea.[6] However, without any of these trappings, you can learn to directly receive intuitive information in a way that is much more portable, versatile, and immediate. Practice this exercise to develop your intuition, and you can receive answers to all your questions.

Exercise for Developing Intuition

1. On five identical, unmarked pieces of paper, write down three questions that you would like answers to, and two questions regarding someone other than you such as a friend or family member. Each piece of paper will have one question written on it when you are done.

2. Turn the pieces of paper over so the blank sides are facing you, and shuffle them around until you no longer know which paper has which question written on it.

Assign numbers from one to five to each page, and write the number on the blank side for each piece of paper.

3. Select the page marked "1," and move it close to you. This is the question for which you will first receive intuitive impressions. Without

looking at the question, imagine that you can easily use your high sensory perception to answer this question. You will receive information in the form of sights, sounds, smells, tastes, and/or feelings for four questions, which you will write answers for on the page in front of you after you receive your impressions: (1) What is the *current situation?* (2) What happens in the *distant future?* (3) How does the situation *evolve?* (4) What significant *changes* will take place?

4. Ask your intuition to show you how the object of question "1" appears right now at this time, and answer the question, "What is the *current situation?*" Don't worry if your mind seems to be wandering—any dreamlike images will have relevance, so note them and write them down.

5. Ask your intuition to show you how the object of question "1" will be in the *distant future.*

6. Ask your intuition to show you "How will the situation *evolve?*"

7. Ask your intuition to show you the answer to the question, "What significant *changes* will take place after these events have unfolded?"

8. Once you've received answers to all four questions for your first piece of paper, set it aside and select another piece of paper. Repeat steps 4 through 8 for each of the remaining pieces of paper until all five of the questions you wrote down have been answered.

9. Once all questions have been answered, flip the pieces of paper over and contemplate how the answers you received make sense for the questions you had originally asked. ◎

For some people, the most challenging part of receiving intuitive information lies in the interpretation of symbols. If you ask a question about how you will do in a new career, and get a visual impression of fish jumping in a stream, you may feel mystified by this answer. Free association can help you better understand the meaning of the jumping fish. You can ask yourself, "What does it mean when the fish are jumping?" and pay attention to every thought that comes to your mind. In the context of fishing, for example, jumping fish are more likely to go after bait.

At spawning time, jumping fish are returning to the place they were born. Your subconscious mind communicates clearly in symbols, which make sense to you on a very deep level.

Intuitive Symbol Interpretation Troubleshooting Guide

Problem:

The meaning of the symbolic object I see is unclear to me.

Suggestion:

Consult a dream symbols book, or free-associate all things, feelings, and activities connected with the image you saw.

Problem:

The only meaning I can find for the symbol makes no sense in the context of the question.

Suggestion:

Mentally step back from both the question and the symbolic answer, in order to get better perspective. You are likely looking so closely at your question that you "can't see the forest for the trees."

Problem:

I don't see any symbols.

Suggestion:

Pay attention to *whatever* you perceive. You might get a bit of tune from a song, or a long-forgotten smell, or a feeling.

Detect and Clean a Weakened Aura

Have you ever suffered a sudden loss of self-confidence? Have you experienced a string of accidents and bad luck? Have you suffered from recurring nightmares? You may have been noticing warning signs that your aura has slipped into a weakened condition. This can happen if you are regularly exposed to any kind of media that includes advertisements, news stories, and commentary.

We often pay little attention to these things, as the daily television news, newspapers, and radio shows are part of our daily routine. While our conscious mind is blissfully unaware of steady comments that we need to buy more things or are somehow not good enough, our subconscious soaks these thoughts up like a sponge soaks up water. We also pick up feelings of dissatisfaction, unworthiness, and uneasiness from our neighbors, family, and friends. As long as your inner energy reserves are strong enough, all this static won't cause you any noticeable difficulties. The trouble begins when you feel tired and your energy body is weak, because all these environmental stressors will tend to further undermine what's left of your aura's strength.

The first step in protecting yourself from the myriad negative thoughts and feelings you are bombarded with every day is to be aware of the warning signs of a weakened aura—in much the same way you keep an eye on the fuel gauge on your car. Your aura is a lot like the fuel in your car because it supplies you with the energy that keeps you going! By learning the top ten warning signs of a weakened aura, you can more readily recognize when it's time to recharge and bolster your auric protection.

If you notice any of the following, you may be experiencing a weakened aura. If you suspect you might be experiencing physical health problems, be sure to discuss your symptoms with a qualified health care practitioner.

Top Ten Warning Signs of a Weakened Aura

1. Feeling like someone is watching you
2. Acting suddenly out of character; big changes in behavior
3. Lapses in memory
4. Inexplicable, sudden, profound fatigue and feeling drained

5. Frequent nightmares
6. Recurring or bizarre accidents; string of bad luck
7. Inexplicable negative or obsessive thoughts
8. Sudden illnesses, aches, and pains
9. Dramatic loss of self-confidence
10. Irrational and sudden emotional swings

If you are experiencing more than one or two of these ten warning symptoms, you will definitely benefit from increased aura protection. If you are experiencing any of these symptoms, it is a good idea to do the aura cleaning exercise described at the end of this section.

Most of us are flooded with unwanted, continuous, and negative messages from many different directions in our daily lives. A person would have to go to elaborate lengths to eradicate all thought-form contamination in his or her life—including eliminating the telephone and answering machine, e-mail, television, and newspapers. Additionally, it would be necessary to look away when driving past billboards, and to somehow ignore anyone who was suffering or in pain. Since few of us are willing or able to go to such dramatic lengths in order to minimize our exposure to negative energies, we need to rely upon self-awareness to help us cope with living in the midst of chaos.

The single most important step in detecting weakening of your aura is recognizing that this could well be happening. There is a common tendency for people to be distracted by *maya*, or the surface appearance of physical situations, and address the *symptoms* of problems rather than their underlying causes. Many of us civilized westerners are used to finding physical solutions to what we perceive to be physical problems. We take pills and have surgical operations when we are sick, and we buy new appliances when the old ones break down. We have long forgotten how energy healers and shamans help people heal and make broken things work again by consciously directing universal life force energies. We have also forgotten that all healings begin from a stable base foundation—from an aura that is not leaking energy like a sieve!

We are each responsible for maintaining our own strong auras, although most of us were not taught this by our parents or teachers when we were growing up. We know that when we work with dirty or greasy things, we need to take a bath. We understand that when we eat candy and soda pop, we need to brush our teeth. We also need to remember that when we venture out into the dirty energy areas of this world (or when they intrude into our homes), we must clean our auras. To overlook this basic responsibility is to risk allowing a minor cleanliness issue to escalate into a major health concern. Since our emotional and physical health depends upon our auric health, keeping our auras clean would naturally seem to be our top priority for overall health. While regular meditation and prayer go a long way toward clearing our auras, they are not always focused on that result. It's therefore useful to know how to give yourself an occasional all-over auric cleansing.

Exercise for Detecting and Cleaning a Weakened Aura: Take an Auric Bath

1. Review the checklist of the top ten warning signs of a weakened aura. If you are experiencing any of the warning signs, continue with this exercise. If you are not experiencing any symptoms but wish to take an auric bath anyway so you can be squeaky-clean, please continue!

2. Take a bath with two cups baking soda and one cup salt to help clear your aura. If you don't have a bathtub, you can achieve the same restorative effects by putting the mixture of baking soda and salt in a plastic bowl or glass, and showering with it. Take care to rub the powdery mix over every part of your body.

3. When you emerge from your bath or shower, get a fresh glass of

drinking water, and intend that it be charged with cleansing energy, which will detoxify you from the inside. Holding the glass in both hands, say aloud, "Healing water, thank you for attracting and removing all toxins that reside within me," and drink this glass of water.

4. Visualize a grounding cord to the center of earth, which will now carry away all extraneous energy.

5. Visualize your aura completely clean. In every place that you sense a "hole" or gap in your energy field, wave your arms upward to "fluff" and in figure eights to "weave" your energy field into one unified, healthy whole. ◎

Clear Out Extraneous Energy

When you master the art of cleaning out extraneous energy, you'll find that you no longer feel compelled to buy things you don't need, do things you didn't intend to do, or take out negative feelings on your loved ones. You will not stand out as a target for being harassed, manipulated, or bullied. You will be better able to withstand corporate and office politics, which can contain a great deal of negative energy.

Others are best able to influence you when their energy fields interpenetrate yours. This can occur through what some energy intuitives refer to as "cording in," which refers to how others can access and affect your energy through auric energy cord strings that constantly act as conduits carrying whatever thoughts and feelings they may be experiencing directly to you. These connections can feel nice, or they can feel very unpleasant, depending on what those thoughts and feelings are. When people feel any kind of negativity and are closely connected to you, they can inadvertently transmit this via the energy cords connecting the two of you whenever they are in a relaxed state.[7]

If you have recently angered someone, and then suddenly experienced a bizarre accident or streak of bad luck, there is a good chance that you can benefit from clearing out some unwelcome energy. There are many ways you might have angered someone recently, and it's not all that important to worry about exactly who it was that sent such anger in your direction. Perhaps you reported someone's illegal activities to the authorities. Perhaps you received special recognition that someone else felt should be rightfully his. Whatever it is that caused so much anger to reach out and attack you, you must stand firm and tell it to go away.

First, tend to whatever physical activities require your immediate attention. Then, once you have a quiet moment to collect your energy, turn your attention to the most probable source of the energetic attack. You need to be consciously aware of the source, even if you don't know the name and location of the individual or individuals, and you will need to demand that it leave you *now*.

Any time you find yourself facing any kind of unwelcome negativity, demand that it leave you immediately. Firmly state your intention that it is not welcome here, and must go. If you feel it resisting, gather energy from all those who love you now, all those who will ever love you, and all those who have ever loved you and the universal life force itself and *push* it back to the sender, or to its original source. If you detect any kind of auric energy cord connecting you to the sender, sever it immediately with whatever visualization that feels right to you for the job. Be creative; think of your favorite tool for clearing your path of obstructions.

Exercise for Clearing out Extraneous Energy: Demand That Intruders Leave

1. Visualize a grounding cord to the center of the earth, which will now carry away all extraneous energy. Visualize your aura and the aura around your home as complete, healthy, and whole.

2. Sense whether there is any trace of an intruder's energy in your field or your home's field. If there is, demand that it leave. If it resists,

gather energy from all those who have ever loved you, love you right now, and will ever love you through all time and space and the universal life force energy . . . and *push* it back to the sender or its original source.

3. If you sense any kind of auric energy cord connecting you to the sender, sever it immediately with the tool of your choice (sword of truth, torch of fire, laser of love). ◎

Generally speaking, it is preferable to remove all energy cords that carry anything other than unconditional love, since the risk of picking up other "vibes" can bring about painful, unpleasant feelings. Your energy body will benefit from carefully reviewing every relationship in your life, and cleaning out all those that primarily bring you feelings of discomfort and unease. Do you remember the importance of the "Roseto effect"?[8] It is very important to keep all energy cords that connect you to genuinely loving and caring individuals who do not harbor resentments toward you, so it's worth spending some time assessing each of your energy cords. You can identify these fairly easily if you do the following "Cast of Characters" exercise.

Exercise for Clearing Out Extraneous Energy: Cast of Characters
In this exercise, you'll step back a bit from your life to get perspective on your story so far, and how the main characters in your life are affecting your energy. As Shakespeare wrote, "All the world's a stage." Now is your chance to review how you, the lead character, interact with all the other characters!

1. Start by clearing your mind, chakras, and body of all pain and discomfort. Feel as loving and loved as possible. This will provide you with a "clean palate" for experiencing the energies of the most important characters in your life.
2. Consider one of the most important people in your life. Feel his or her presence near you, and notice how your body responds. How do you feel?

3. Use your high sensory perception and intuition to receive any additional information about what gifts this person brings to you—what have you learned and gained from your connection to him or her?

4. Now ask what further gifts/messages you will receive from this person.

5. If you find that the gifts and messages are highly unpleasant and without much value to your life, then sever the energy cord(s) between you with the tool of your choice (such as a sword of truth, a torch of creation's fire, or a laser of love).

6. If the connection to this person feels good and healthy, thank him or her for being in your life, and offer him or her whatever form of energetic support or offering feels most appropriate.

7. Repeat steps 2 through 6 for other important people in your life. ◎

Post Aura Sentinels

If you had an imaginary friend or friends when you were growing up, chances are extremely good that they were acting on your behalf as guardian angels. Aura guardians or sentinels offer help for keeping your energy field clean and inviolate. By simply imagining any of a wide variety of aura sentinels, you can quickly and easily bolster your auric defenses. Everything from the staunchest warriors to the prettiest flowers can act as energy field sentries on your behalf. All you need to do is decide what kinds of guards most appeal to you and welcome them to your energy field. Since their energy presence can be seen by intuitive clairvoyants, choose accordingly; select only those you don't mind being seen with. Whatever you select, your energy field guardians will thrive most when you tend to them with daily affection. All energy field guardians provide help only when requested, allowing people to exert free will in welcoming or ignoring them.

It is wise to screen all potential spirit guardians by checking to make sure they only bring unconditional (non-controlling) love and that their presence does not create rogue thought-forms in your energy field. You may well have such spirit guardians with you at this very moment. They may be angels, or people who have loved you or will love you very much. You may feel their presence when you meditate, or when you are in between waking and sleeping in the hypnagogic state of aware-ness. If they are present in your life, you may find yourself gifted with their wisdom whenever you need it most.

You may already sense that you are surrounded by aura sentinels and guardians. If this is the case, you may not need to visualize additional sentries of your imagination. If you have some sentinels but would like to add some additional ones, that's fine, too. The main idea to master here is to become aware of and comfortable with your aura sentinels. They are here to help you, and will reflect your character and personality when they meet and greet the outside energies of the world. Once you've selected and energized your sentry with gratitude and appreciation, be sure to ground it so that all unwanted energy from the outside world can be intercepted by it and released to the center of the earth.

Exercise for Posting Aura Sentinels: Choose and Thank Your Guardians

What kind of guardians would you like to employ? In the realms of energy and imagination, anything is possible. This exercise will give you a chance to acquaint yourself with your own personal energy guardians.

1. Find a quiet spot where you can be uninterrupted for twenty minutes.
2. Close your eyes, and imagine what you would most like to have alongside your energy field, meeting and greeting the world for you. Keep your eyes shut until you have imagined something you'd be happy to have as a guardian. This could either be someone familiar who comes to you or someone completely new.

3. Open your eyes and stretch your arms out in front of you. Imagine that just past the ends of your fingertips is where your guardian now stands. Whether your guardian is a plant, an animal, a crystal, or anything else, welcome it into your energy field and thank it for being here with you.

4. Ground yourself and your guardian, by visualizing energy cords running deep down into the earth that carry away all unnecessary and unwanted energies.

You've got a guardian! Thank your guardian every time you remember it's there, and check on how it's doing. ◎

Protect Yourself from Psychic Attack

In much the same way as we can be healed from a distance by people who send feelings of love and affection our way, we can also be injured non-locally. Sometimes people intentionally curse others who they perceive to be very different than they are, or responsible for some injustice, or simply in competition with them. These kinds of psychic attacks can happen suddenly and without warning.

If you feel you may be under psychic attack, it's a good idea to get assistance. Some psychic attacks occur with such sudden ferocity that the recipient feels completely overwhelmed and at an emotional, intellectual, and physical disadvantage for dealing effectively with the situation. In very severe cases of psychic attack, the aura is so damaged that physical pain, illness, and even death can result.

Your greatest protection from psychic attack is to maintain a strong aura and strong auric cords of love to others that are as free as possible from guilt, doubt, loathing, and fear. Intentional curses only have power to seriously harm people who *believe in the power of the attacker* to cause serious harm, and allow such harm to occur by *sharing the attacker's dream vision.*

If you ever find yourself feeling that you are under psychic attack, immediately reinforce all auric cord connections to others who have ever loved you, will ever love you, and love you right now. Remember to ground your energy body, and thank all your auric sentinels and guardians for their assistance. If you do not feel strong enough to push the psychic attack away, call for spirit/auric helpers with all the strength you have left. Resist whatever negative imagery and feelings are being projected at you, and do your best to recall that these are only *maya*—only illusion. As long as you do *not* accept the unpleasant vision of the future that is being forced upon you by an attacker, and you remain connected to those who have sufficient energy to push this attack away, you go untouched by a psychic attack.

Research has also yielded additional remedies, such as crossing over running water—even running water from a garden hose will do[9]—or smudging yourself with sage or other herbs that can offer assistance for resisting psychic attacks.[10] No matter what the circumstances of the attack or your chosen remedy, you must always remember to feel connected to all who love you through all time and space, and believe that this attack will not seriously harm you (see yourself in a positive vision in the future).

In the martial arts, there is a way of standing called a "horse stance" (because a person in this stance appears to be seated on an imaginary horse). This stable yet protected standing position allows a person to be prepared for attack before it comes. It relies upon two things: a low center of gravity for the best connection to the earth, and bent knees that cannot easily be broken or moved. Just as martial artists practice this stance for hours before ever using it in sparring or fighting, you will be better prepared to face an actual psychic attack when you practice the energy body version of the horse stance. To stay grounded and supported, you need to practice feeling energetically connected to everyone and everything that loves you. To prevent injury to yourself, you need to practice visualizing a positive future for yourself. This exercise may seem trivial or overly simplistic, but do not underestimate its power. The more often you practice this, the stronger you will become.

Exercise for Protecting Yourself from Psychic Attack: Auric Horse Stance

1. Feel connected to everyone and everything that loves you through all time and space. Imagine their faces, feel their love; see their smiles.

2. Visualize a positive image of yourself, doing your best at what you do best and being recognized for who you are and what you do.

3. Now feel both your aura and auric cord connections simultaneously. Feel your positive image of yourself and your connections to everyone who loves you at the same time. Hold this vision of yourself and how you relate to the world in place of any other thoughts or feelings that may try to intrude.

4. Be ruthless if you sense any such intruders, and toss them out. You are strengthening yourself and need only concern yourself with this vision of you doing and being your best, surrounded by the love of all who have known you and will ever know you. ◎

Chapter 7 Questions for Review and Reflection

1. What question would you like your intuition to answer for you today?

2. What intuitive insights have you had that helped to protect you?

3. What signs (if any) of a weakened aura do you notice in your life?

4. Think of one thing you can do today to help protect your energy body.

5. Have you ever felt someone "cording in" on you? How did it feel?

6. What kind of external energy do you feel uncomfortable keeping inside your aura?

7. What kind of aura sentinels/guardians do you feel most comfortable with?

8. Why is it so important that you remember to ground your sentinel/guardian?

9. Which of the two components of the Auric Horse Stance is easiest for you (seeing yourself in a positive future, or connecting to those who love you)?

10. How long can you hold a vision both of connections to loved ones and yourself in a positive future simultaneously?

Part 3

Chapter 8

Aura Photography and Imaging

The very earliest images of auras were captured in religious and spiritual depictions as halos. Bright, radiant crowns of light have graced portraits, coins, statues, and carvings of saints and deities in many different cultures around the world since the dawn of recorded history. These halos depicting spiritual enlightenment were the most typical images of auras to be found in ancient artwork, and remain prevalent in religious and holy artwork today.

Ever since the photographic process became public in 1839 and X-ray pictures, or "shadowgraphs" as they were originally called, were introduced in 1895, interest in aura images has been slowly and steadily increasing. Aura photographs and portraits provide us with a recorded history of how our inner light shines for all the world to see. While ordinary photographs display what people with normal vision can see, aura photographs capture that which usually goes unseen. We crave confirmation of who we are and what we truly look like on the inside. With before and after photos, energy healers visually demonstrate the effectiveness of their work. People like to have aura photographs taken at special times in their lives, such as when they have graduated from school or fallen in love.

Aura photography began in 1777, when German physicist Georg Christoph Lichtenberg was the first western scientist to observe a corona discharge from a person's hand. A relatively short 111 years later, Czech physicist Batholomew Navratil, working with Polish-Russian physician Yakov Narkiewicz-Yodko, coined the term "electrography" in 1888 to describe the process of using the then brand-new photographic process to record electric discharges from both animate and inanimate things. Inventor Nikola Tesla took the first X-ray photographs in the late 1800s, and demonstrated how luminous discharges appeared around him when he ran 50,000 volts through his body with his recently developed Tesla coil in the 1890s. Few people shared Tesla's hands-on enthusiasm for directly handling high-voltage equipment, however, so this method for obtaining aura photographs did not catch on with the general public. The first American electrophotographs were taken in 1917 by F. F. Strong of Tufts University Medical School, who used Tesla's coil to photograph his hand as he placed it directly over a sheet of photographic film.[1]

Drs. Pratt and Schlemmer experimented with electrographic images from living tissues in the 1930s, and published their results with corona discharge photography in the *Journal of the Biological Photographic Association*.[2]

The first truly practical images of auras to be recorded for the general public were likely the aura sketches created by Dr. Walter Kilner in England in 1908. Kilner was in charge of medical patients at London's St. Thomas Hospital in the X-ray department, which was the first London hospital to have a demonstration of the roentgen rays in 1896. By 1897, St. Thomas' X-ray department was very busy. Dr. Walter Kilner's familiarity with the medical value of the X-ray photographs prompted him to see what other new kinds of imaging might prove useful for doctors. Kilner's breakthrough came when he discovered that human auras are visible through glass screens coated with dicyanin, a coal-tar dye that made human observers short-sighted and more able to perceive radiation in the ultra-violet band. With Kilner's viewing apparatus, patients could be scanned through the specially coated screens, which showed the size, location, color, and texture of their auras. Kilner was fascinated by changes in the aura, and he conducted many different kinds of experiments to see how gaseous vapors (including ammonia, bromine, chlorine, and iodine) changed the color of the aura and sometimes caused the inner layer of the aura to constrict in toward the body. Kilner also worked with subjects who could voluntarily change the color of their inner auric fields to match colors of objects in the room, and could do so for very small, localized areas of their auras. Kilner observed how the aura is smaller for children under the age of fifteen than it is for adults, and he also noted how teenagers have transitional auras. Kilner conducted a number of aura studies on people who suffered from a wide variety of illnesses, and he became so confident of the accuracy of his interpretation of healthy auras versus non-healthy auras that he wrote in his book, *The Human Aura,* "Examination of their aura has been the means of reassuring not a few people who had come up under the impression that they were suffering from cancer."[3]

Kirlian High Voltage Electrical Photography

Aura photography took an exciting step forward with the development of high voltage electrical photography in the 1940s. Soviet Semyon Davidovich Kirlian, a professional electrician and amateur photographer, and his wife Valentina built a simple photographic device that ran electric current from a high-frequency spark-generator (75,000 to 200,000 electrical pulses per second) across plates that sandwiched a sheet of photographic film. This device took luminescent photographs, which showed glowing auras without need of lenses or traditional cameras. Their new photographic technique was tested one night by a Soviet official who requested that Kirlian photos be taken of two nearly identical leaves, which had been plucked from plants in a Moscow greenhouse. The Kirlians were thrilled to be given such an exciting opportunity to demonstrate their new photographic technique, and worked through the night to make the best possible photographs of the leaves with their auras.[4]

By morning, the Kirlians were feeling disheartened, because only one of the leaf photos showed the kind of bright luminescence that was characteristic of Kirlian photographs. The bright leaf image had roundish spherical flares scattered symmetrically over the entire leaf image. The other photo was dim by comparison, with tiny geometrical dark figures sparsely scattered across the leaf image. When they showed these results to the scientist from Moscow, he exclaimed, "You've found it! One of those plants had already been contaminated with a serious plant disease. You've found this out immediately!"[5] He continued to explain that the leaf with glowing luminescence in its photograph was taken from a healthy plant—the other leaf whose photo showed little glow was from a diseased plant. While the two leaves appeared similar in terms of being fresh and green, their energies were very different, and illness would soon manifest in physical form in the diseased plant if it did not receive immediate care.

As researchers investigated auras with Kirlian photography, some found that damaged leaves sometimes appeared whole and healthy in Kirlian photographs. This "phantom effect" produced ghostly images of intact leaves around leaves that were obviously missing parts. Apparently, the energy field around living things can sometimes continue on even when the physical body has been damaged. In the 1960s, a group of Soviet scientists at the Kirov State University of Kazakhstan from a wide range of disciplines (including biology, biochemistry, and biophysics) combined Kirlian photography with electron microscopy and witnessed the energy body "double" of a living organism in motion. When asked to explain what this energy body double was, exactly, they described it as being "some sort of elementary plasma-like constellation made of ionised, excited electrons, protons, and possibly other particles. But at the same time, this energy body is not just particles. It is not a chaotic system. *It's a whole unified organism in itself.*"[6]

Kirlian photographs continue to prove themselves useful in showing levels of Qi in humans. While some scientists claimed that moisture was the actual variable being measured in Kirlian photographs,[7] they did not consider the effects of Qi. One such study published in *Science* in 1976 found that people who exercised until they got sweaty had strong Kirlian images, whereas those who sealed their hands in airtight plastic bags or dipped their hands in regular tap water had weak Kirlian images. Researchers knowledgeable in Qi, such as Richard Lee,[8] have reproduced similar results as the ones described in *Science*, but with the understanding of a QiGong practitioner. Lee saw the reasons for confusion when only *water* (wet hands) is considered a variable, so he conducted further tests, which showed how exercise increases Qi, and washing hands with magnetized water instead of regular tap water also increases Qi.

Kirlian Photography Today

Kirlian photography is still being utilized today. Researchers seek to understand how to detect signs of illness with Kirlian photographs in a timely fashion, and how a variety of energetic practices (such as QiGong and meditation) affect the aura. Kirlian researcher Thelma Moss of UCLA's Neuropsychiatric Institute conducted extensive research on how fingertip coronas correlate to a variety of emotional states. Moss found that the coronas of people who were photographed feeling strong emotions such as anger appeared red, while the coronas of relaxed people appeared blue. She also noted that occasionally when two or more people's fingertips were photographed simultaneously, one person's corona disappeared entirely. Moss and her colleagues considered several possible theories for the vanishing coronas, and felt the most likely explanation was that the energy fields of people with less dominant personalities were occasionally over-shadowed by those who were more dominant.[9] Whereas healthy, relaxed individuals typically have blue-white coronas, which appear on the Kirlian photographs between one sixteenth to one quarter of an inch, anxious or ill people usually have red blotches, which often somewhat dissolve the coronal boundary.[10]

Kirlian photos show fascinating glimpses of how peoples' auras intermingle: a couple who are photographed while thinking unpleasant thoughts toward one another while their fingertip coronas are photographed will appear to have two separate coronal images, whereas a Kirlian photograph of the couple's fingertips while they are feeling loving toward one another appears as a blur of energy as the two fingertip fields merge into one. Kirlian photography can also record the true states of interpersonal relationships. When two people like one another and are in close physical proximity to each other, their skin resistance drops and their energy fields intermingle affectionately. When two people do not feel attracted to one another, their skin resistance increases, and the auric field membranes separating them form something of an energy wall between them. Naturally, these feelings of attraction or resistance that people feel for each other can change over time, and Kirlian photography is capable of recording those changes. One Kirlian photographic study showed how a man and a woman's combined Kirlian photos progressed from the separate coronas of strangers to bright coronas of intense interest, to blended coronas of mutual affection over a period of three weeks.[11]

Kirlian photographs have proven themselves to be indispensable for a wide variety of practical applications. They help engineers to identify structural defects, such as tiny impurities and cracks. They help food science engineers find ways to keep produce fresher longer. They even appear to show tremendous potential for detecting life-threatening illnesses in humans. Kirlian researcher Dr. Loan Dumitrescu scanned 6,000 Romanian industrial workers for cancer, and found a 100 percent success rate in detecting breast cancer early and 74 percent success in detecting all cases of malignant cancer. In three cases of sarcoma, the tumor was indicated in the electrographic image, and the corresponding X-ray photographs showed no indications of cancer. Equally impressive was the finding by P. S. Chouhan that coronal fingertip images for 246 patients with cervical cancer could be sorted readily into groups of varying severity of illness. Chouhan found increasing density in images as patients suffered from higher stages of cervical cancer, with stage four cancer patients having the densest images on their Kirlian photographs.[12]

There is a great need for standardization of Kirlian photographic techniques and apparatus, in order that photographic results may be composed for scientific studies. Kirlian researcher J. Gordon Gadsby reports in *Complementary Therapies in Medicine*, "There are no international or local standards relating to the technical specifications for Kirlian cameras at this time."[13] Clearly, this is an oversight that deserves to be remedied, so that we may benefit from further Kirlian research into medical diagnosis.

Aura Imaging Today

Guy Coggins, founder and owner of Aura Imaging Systems and inventor of the Aura camera and the WinAura video system, first became interested in aura photography in 1970 when he saw a Kirlian camera at a holistic health event. Coggins was fascinated by the Kirlian photography and dreamed of one day building a camera that could photograph the aura around a person's body. The Aura camera, which Coggins subsequently invented and refined over the past thirty years, transmits radio waves through a person's energy field, which are detected by electrical sensors on an antenna grid receiver system behind the person and translated by a computer into colored lights that appear around the person's head and shoulders in the Polaroid photograph.[14] This Aura camera and his newer computer/video WinAura system have made practical aura viewing a reality, helping people get instant feedback about their auras. They have helped to demonstrate the effectiveness of energy healing to transform auras, and have changed thousands of lives as people become more conscious of their light shining within.

There are several ways to obtain a photo of your aura. For example, you can arrange to have your aura photograph taken at most psychic fairs. You can also have your aura photograph taken by energy healers who provide clients with before and after aura photographs. The images you will see in your aura photograph depict an approximation of what energy intuitives and aura viewers see when they view your aura. If your auric energy is primarily focused on thoughts and ideas, you'll likely see a lot of yellow and green in your aura. If your feelings are passionate and they dominate your thoughts, you'll see red or orange. Your mood can affect your aura photograph, so be sure to note exactly how you were feeling overall at the time of your aura photograph, and compare your self-assessment with that of the aura camera image. Many aura photographers are also energy intuitives who can help you understand the significance and meaning of the colors in your aura photograph.

Although aura cameras are not yet officially being used in

most hospitals and medical clinics, many alternative healing centers do utilize aura photography as a useful addition to their diagnostic services. Since persistent dark areas in aura photographs can indicate problem areas well in advance of physical ailments, aura photographs can help medical practitioners zero in on possible causes of medical problems. This approach is especially useful for medical patients whose medical complaints have no known cause. By localizing possible problem areas, aura photographs provide healers with much-needed information in a timely manner. While Guy Coggins and the staff at Aura Imaging Systems are careful to state that their cameras are not intended for use as medical devices, many people seeking additional insight into how they can improve their health are grateful for anything that can provide them with new clues. Aura Imaging Systems continues making new strides in aura photography, such as developing an aura system for pets, and Coggins is currently working on creating a much more sensitive large-scale imaging system for viewing entire human auras.

Schlieren Photography

Another kind of aura imaging photographs the human thermal plume. Schlieren photography was originally created in Germany in 1864 to detect flaws in glass. "Schlier" means "streak" in German. All changes in air density appear as being either brighter or darker than the background, so schlieren photography has been used extensively for wind tunnel disturbance studies of aircraft and projectiles. The human thermal plume was first photographed using schlieren equipment immediately after the end of World War II by a group of British scientists who were startled by what they saw.

Researchers at the City University of London have used schlieren photography to examine currents around the human body. They report, "Starting at the soles of the feet, the air layer moves slowly upward over the body. At the groin and under the armpits, it reverses direction briefly. At the shoulders, it spurts upward to dissipate in a feathery plume about five inches above the head."[15] This "plume" above the head sounds very much like the halo so familiar to us from ancient spiritual and religious art!

Using schlieren techniques in which people are photographed in front of a parabolic mirror that bends light, these images reveal the waves of heat, chemicals, and even flecks of skin that become airborne around our bodies. American chemist Gary Settles has patented a device that analyzes the human thermal plumes for airborne chemicals, such as explosives or drugs. He believes his device will prove useful for airport security and medical diagnoses. Any illness that causes people to produce unique and identifiable chemicals, such as the way diabetics produce a lot of acetone, could be easily detected with these photographs.[16]

While photographs of the human thermal plume are not photographs of the human energy body, they seem to be capable of providing similar information, such as early signs of illness. It would therefore be interesting to see side-by-side photographic studies of schlieren photographs, Kirlian photographs, and aura photographs taken at the same time and under the same conditions. It would be especially interesting to see whether various emotional and physical conditions appear similarly for all these photos.

Photographing Water Crystals

There is a lot we can learn from looking more closely at the pictures we take every day. Sometimes we can see signs of subtle energies at work in the simplest things, such as drops of frozen water under great magnification. When Japanese researcher

Masaru Emoto and his team of researchers photographed tiny ice crystals under high magnification, they discovered that something truly amazing happens. Emoto collected water samples from all around the world, and was able to demonstrate that water crystals from polluted locations look dark and gloomy with poor crystalline lattice structure when magnified between 200 and 500 times, whereas water from pure sources looks sparkling white with clear and beautiful crystalline structure. More amazingly, Emoto showed that water from polluted areas can be improved when prayed for,[17] as can water that is exposed to music by composers such as Beethoven or Mozart.[18]

The "message from water" that Masaru Emoto brings to us is that our thoughts and feelings have a visible effect on how clear, crystalline, and beautiful water drops will be. In a variation on his earlier trials, Emoto photographed water crystals that simply had words taped to their sample containers such as "beautiful," "dirty," "angel," and "devil." The differences that one can see between these drops of water that came from identical sources are simply amazing. While the "angel" water crystal looks something like a garland of beautiful white flowers arranged in a halo pattern, the "devil" crystal has a texture that looks something like scales.[19] The crystal from the vial labeled "beautiful" indeed looks beautiful, with lovely fronds of crystals that resemble a flower, while the crystal from the vial marked "dirty" looks dirty.[20]

When there is such a big difference in photographs of water crystals taken under very high magnification, it becomes obvious that even regular cameras can sometimes capture the influence of subtle energies at work.

Spirit Photography: Revealing God's Universe

Conventional photographs can sometimes contain very unconventional images, such as the visages of deceased people. These images are called "psychic photographs" by some, as a way of indicating that normally hidden things have become visible. Boston engraver William Mumler took the first known psychic photographs in 1862, when he was startled to see images of dead relatives appearing in the photographs he took of family and friends.[21]

Harriet Boswell describes how some normal photographs become psychic photographs many weeks or months after the photographs have been developed. In Boswell's experience, "extras" appeared on previously processed prints, which had looked normal when viewed for the first time.[22] These "delayed photo impression phenomena" and the psychic photographs that include dead people seem to indicate that the photographer's intention and energy field can transform ordinary, run-of-the-mill pictures into extraordinary photographs.

Madge Donahoe of Hampstead, London, discovered that she didn't even require cameras to produce images on non-exposed photographic paper or plates. In the 1920s, Madge Donahoe believed that she was able to facilitate these photos, called "skotographs," with assistance from spirit guides. While holding the unexposed film, Madge would feel that an image was being created, and the resulting blurry images at times ended up looking like dreamy impressions of things, such as a bouquet of flowers.

Chicago bellhop Ted Serios not only produced psychic photographs when he pointed a Polaroid camera at a blank wall, but he performed demonstrations for scientific observers in the 1950s.[23] In one such demonstration, Serios produced a photograph of a composite of two images that the researchers requested: the old Opera House in Central City, Colorado, and the medieval town of Rothenburg. Serios' resulting image is astonishing; it shows strong resemblance to the livery stable across from the old Opera House, but the bricks have been replaced by the kind of stone walls that are typically found in the medieval town of Rothenburg. On another occasion, psychiatrist Dr. Julie Eisenbud held the Polaroid camera and aimed it at Serios' forehead, while Serios focused on the intention to produce a photograph of the Chicago Hilton. That photograph, although somewhat blurry and out of focus, appears to have been taken from above the tops of the trees, higher than any camera angle commonly utilized by pedestrians, but a typical vantage point for someone engaged in an out-of-body astral travel experience!

Some people claim that their very presence around cameras can alter the way those cameras take pictures. In the mid-1970s, Dr. William Tiller conducted a dual-camera study with one such man, named Stan. Whatever camera Stan carried close to his body for several days became sensitized so that it would produce photographs in which people appeared somewhat transparent with occasional streaks of light. Stan's film and camera were sent to Kodak specialists, and determined to be in good working order. The peculiar photographs taken by whatever camera was sensitized by Stan did not fall within any of Kodak's standard error-mode categories. Stan could sensitize other peoples' cameras too, yet within a time period of between one to ten hours, the anomalous effects would end.

The dual camera study in which Dr. Tiller photographed the same scenes with an unsensitized camera alongside Stan's sensitized camera show some amazing differences.[24] People in Stan's photographs appear luminous and blurry, and sometimes quite transparent, while ordinary objects such as tables and chairs appear the same in both photographs. Light fixtures in the room seem to be generating streams of light in Stan's camera's photographs. Stan reported to Dr. Tiller that when he felt a sensation in his seventh cervical vertebra and his fourth thoracic vertebra, the camera he was using would take unusual pictures. The only other thing that Stan was doing differently than other photographers was that he prayed daily in accordance with his Bahai beliefs, with the intention "to reveal God's universe." Stan found the most pronounced effects occurred at spiritual or metaphysical locations or events.

As unusual as Stan's story may sound, it is possible to charge a camera with subtle energies and end up with rather unusual photographs. High Qi energy and exuberance may create this kind of energy photograph, and you can test it out for yourself. If you are interested in photography and have an adventurous spirit, chances are good that you'll have fun with this next exercise!

Exercise for Spirit Photography: Taking Pictures of Subtle Energies
This exercise requires only that you have a camera, a willingness to try an experiment with several rolls of film (be sure to have extra rolls, since there are no guarantees that your photos will show subtle energy right from the start), and are willing to keep your camera close to your body for several days while doing energy exercises.

1. Keep a camera close to your body, hung on a strap around your neck or at your side, for a period of several days, taking twenty minutes or more each day to meditate and/or pray to see the true nature of reality.

2. Focus on the area at the base of your neck (vertebra C7; the bony bump you can feel when you bend your head forward), and your heart (vertebra T4; near where your shoulder blades meet your spine).

3. Open your heart and throat chakras, by feeling warmth at both areas. You can put your hands over your heart and throat to help you feel your chakras. Working on one chakra at a time, slowly move your hand in a circular motion with the palm of your hand open and positioned a few inches away from your body. The circular motion of your hand helps to open your chakras.

4. Pray and/or meditate with the intent, "Show me the true nature of reality."

5. Take pictures with your camera after several days of sensitizing your camera, especially when you feel a sensation of energy around your seventh cervical vertebra and your fourth thoracic vertebra. The most interesting pictures indoors are ones with people in them as well as objects that provide points of reference.

6. Develop the pictures, and see whether you got photographs of subtle energy!

7. If you don't get anomalous effects the first time you try this exercise, do not be discouraged. Simply try it again, changing your photographic subjects to select times when Qi is naturally high (such as children photographed during the holidays). ◎

Aura Portrait Artists

Sometimes, a person's true personality can be conveyed most clearly in a painted portrait or sketch. Their inner qualities of being and essence are often clearly conveyed by the hand of a gifted artist. This becomes even more true when the portraits being created are aura portraits. Professional aura artists paint portraits of peoples' auras in many different ways. They can work from photographs, since the information they receive is highly clairvoyant. They can also work directly with subjects in person, which is generally best, since peoples' energy can change dramatically in just a few weeks. Just as the best painters and photographers will capture very different perspectives and views of their subjects, so too do aura portrait artists see subjects with unique artistic vision.

There is tremendous diversity of artistic styles available in aura portraits. Some artists, such as Carol Skylark, combine symbols, photographs, and a vision of auric colors into beautiful computerized aura portraits that have been used for CD and book covers, brochures, and signs. Skylark paints peoples' portraits with colors and symbols superimposed over the image of their head and upper body. Other artists, such as Bobbie Bowden, work with watercolors, pastels, and acrylics to depict brilliant plumes of color over peoples' heads to illustrate how their crown chakras appear.

Every sitting is a unique experience in which the artist might see something quite unexpected. For example, aura artist Carol Skylark, while doing a portrait of healer John Pollack, saw a white dove fly out of his heart as he did an energy healing for a man with a backache.

Aura portraits can also change peoples' lives. Aura portrait artist Elke Macartney has received hundreds of grateful letters, phone calls, and e-mails over the twelve years she's been doing aura portraits. Her subjects have reported profound changes in their lives immediately following the painting of their aura portrait. "All the changes boiled down to the one aspect of the aura portrait that they responded to: they got to see their true selves in all their radiant color and purpose. That changed their perception of themselves from one of a human stumbling through life, to a Being with a purpose, even if the purpose is to pose as a human stumbling through life."[25]

Aura portrait artists have a responsibility to show people their inner light, and focus on the positive rather than the inevitable dark spots and smudges that all of us have. Sitting for a portrait with any artist is an act of baring one's soul, and sitting for an aura portrait is the barest one can possibly get. Compassion and respect are essential qualities to look for in an aura portrait artist, as well as an understanding that the artist does not push or force his or her subjects to change. Elke Macartney explains, "Sometimes people come to my sessions crying, because the 'great so-and-so,' almighty seer, saw 'darkness' in them, and they needed it 'purged.' I bless the original reader's earnestness, but it is where I beg to differ: everyone has beauty inside, and everyone has a 'smudge' or two in their aura. Everyone."

The value of having your aura portrait done is the opportunity it provides to see yourself as the being of light you truly are. Your radiance is unique in its color and brilliance, and as you learn and grow in love and compassion, these changes shine forth around you, illuminating everything around you. When you see human energy fields, you may wish to share your vision in the form of colorful sketches or paintings. Using colored pencils or crayons, oil pastels, or paints, you can create beautiful works of art for family and friends when you draw their auras for them. If you feel unsure of your ability to draw the human figure, you can draw a simple stick figure that you surround with auric colors.

Exercise for Aura Portrait Artists

1. For this exercise, you'll need a piece of drawing paper, a recent photograph of a friend or family member, and some colorful pens, pencils, pastels, or paints. You can also do this exercise with a live portrait model, if you prefer.

2. Find a work area where you can comfortably sketch or paint your auric view of your subject.

3. Before you begin your portrait, close your eyes and exhale any tension and stress you are feeling. Inhale deeply, and feel energy rise up to you from the earth. Ground along an energy cord to the earth, and feel your intention that you will sketch, draw, or paint what you see.

4. Using clairvoyance and your artistic eye, paint any symbols or images that appear at each particular place where you see or feel them. Chakras often contain symbolic information, and the area above the head and around the upper body are often quite active with colors and symbols.

This exercise is especially interesting to do when you work on a picture of yourself. You can also paint an aura portrait of yourself by working with your mirror image. When you examine your own auric light, pay special attention to areas on which you may need to focus your attention for self-healing. These might appear as dark swirls or clouds, or places that are lacking in color. ⓞ

Remember, the whole point of this aura portrait exercise is to develop your confidence in seeing and drawing auras. Do not worry if your portrait is not as polished as you may have envisioned. Your art is valuable because you invested time and energy into it, and it is intrinsically good. The more you practice your art, the easier it will be.

Chapter 8 Questions for Review and Reflection

1. What is the first image of an aura you ever saw?
2. What do you want to learn from your aura photograph?
3. If you could have your Kirlian fingertip photograph taken with someone else, who would you choose to ask?
4. Which method of aura photography most interests you?
5. What special occasion would you want to commemorate with an aura photograph or portrait?
6. Remembering the research results from photographs of water, think of something kind to say to your body (which, after all, is mostly composed of water).
7. When you chose a photo to do an aura portrait sketch of, did the result look and feel true?
8. If your medical caregiver asked if you would like to have your energy field scanned in order to collect more information about your overall health, would you be interested?
9. Would you rather have your aura painted or sketched, or would you prefer to have your aura photographed?
10. Have you ever taken a picture that seemed to include subtle energies?

Chapter 9

Aura Meditations for Everyday Life

Meditation has existed since the birth of humankind, and there are as many different kinds of meditations as there are different kinds of people in the world. Meditation does not require any particular spiritual or religious beliefs, nor is there any one "right" way to meditate. Some meditations are walking meditations, some focus on clearing the mind, some emphasize breathing and breath control, some involve silently repeating a secret mantra over and over again, and some involve carefully sensing one small thing (like slowly rolling a grape in your mouth and tasting it). If you have tried a variety of meditations, then you might already know which kinds of meditation work best for you. If you are new to meditation, then you can try a variety of meditations in this chapter, and hopefully at least one of them will appeal to you.

Many studies have shown the benefits of meditation to be real and profound. Simply by meditating, people have been able to reduce the amount of stress they feel in their lives, alleviate physical pain, deepen awareness, relax muscle tension, improve mind-body coordination, achieve a sense of peace and joy, see more possibilities, and even reduce biological age.[1] In this chapter, different kinds of meditations are provided for assessing and transforming your aura to better suit the life you most wish to live. When you choose the area you most wish to improve (love, money, stress-relief), you can keep track of your progress in a journal by recording your observations as you undergo the process of changing your aura to change your life. Meditations can be done alone or in a group in which one person guides the meditation process and facilitates the sharing of experiences.

Have you ever been awakened in the middle of the night and not been able to fall back asleep again? Sometimes when you are under a great deal of stress, your mind will focus on problems so much that your sleep may be disrupted. Even when you know that such worries are a waste of your time and energy, they can seem to take on a life of their own in the wee hours. At such times, you may find yourself compelled to wake up and do something active, because so much adrenaline races through your system. In these situations, remember that the best solution might be to meditate. It may take some effort for you to remember that meditation is an option, because the urgency to *do* something can be so powerful.

Another time when you can greatly benefit from meditating, but probably forget to do so, is when you're frantically trying to get as many things done in as short a time as possible. Like a many-headed Hydra, you can lose your sense of unified vision and feel like you're being pulled in several different directions at once. It can seem crazy to set aside twenty minutes to meditate at such times, since you are keenly aware of how much needs to be done. Try meditation out some time, and see if the twenty minutes you invest in meditation and/or prayer reaps returns that compensate for the delay and inconvenience involved. Instead of feeling stressed and tired, you can be feeling relaxed and energized. Instead of thinking you have few or no options available, you can see a wide variety of choices you can make. Instead of feeling confused, you can feel focused and centered. There are even times following meditation and/or prayer in which you might feel you are guided to do exactly the right things at the right times, and everything you do feels effortless—like you're being assisted by fairies, elves, and angels!

If you are looking for the best way to enhance your aura and turn your life around, studies have shown that meditation might be the best thing you could do. A five-year study of male felons who were paroled from federal prisons showed that those parolees who practiced meditation were 35 percent to 40 percent less likely to return to prison or be sentenced for a new crime than otherwise similar parolees who didn't meditate. Meditation was proven to be much more effective than vocational training, psychotherapy, and prison education for helping parolees break free of a life of crime.[2] While your problems may not be quite as severe as those of federal prisoners, it's still good to know that such a powerful tool exists for making sweeping changes in your life.

Most of the following meditations require that you have some quiet space to yourself for about twenty or thirty minutes. You can read through all of them to get an idea of which ones might be most helpful or interesting for you, and get a sense of what's involved before you take the time to try them out.

Perceiving Auric Space Meditation

The space you take in this world is a relative thing. Your energy body can expand for miles around your physical body, or it can collapse in such a small space inside your body that it is nearly invisible. It is your perception of auric space that gives you a feeling of being expansive, or of feeling constricted. This meditation will help you broaden your horizons and become more conscious of space in your life.

1. Imagine your auric field wrapped tightly near your body, barely extending out from you at all. This is how your auric field hugs closely to you whenever you are sick, and at times when you feel scared. Notice whether you can perceive much of anything around you, using your high sense perception through your auric field. Notice where your attention tends to focus (such as on your physical self).

2. Now, pay attention to how your auric field expands slightly as you exhale, and give it a gentle push so it extends just a bit farther from your body with each breath you exhale.

3. Continue expanding your aura until its outer boundary extends farther than one arm's length away from your body. Keep breathing slowly and deeply, and watch your auric field continue to grow and expand.

4. See how far you are comfortable extending your aura. Do you wish to see if you can extend it even farther than that?

5. If you wish to keep extending your aura, watch your auric field reach out toward things far away from you. See it fill the space for feet, yards, and even miles around you with the brilliant colors of your auric field. Very large auric fields are common among enlightened masters and people who feel tremendous passion and compassion and love for life.

6. Bring your auric field back to whatever size feels most comfortable for you.

7. What difference (if any) did you notice between the time when your aura was very close to your body, and the time when it was extended?

Best Possible Life Chakra Meditation

This meditation is a powerful one, capable of changing your life for the better in every possible way. It can require a commitment of a great deal of time at first, but as your focus and attention improve, it will become easier and less time-consuming. The goal of the best possible life chakra meditation is to envision your best possible future self while viewing all seven of the primary chakras—and to align your chakras with this ideal arrangement.

As you begin this meditation process, you may experience some difficulty remaining focused on each chakra. The most important element and success factor for this meditation is that you *strongly desire* to align your chakras with your highest potential, and *remain focused* on each chakra as it feels and appears to you—waiting until your chakra changes to match the ideal configuration for you.

1. Imagine your best possible future self in energy form, with all seven primary chakras shining brightly. Feel your love for taking the path to becoming your best possible future self, and through this connection cord of love, sense your future self as if it were your own energy body right now through this energy cord.

2. Starting with the seventh chakra, the crown chakra, compare the way your best possible future self's crown chakra feels with how your current energy body's crown chakra feels. Especially note any differences in energy flow, color, and texture. If there is a big difference between the way your crown chakra feels now and the way it feels in your best possible future self, savor the feeling of your future self's crown chakra. Bask in it; notice every nuance and detail of the experience.

3. Feel the energy line of love connecting your current energy body and your best possible future self's energy body. Notice how the crown chakra on your best possible future self feels, and bring your current crown chakra up to feeling exactly like it. You may notice that other chakras in your energy body are affected by this change, and if this happens, relax in the knowledge that you are attuning your own energy body to its ideal configuration. Each chakra does affect its neighbors and is

sensitive to changes. Go slowly and savor the way your crown chakra feels now.

4. Repeat steps 2 and 3 above for the sixth chakra, the third eye chakra. Feeling love for becoming as much like your best possible future self as you can, sense how the third eye chakra will feel when it is optimally configured for you. Take your time and use all your senses to savor this moment, and when you have noticed every important nuance of feeling, allow your current energy body's third eye chakra to make the transition to its best possible configuration.

5. Repeat steps 2 and 3 above for the fifth chakra, the throat chakra. Feel how much you would love to have a perfectly configured throat chakra, and sense what this feels like. When you have a clear and complete feeling of this, bring it back to your current energy body's throat chakra.

6. Repeat steps 2 and 3 above for the fourth chakra, the heart chakra. This is your chakra of love and compassion, and these are the feelings to focus on now for your best possible future self. How will your heart chakra feel when you are the living embodiment of your best possible future self? Bring this feeling back to your current energy body's heart chakra, and hold that feeling—savoring and embracing it.

7. Repeat steps 2 and 3 above for the third chakra, the solar plexus chakra. This is your communication center between you and the outside world, and a powerful energy center for manifesting what you want in your life. Feel how your best possible future self is holding this solar plexus chakra energy—is it clear and strong, and vibrant and clean? Most likely it's in a lot better shape than your current solar plexus chakra energy! You can remedy this by transforming your existing solar plexus chakra to match that of your best possible future self.

8. Repeat steps 2 and 3 above for the second chakra, the hara chakra just below your navel. This chakra is also known as

the "dan tien" chakra, and it is a place you may be inadvertently picking up and carrying other peoples' "stuff." Feel how different your best possible future self's second chakra is compared to your current energy body's and allow your chakra to change to match your ideal self.

9. Repeat steps 2 and 3 above for the first chakra, the root chakra at the base of your spine. Feel how well grounded your best possible future self is, and how that allows you to stand up for yourself and feel centered and an important and integral part of all that is. Notice all the sensations in your best-balanced root chakra, and bring those qualities back to your current energy body root chakra.

10. Once you've viewed and transformed all your chakras, take a few more minutes to feel your chakras integrating with one another and interacting with the world around you. Pay attention to how your day goes differently than usual—hopefully in enjoyable ways, and in how you feel about yourself and events that unfold around you.

The first time you do this, it's a good idea to draw what you see and take notes about what you observe in this exercise. Your notes will help remind you of your highest energetic goal.

Fast Aura Meditation

You can use this fast meditation when you don't have a private place or time to meditate, but wish to calm yourself and enhance your aura quickly. If you don't have large blocks of uninterrupted time and find yourself in need of a quick energy pick-me-up, this is a great meditation to do wherever you may be.

1. Ground yourself, imagining an auric cord of energy running down to the core of the earth from your root

chakra. Let all worries and resentments drop away.

2.   Feel your crown chakra open to receive love and divine inspiration and guidance from the source of all creation.

3.   Sway your body gently as you visualize all your chakras aligning with one another and your divine purpose. Softly roll your head, shrug your shoulders, lift and gently roll your left shoulder and then your right. Visualize each chakra shining brightly as it opens to receive healing energy from the sky above and the earth below.

4.   Inhale deeply, breathing in love and appreciation for who you are. Exhale deeply, releasing everything inside you that is not part of you and your energy.

While this fast aura meditation can be done in a short amount of time, you can also take your time with it if you prefer. It is elegant in its simplicity, since it provides you with the tools for establishing and maintaining a healthy flow of Qi. Best of all, it's versatile. It is a good meditation for doing while riding on public transportation, standing in line, or lying in bed.

Good Health and Healing Meditation

Just as chronic worry and stress first cause damage to one's aura and then create problems in one's physical body, freedom from stress can eventually clear one's aura and reverse physical health problems. All meditations that increase an overall sense of being simultaneously energized and relaxed are therefore good for one's health. The following meditation is especially good for improving one's physical health, since that is its primary emphasis and intention.

1. Find a quiet time and space where you can have twenty

to thirty minutes alone. Sit or lie down in the most comfortable position for you.

2. Close your eyes and feel your energy body around you. Notice if you can see any dark areas, holes, tears, rips, or sections of grainy energy.

3. Imagine that you are now calling on a brilliant angel/energy being of love to help you repair the damaged areas in your aura. (*Important: When you first call on angels, be sure to state that you only invite those who come in the purest form of unconditional love. Do not invite any energy beings who make demands upon you or do not feel completely loving.*) This energy being is an expert at strengthening your energy field, and when you request assistance will immediately begin repairing all damaged areas of your aura.

4. If your energy body requires extensive assistance, call on another angel/energy being or two . . . or three! Know that whatever you need will be provided, as long as you ask with all your heart and feel grateful for the help you receive.

5. Observe what these angels are doing, and how much better you feel as they work to fluff, clear, and repair your aura. Note whatever physical sensations you feel as this healing continues.

Integrated Across All Possible Universes Meditation

This meditation may seem rather exotic and unusual, because it involves visualizing all your possible selves. There is special value in this meditation, for it works to bring increasing order to the universe across all possible realities. As you find yourself becoming consciously connected to all your possible realities and becoming more relaxed and energized through this meditation, the benefits will be far-reaching and profound.

1. Imagine for a moment that you exist in many different forms across an infinite number of parallel universes. In one universe you are poor, in another you are wealthy, and in yet another you are the opposite gender from what you are today. What remains the same in every universe is some quality of uniqueness about your energy essence and who you truly are.

2. Imagine that as you become aware of all your possible selves, they become aware of you. When you intend to become more energized and relaxed through meditation, so will each of them.

3. Imagine that you and all your possible selves are grounded, so all negativity, stress, and tension slips down and away.

4. With each inhalation of love, all of your possible selves will feel loved and connected. With each exhalation of worries, doubts, anger and fear, all your possible selves feel stronger and more centered.

5. Imagine that you and all your possible selves are connected to a divine source and are receiving inspiration that will allow you to fulfill your unique purpose and special destiny.

6. As you finish this meditation, thank all your possible selves for joining you in this meditation.

Prosperity Meditation

You are already prosperous in many ways. This meditation will help you recognize how well you are doing, and increase your confidence that you are attracting all you desire to you right now. The key to success of the prosperity meditation is the feeling of it. It depends on your ability to feel gratitude and love, and to let go of fears and resentments.

1. Close your eyes, and see yourself as spirit or God would see you—shining brightly, like a star. You are surrounded by

love and were created from love. You are precious beyond measure. You are blessed with the ability to help yourself and others in many ways. You have great potential within you to shine more brightly than ever before. The only things that have ever stopped you from shining so brightly have been your fears and resentments. Let go of all blame and anger, and all doubt and worry. You are a divine being of inner light who has become manifest in physical form. As you more fully embody this divine light, you will be blessed with abundant prosperity. Help is always here for you. All you ever need to do is ask spirit for guidance.

2. Open your eyes and say aloud three times, "The source of all prosperity is infinite, and blesses me with abundance. Thank you for fulfilling my every need today and always."

3. Feel the loving energy of all those who support your endeavors.

4. Using all your high sensory perceptions (clairaudience, clairvoyance, clairsentience, clairgoutance, clairolorance), imagine your best possible future as fully and vibrantly as possible. See and feel yourself immersed in every aspect of life as you most need it to be. Say aloud, "All my favorite dreams have come true!" and feel the joy and exuberance of this being so.

Summoning Your True Love Meditation

This summoning your true love meditation can be used to call your true love to you. By visualizing his or her presence in your life, using your high sensory perception, and feeling your need for her to be in your life right now, you will send out a very strong auric cord to the one who is best suited to you. She will feel this pull of attraction, and be drawn into your life. You will then simply need to recognize her when she arrives.

1. Feel your genuine heartfelt desire to know your true love. Let this feeling of love open your heart chakra, and send out a greeting to your true love.
2. Shut your eyes, if you like, and hone your high sensory perception. Notice every nuance of a vision, smell, and feeling you receive.
3. When you sense your true love's presence near you, ask for a hug, so you may know how to recognize this person in the way she interacts with you. Pay attention to how this hug feels different from every other hug. Notice additional aspects of how this person feels when she is so close to you.

Once you've done this summoning true love meditation, you have established a strong, conscious energy cord link to the one your spirit knows as your true love. You have felt how this person feels near you and while hugging you, and you can repeat this meditation at other times if you wish to gain additional information. By contacting this person with so much love through an auric cord, you have initiated a call that is even now summoning him or her into your life. She may or may not be easy to recognize in physical form, but at least you now know that she exists, as well as knowing a little bit about how she feels when close to you.

The Star You Are: Eternal Connection to Cosmic Source Meditation

Each of us energy beings arose from a common source. In this meditation, you will experience your connection to the cosmic source of all that is, and observe how you are uniquely created from love. When you recall your divine connection to the cosmic source, you strengthen your energy field and gain important knowledge about who you are in your pure energy form.

1. Close your eyes and imagine that you are at the center of all universes, at the place and time where all life and consciousness begins.
2. Imagine that you can see yourself as a very small, yet important piece of all that is. Your energy body emerges slowly from the source of all creation, shining softly at first in a cloud of gentle light, and then more brightly as your unique role in the universe is made clear.
3. Slowly you emerge as a shining star of brilliant light set against the background of darkest night. Other lights shine around you, welcoming you.
4. Your connection to the cosmic source is the tap root, or primary source of sustenance, of the essence of your being. That multidimensional silvery thread of energy is nearly invisible, but infinitely strong. You are connected through it to all possibilities, to all universes, and to all loves past, present, and future. You are a unique creation of cosmic love with divine purpose.
5. You are an energy being of light, and you vibrate as both music and light. Listen carefully to hear the sound of your soul, and hear how it plays in harmony with the sound of cosmic creation.

You-niversal Energy Body Meditation

Visualize your aura as being very, very large—the size of an entire universe! Imagine that your consciousness is as small as a single ray of light, and that you will be traveling across the great expanses of your aura to more fully explore it. Like a single photon, you take up no space at all and although human consciousness observes that you travel very fast, from your point of view, you proceed at a slow enough pace to observe everything around you.

1. Begin your voyage across your energy field by approaching yourself from a long way away. At first, all that you can see of your aura is a gentle glow in the distance.

2. As your photon ray of consciousness approaches your energy body, notice the shapes and colors you see that encircle the physical form.

3. Come close enough to see the outer auric field membrane, and circle around it. Make several complete rotations around the energy field, noticing any variations in color, texture, or shape.

4. When you feel ready, pierce the outer layer of the auric membrane and travel through the layers inside. Each layer is huge, and you are free to look around and see how each auric layer meets its neighbors, and what is going on inside. Notice any visual symbols you see, in addition to the colors.

5. As you approach the innermost layers of the auric field, look to see if you can observe the chakras. Notice what colors and brightness they have, and look to see how open or closed they are. If you wish, you may travel through one of the chakras to the other side (from front to back, or from back to front). Pick the one that most appeals to you.

6. Now, travel to the center of your energy body. Observe the entire universe of energy all around you, moving and flowing in brilliant colors of light. You are a universe of light.

Aura Texture Healing Meditation

There are many different possible textures in human auras in general, and within your own aura in particular. You can learn to identify areas of your energy body that are in need of clearing or cleansing, by becoming adept at recognizing the difference between healthy and unhealthy energy fields. Whereas healthy energy fields typically feel smooth and vibrant, unhealthy ones can feel clogged, sticky, prickly, grainy, heavy, or thick.

1. Sit down in a chair in which you can comfortably move your arms around your entire body. You will use your hands as sensors for this meditation to feel the energy field all around your body.

2. Beginning at the top of your head, place your hands on either side of your head, situated several inches to a foot away from your ears. Slowly move your hands around your head, feeling the texture of your auric field.

3. Move both hands together without touching each other or your physical body—wave your hands slowly and sensitively through your auric field to feel whatever you can feel. Move your hands in close to your body and out far away from your body. Move them in front of and behind your body.

4. Continue moving your hands slowly around your entire auric field, noting what you experience as you go. If you find areas of missing aura, wave your hands in a figure eight shape to reconnect your field in that location. If you find heavy, sticky, or otherwise unhealthy energy, use your hands to pull it out of your energy body as you exhale the negative energy and inhale love and healing energy. Continue exhaling and releasing disease, and inhaling love and good health.

A Fresh Start: Tabula Rasa Meditation

To a large degree, your life is exactly what you create it to be. By virtue of your daily habitual thoughts and feelings, you create the foundation upon which the house of your life is built. The advantage of cleansing the foundation of your life of energetic clutter is that like a blank slate or tabula rasa, anything at all can be possible for you. This meditation is recommended for you if you have faced persistent problems in life, and wish to find an energetically clean point for starting fresh.

1. Do you remember a time when you were a child and felt wonderfully excited about something? You were not concerned with practicalities, and had not yet told anyone of how you were feeling and what you were thinking about. You were experiencing a moment that contained all possibility and tremendous enthusiasm.

2. Smell the smells around you as you feel this joyous state of being. You know in your heart and soul that anything is possible, and can look around at the world and feel your heart sing. See the colors and shapes of energy around you; feel their textures.

3. Wrap this special moment up energetically as a present from your past, and bring it to your life in this moment now. Feel the joyous sense of wonder you had and the sheer delight in being alive. This is the energy you can now bring to anything in your life you need it for—anything at all! With childlike wonder and creativity, you can face every situation with love, awe, and fearlessness. You are meant to succeed at bringing your special gifts to the world, and you can feel the sheer joy in reveling in the essence of all you are.

4. If you feel any negative thoughts or feelings, ground yourself and let them go down an auric energy cord to the earth. Look at that present of the bliss of your youthful excitement, and feel once again the sense of joy and wonder it brings to you. You are a whole new person today, refreshed with the youthful vigor of your spiritual energy and ready to do anything you put your mind to!

Fetal Memories Meditation

In this meditation, you will re-experience your birth as an energy being inhabiting your physical body, and will view yourself as a baby inside your mother's womb. The purpose of this meditation is to more fully regain your auric viewing and sensing abilities as you get a chance to see yourself as the adorable baby you once were.

1. Close your eyes, and imagine the time when you were a fetus in your mother's womb. All is dark and warm and safe, and you are able to see colors and shapes and sounds around you. You can feel your mother's heartbeat and see waves of colored light wash over and around you.

2. When you are ready, let your awareness move as you "fly" above yourself and your mother and look down from above to see both of you.

3. Observe the light shining from your mother's womb, where your tiny body grows. See your light and its soft colors blending with your mother's aura. Feel how the waves of color and light wash across each other and combine occasionally, like waves in the sea.

4. As your mother goes about her daily activities, your light combines with hers, touching what she touches, feeling what she feels. See how the colors of your aura look similar to your mother's, and also how they are so very different. Sometimes you have the same reaction to people and situations, and other times you respond quite differently. Observe what is going on around the two of you, and watch your auras in action.

5. See how your aura grows and responds to your mother and everyone and everything around you. Before you are even born, you are perceiving the world around you and getting to know your body, your home, and your family. You are

establishing a sense of who you are, and how you will fit in to this life, to this environment.

Perceiving Consciousness Meditation

Imagine for a moment that everything around you is conscious, and is aware of your thoughts and feelings even when you don't say a word. The floor, the walls, the birds, the grasses, the trees, and every man-made thing is observing the effects of your energy. This meditation will help you perceive this consciousness all around you so that you may more effectively interact with the world.

1. Shut your eyes, and clear your mind. Let all thoughts, worries, fears, and mental clutter fall away to the center of the earth. Listen to hear if the earth makes any sound, using your clairaudience. Thank the earth for helping clear out your energetic clutter. Notice if you feel or know any response from the earth, using your clairsentience. Open all your high sense perceptions, and observe anything at all that earth says to you.

2. With as clear a mind as possible, note any feelings or thoughts that drift your way and you are fairly sure are not your own. When you feel one, ask, "Whose feelings and thoughts are these?" Listen for a response. Keep listening and reaching out with your auric membrane to sense the consciousness of all things around you.

3. If you find your mind getting cluttered again with your own thoughts and feelings, repeat the grounding exercise as often as necessary. Continue listening for feelings and thoughts around you, and asking, "Whose thoughts and feelings are these?"

4. When you hear silence and quiet, reach out to talk with something near you, using just your mind and energy body to make a connection. Say, "Hello!" and ask, "How are you feeling?"

and wait to receive a reply. Some things don't say much, and feel deeply and slowly, while others chatter and race from topic to topic.

5. Say, "Hello!" and "How are you?" to other objects around you, waiting for responses from each one before proceeding to the next. If you are pleased with the answers you receive to these questions, feel free to ask more questions, such as, "What would you most like me to know?"

Nothingness Meditation

This is an ultimate cleansing meditation that is designed to help you clear out all negative influences, and fully connect to your innermost essential self. The experience of nothingness is one that takes us back to our primordial beginnings, to the nothingness from which we arose. The nothingness is the mother of us all, the place from which we cannot fall. It connects all dimensions of existence across all realities, and has the ability to restore our vision of ourselves as who we truly are.

1. Imagine a sense of absolute emptiness, devoid of all sound, smell, tastes, touch, and visions. Here is a place of absolute tranquility that transcends space and time. Eternal and everlasting absolute silence abides here.

2. Feel yourself embraced by this nothingness, and calmed and soothed by it. It is your birthright as a spiritual being to enjoy the peace and tranquility that is found here, as everything that is not your true energy essence is stripped away from you, absorbed into the infinite expanses of nothingness.

3. As you rest in this nothingness, feel yourself returning to your own natural rhythms of existence. You are no longer affected by the comings and goings of others, nor by their thought-forms. Your every thought and feeling arises like a flash

of brilliant light, alone and spectacular against the background of nothing in all directions.

4. Watch the sound and light show of your energy body essence as each and every thought arises, takes shape, and drifts away. If you reach a moment of stillness in which no further thought-forms arise, feel the beauty of yourself and see yourself as who you truly are: resplendent with light, a bright shining star.

Bringing Meditation Home

Once you make meditation a regular part of your daily life, you may notice that you feel at home wherever you may be. If you want to know how much of a difference meditation can make in your life, keep track of how often you meditate in a journal. When you feel rushed, meditation can bring you back to a sense of living in the eternal now. When you feel tired, meditation can refresh and renew your body and spirits. When you feel confused, meditation can bring you clarity. When you feel defeated, meditation can bring you inspiration and new ideas.

Chapter 9 Questions for Review and Reflection

1. What benefits can meditation bring you that you feel most in need of?

2. When can you regularly devote time, space, and attention to meditation in your daily life?

3. How did you visualize yourself in the best possible life chakra meditation?

4. What kind of meditation feels most comfortable to you?

5. What meditation are you most in need of at this time?

6. What did you discover in these meditations that surprised you most?

7. Which of the meditations in this chapter would you most like someone to guide you through?

8. Which of these meditations would you like to guide others through?

9. Which of these meditations helped you know yourself better? What did you learn?

10. Did any of these meditations feel familiar to you, as if you've done them before?

Chapter 10
Color Assessment and Therapy

Color has a tremendous physiological and psychological impact on people, though we often take its powerful effects for granted. Color can soothe or excite us, please or upset us, alert or distract us. Color is capable of grabbing our attention with dramatic force, or exerting a much more subtle effect on our psyche. If you ever spend time in a room lit by red light, for example, you may notice how your blood pressure increases and you begin to breathe and blink more rapidly. If you spend time in a room lit in blue, you will probably notice feeling much more relaxed.[1]

Psychologists, interior and exterior designers, product designers, human factors engineers, and alternative health care providers are just a few of the professions that rely upon knowledge of the powerful effects that colors have on people. They use color to sell products, improve work productivity, clarify communications, assess personality characteristics, enhance physical therapy treatments, and ensure safety around hazardous places and machinery. Consumers are so fascinated by colored foods such as green and purple ketchup that ketchup sales increased by 14 percent in the first year these products were introduced.[2] Some of the effects that color has on people are so remarkable and well-documented that entire nations have changed the way they do things to take advantage of color's tremendous power in our lives. After the U. S. Navy hired a color consultant to improve safety in the 1940s, there was such a significant reduction in accidents at naval shipyards that safety color codes were soon adopted as international standards worldwide.[3]

Color assessment therapy is an age-old practice of utilizing colors in ways that help people feel healthier by assessing their need for colors and providing treatments for color imbalances. Ancient Egyptian healers placed their patients in colored rooms, and prescribed colored gems and perfumes for them to wear.[4] The ancient Greeks and Romans also extensively practiced similar kinds of color therapy. In Europe during the Renaissance, colored clothing, ointments, flowers, and salves were recommended for people who requested medical assistance. In the late 1800s, Edwin Babbit's "Thermolume" color treatment cabinet and funnel-shaped color treatment "Chromo Disk" provided some of the first color light therapy for people.[5]

Some children now attend schools that surround each age and activity group with the most helpful color for who they are and what they are doing, such as the schools designed by Rudolf Steiner. Students move from beginning-year pink classrooms through the subsequent orange, red, yellow, and green classrooms. Warm colors for stimulating activities are found in the orange and red handicrafts room. Cooler colors that have a calming effect, such as blue, are used for the stage where assemblies, group presentations, and performances take place.[6]

Many medical studies in the 1980s indicated the tremendous potential that color therapy has to improve our lives. Rodent studies showed that exposure to red or pink light increased appetite and growth rate, and exposure to blue light caused their fur coats to grow thicker. Human studies showed that colored lights can relieve jaundice, arthritis, migraines, and dyslexia, and full-spectrum or blue light treatment brings jaundiced babies' bilirubin levels down to safe levels.[7] Blue light has also been found to be useful in relieving pain for women who suffer from rheumatoid arthritis,[8] while red light has been found effective for treating migraine headaches.[9] Colored contact lenses have been found to help dyslexics instantly improve their reading abilities.[10]

While there is a growing body of evidence to suggest that bringing needed colors into one's life can positively affect one's emotional, intellectual, and physical health, medical studies have not fully explored the health effects of color treatment. Doctors know that people's health can be profoundly affected by light, yet there is a need for further research into the effects of colored light. Since the American Medical Association feels there is still insufficient evidence that color can consistently assist people heal, it has actively discouraged color therapy in America. Many color therapists therefore continue their specialized form of alternative medicine in other countries, such as England.

Color Therapy Self-Assessment

Do you feel like the demands of your life are pushing you off center? You might be subconsciously expressing the need for a certain color in your life. For example, if you are feeling unbalanced, you will probably benefit from introducing green into your life. Wearing green clothes, wearing green eyewear, visualizing green, eating green food, or putting green decorations or colored lights in your home or office are all good ways to help bring green into your life. Remember to trust your own intuition and "gut feelings" (do a chakra check!) when making any such color changes in your life, because color therapy can greatly affect you on all levels. If you would like a full assessment of your colors, you will benefit from visiting a color practitioner. Color practitioners help you assess your color needs and aid in correcting color imbalances in the aura by using a variety of techniques. Full spectrum lamps, colored crystals, and colored massage oils are some of the many treatment options provided by color therapists today.[11]

If you're curious about the benefit of particular colors in your life, and can't visit a color practitioner, you can assess your color needs by looking at the following table and noticing if anything listed on the left-hand side is troubling you. You can trust your own intuition for selecting the colors that will be most helpful in your life. Studies have shown that if you are feeling stressed and tense, you will naturally tend to prefer darker colors that help soothe you, while if you need to burn off excess energy, you will tend to select brighter colors that stimulate you to exercise.[12] If you notice you often feel apathetic, for example, you can bring more red into your life. If your need for the color is situational—such as you only feel rushed while you are driving on the freeway to work each day, or you only feel depressed when you first start work on Monday morning—you can even think of creative ways to bring the color you need to the time and place you need it most. You can reduce your feelings of stress on the freeway by adding a few blue accessories to the interior of your car (such as blue floor mats), and an orange coffee mug on your desk can bring you more joy at the beginning of each week when you need it most.

Color Therapy Self-Assessment

If you are feeling:	*You may benefit from more:*
Apathetic	**Red** for exciting energy
Depressed	**Orange** for joyful celebration
Confused	**Yellow** for creative clarity
Unbalanced	**Green** for healing balance
Rushed	**Blue** for calm dependability
Socially pressured	**Indigo** for sensitive individuality
Inferior	**Violet** for inspirational respect

The colors you need are a matter of your individual require-ments at this particular time in your life. Colors that are right for someone else may not be best for you, and even colors that were right for you several years ago may no longer be what you need most right now. Your favorite color is probably the one you feel comfortable having near you most often, although a color you don't like very much may well have the benefits you need the most. Once you have identified a color or colors you feel you can benefit from, all you need to do is find fun ways to bring more of that color into your life. Some relatively easy ways to satisfy your color needs are by changing the colors of your clothing, your home, the food you eat, and your meditations. Every time you notice colors in your life, ask yourself if there is a way to introduce a bit more of the color(s) you feel deficient in. Most of all, make sure you have fun with color!

You will likely notice emotional and physical effects on you when you add a new color to your life, as it influences your entire energy field. Colors that you find most unpleasant to look at tend to be the ones you most need in order to restore balance to your life, although seeing those unpleasant colors may cause you to feel additionally stressed.[13] Your particular need for a certain color will likely be related to an area of your body that has been sick or injured, or a chakra that holds a lot of trauma. As you may recall, each chakra has its own color that is typically associated with it, and when the chakra gets "muddy" or dark, that area of your life also suffers. When you gradually introduce the colors you need to your life, make sure that you keep lots of your favorite colors nearby, so you can ease yourself into the benefits of the new colors without feeling a need to resort to old vices (such as smoking, drinking, or eating sweets) for emotional support.

Clothing Color Therapy

When you look at your wardrobe, do you notice a greater abundance of one or two colors? These are most likely the colors you like the best, and with which you resonate most strongly. If you have discovered a need for more of a given color in your life, you can start wearing more of that color. Pay attention to how you feel when you wear the "new" color, and note if it brings you the desired changes in your life and aura over time. The color of the clothing you wear can have a big effect on the people around you, and an even bigger effect on you, when you wear that same color for extended periods of time. Colors that you wear a lot become part of your own energy field, where they persist in your aura long after you've taken the clothing off.

Now that you're looking at the effects that color has on your life, you can try color-coordinating your closet, so each color is grouped together, creating a rainbow effect. This organizational system will make it easier for you to quickly coordinate your outfits, and it also gives you a chance to consciously consider which colors you need the most as you get dressed. When you find you need more of a color you don't have much of, you can remember that color the next time you go shopping. You can also learn a lot about yourself while color-organizing your closet. For example, you may notice that you've gone through phases of color preference in your life, which says a lot about how you were feeling at the time you had those color preferences.

Exercise in Clothing Color Therapy

1. Take a look at your clothing and find out whether it covers the entire spectrum of the rainbow, or consists of mostly one or two colors.

2. If you feel a need to wear different colors of clothing than what you currently have, take an inventory of what colors of clothing you would most like to add to your wardrobe in the future.

3. Try wearing the color you selected as needing more of in your life. Notice if you feel any different wearing that color after a day or more. You can make notes in your journal about how you feel each time you try a new color, so you can keep track of your wardrobe color experiment. ◎

Eyewear Color Therapy

A relatively easy way of receiving color therapy benefits is from wearing colored eyewear, such as colored sunglasses. The only challenge is in finding glasses that you feel will work best for you, and then wearing them at times when they won't adversely impact your activities (such as driving a car). You can find out whether or not your worldview changes when you wear "rose-colored glasses," or you can try violet, green, indigo, or blue glasses.

The advantage of this form of color therapy is that you can wear a certain color for however long or short a time you feel you need it. The disadvantage is that you may find yourself needing to try several different colors, and not knowing exactly which ones will work best for you. You can use intuitive methods to find out which color will be best for you, or you can get several different kinds of glasses and see how you feel when you try different ones on. While there are currently about 140 different possible choices for prescribed tinted lenses, there are seven choices of rainbow-hued non-prescription colored glasses.

A relatively new trend in eyewear is the use of colored contact lenses. If you choose to try these, make sure that you wear lenses that have been tested (don't make your own colored lenses at home), and consult an eye doctor regarding whether such lenses are safe for you to wear. You need to consult an eye doctor even if you don't require prescription glasses, because some peoples' corneas get scratched easily if they wear contact lenses. In any case, you will need professional advice on wear schedule and proper fit.

Exercise in Eyewear Color Therapy

1. Determine which color you'd like to have more of in your life by how you feel toward the wide spectrum of colors.

2. Find colored glasses in that shade of color that you need. Several shops sell these kinds of eyewear on the Internet, and you can also find them at many places that sell sunglasses.

3. Try wearing the colored eyewear for twenty to thirty minutes a day, taking them off when you feel a desire to remove them.

4. What difference (if any) do you notice after wearing the colored glasses? ◎

Home Décor Color Therapy

Your home living environment is another great place to introduce color changes, if you wish to bring more of a certain kind of energy into your household. Since colors in your home affect everyone who shares your living space, it is wise to assess individual needs before making large changes in your interior color scheme. What helps one person might aggravate another, so it's good to compartmentalize color changes whenever individual needs are different.

Many people who work in the field of graphic and visual design are aware of the powerful effects of colors on interior décor. Shades of yellow-green are banned from aircraft interiors and avoided on boats, because they have been known to induce nausea.[14] Bubble gum pink, or "drunk tank pink" as it has also become known, commonly appears in jail cells, where it is used to help calm potentially violent prisoners, who feel tranquilized by spending time in pink rooms.[15] Clever sports coaches also use this information to their advantage by painting the visiting team's locker room pink.[16] Red has an appetite-inducing effect in kitchens, so color consultants generally advise clients to use other colors in eating and food preparation areas, unless one intends to increase one's food consumption. Fast-food restaurants often take advantage of the way red influences people to eat more, and use red on their walls, floors, counter tops, tables, and chairs. You can help reduce your appetite at home by removing the color red from your kitchen and dining area. If you want to introduce a more respectful feeling at your dinner table, you can purchase violet placemats or a violet tablecloth. You will find that your family will be more polite to one another, even when you're not entertaining company!

Feng Shui

One of the most disciplined methods for carefully utilizing color in interior spaces is the ancient Chinese art of feng shui. Feng shui translates from the Chinese to mean "wind and water," and is the Chinese art of harmonious placement for the best flow of Qi in a given environment. This ancient Chinese practice of balancing Qi is based on the concept that each and every one of us affects the energy of everything around us. The Qi of our home affects our own personal Qi, which in turn affects our physical body. Feng shui helps us better understand how our human energy field is linked to the energy of all other things in the universe, as we pay close attention to the interior décor in our surroundings.

Feng shui practitioners associate colors with the magnetic compass directions in a room or space. Since feng shui also assigns certain attributes such as fame or marriage to each direction in a room, the colors also become important for helping to improve those areas in one's life. Certain colors are considered to be particularly auspicious for improving whatever attribute is located in that direction, such as red being recommended for enhancing fame, when something red is situated in the south side of a room. Each area of a room is therefore considered to be representative of a particular function in one's life (such as marriage, friends, family, wealth, knowledge), and an important part of aligning the Qi properly in the room is selecting the appropriate colors to be situated in each of these areas.[17]

Optimal Feng Shui Colors in a Living Space

Direction	Color	Influence
South	Red	Fame
Southwest	Pink	Partnership/marriage
West	White	Children
Northwest	Gray	Helpful people
North	Black	Career
Northeast	Blue	Knowledge
East	Green	Family
Southeast	Purple	Wealth

Exercise in Home Décor Color Therapy

1. Take a look around your home, and see what colors you notice as you walk from room to room. Unless you've already given a great deal of thought to your interior décor, you may be surprised at what you see. How do the colors in your home relate to the feelings you experience in each room?

2. Ask yourself what you would like to change in order to create a new atmosphere in your home that is more enjoyable for you. Keep in mind that color changes can be easily implemented and don't have to be costly, either. Accessories like artwork, pillows, throw rugs, and curtains can be changed with relative ease and not too much expense.

3. Choose some simple color changes you can easily implement. Notice whether you and those who live with you feel any differently after you've made the changes. ◎

Exercise in Feng Shui
1. Choose an area of your life you would most like to improve, by finding a corresponding influence in the Optimal Feng Shui Colors list (such as fame, marriage/partnership, children, helpful people, career, knowledge, family, wealth).

2. Choose a room in your home in which you will introduce a color change in the appropriate part of the room (such as south, west, north, or east).

3. Add something in the appropriate color to the specified area of the room you have chosen. It doesn't need to be something very large; the most important thing with feng shui is neatness and attention to the Qi of the item. Make sure that the change you make is an overall improvement in the look and feel of the room, and that the colored item you add properly expresses your personality and taste.

4. After several days and weeks pass, notice if there have been any significant improvements in the area of your life you sought to improve, and in your energy field and the energy field of your home. ◎

Food and Water Color Therapy

When you buy food at the store, consider making some of your food purchase decisions based on the color of each food. For example, you can give yourself strong subliminal messages of bringing more clarity into your life when you eat yellow bananas and corn. You can benefit from the joyous quality of orange when you buy carrots and oranges. Natural foods will be best for your body. Look at the color of the food you eat, and be aware of the special qualities it brings you. Calm comes from blueberries, energy comes from red apples, and respect can be felt in purple eggplants. You can also colorize food by placing it inside colored containers for a while. This is one time when it's a good idea to play with your food, and have fun with it!

You can "colorize" water that you drink by placing it in a

colored glass for a period of time. This process gives the water the essence of the color of the glass, and as you drink it, you will also be seeing the color of the glass. Do you feel a bit skeptical that simply exposing some water to a certain color will make any difference at all? You might be reassured to recall that Masaru Emoto has shown us how our thoughts have huge visible effects on water when printed labels are placed on water containers,[18] and Bernard Grad's experiments with plants and animals have clearly indicated that plants grow more slowly when watered by depressed people than cheerful people.[19] How we feel matters a *great* deal, so you can rest assured that by intending to receive beneficial effects from your colorized water, you certainly will.

Exercise in Food and Water Color Therapy

1. Plan to create a meal of foods based on the color or colors you selected that you feel you can benefit more from in your life.

2. If you find it challenging to find certain colors of food, use food coloring. You can easily cook and then dye white foods such as mashed potatoes or pasta, and with some imagination and creativity, you can put together an entire meal that matches the color you need more of. Don't do this too often if you are using artificial food color dyes, but if you create your own dyes from natural food sources, you can enjoy colored foods as often as you like.

3. Serve the meal on colored dishes, if you have them. Colored paper plates can be found at most party goods stores, along with matching napkins, silverware, and cups.

4. "Colorize" water in appropriately colored glasses prior to serving your colorful meal. ⦿

Light Color Therapy

Light color therapy is perhaps the most powerful form of color therapy currently being practiced today. People respond very quickly to colored light, and the effects of the colors are often felt much more strongly than with other forms of color therapy. While professional color therapists can be hard to find, you can do some rudimentary light color therapy in your own home or office. You can change the color of your indoor lights by purchasing special colored lights, or by changing your light fixtures to colored shades and lamp covers. After making a change to your living environment, pay attention to how you are feeling and be prepared to return to white or more full-spectrum light if you feel uncomfortable in any way. When you make a change to your living environment, it is important to consider the needs of others who share the space with you.

Caution is advised for those using light color therapy, especially in shared living or working areas. Light that is less than full-spectrum has been shown to contribute to hyperactivity and learning disabilities in children who have prolonged exposure to it,[20] and to irritability in adults. Radio station personnel at WILZ in St. Petersburg, Florida, found out the hard way that colored light in shared areas can create problems, when their management replaced white fluorescent lights with pink ones. Employees threatened to resign after a couple of months working under pink lighting, with peace being restored only when the original white lights returned.[21] If you plan to utilize light color therapy, it is therefore best to use it for limited times in small areas, since it appears to be quite potent.

Much more sophisticated forms of light color therapy than colored light bulbs and lampshades do exist, and they are the preferred methods of treatment by color therapists today. Color therapists such as Theo Gimbel utilize boxes in which people can place arms or legs for color treatment, as well as large-scale light treatment structures that accommodate a person's entire body, and color treatment bathtubs. Gimbel advises that people seek expert guidance when using light color therapy, because the effects from such treatments are often felt quickly and deeply. Additionally, Gimbel points out that there is a need for complementary color in any program of light treatment. Gimbel has found that treatment with only one color does not produce healing results, so he includes the complementary color in an alternating pattern. For example, if the treatment color is orange, its complementary color of green is also included. Violet and yellow are complementary colors, as are red and turquoise. Gimbel carefully times the exposure of light for each treatment according to "golden mean" proportions, where the exposure time to the complementary color gradually decreases as the exposure time to the treatment color increases. Gimbel also uses shapes that enhance the color's effects, and makes sure that the person being treated wears white, which does not interfere with the color treatment he provides.[22]

Gemologist and Vedic astrologer and Ayurvedic practitioner Howard Beckman describes two kinds of equipment used in light color therapy in his book, *Vibrational Healing with Gems*. One is a precision electronic device connected to lamps with removable outer lenses that can accommodate colored gems. Beckman states, "This type of machine is being used today in many clinics throughout England and other places in Europe with great success, and the use of both low voltage and low heat makes it extremely safe to use with any patient. An added benefit to using gems is that they will never lose their potency regardless of how long or how many times they are used in treatments." Another system utilizes a bio-circuit method for making gem elixirs in an hour or two, and also involves crystal quartz pyramids, which are positioned over storehouses of gems for radiating gem frequencies throughout a room or to a distant location where healing is required.[23]

If you have no access to light color therapists, and no idea which colors you would try out in your environment, you can benefit from the full-spectrum light of the sun. Many health benefits have been attributed to sunshine, such as a decrease in dental cavities in the summer months and in areas that receive more sunlight. Sunlight has also been proven to be effective in treating infection, anemia, psoriasis, arthritis, rheumatism, jaundice, wounds, gout, ulcers, acne, and cancer (including a form of malignant skin cancer).[24] Since sunlight contains all the colors of light you need, you may find that simply spending half an hour each day in the light is the best way to fend off a wide variety of chronic degenerative diseases! Sunlight is also widely used to treat SAD, Seasonal Affective Disorder, a form of depression.

Exercise in Light Color Therapy

Even if you don't have access to a color therapy clinic, you can see for yourself if the use of colored light helps you feel any better. If you are planning to experiment with color treatments to find out if they can help improve an existing medical problem, be sure to first consult with your medical caregiver. Once you've chosen a color to increase in your life, see if you can find a light bulb or lampshade in that color. If you find one of these, go ahead and try it out somewhere in your home or office. If you can't purchase a colored bulb or lampshade, you can make your own papier-mâché lampshade rather simply.

1. Find or purchase a simple lampshade that you can cover with colored tissue papers and a paste solution of flour and water.
2. Choose colored tissue paper in the colors you prefer, and tear little pieces into one-or two-inch squares.
3. Mix a batch of flour and water into a smooth, runny paste, and drip the papier-mâché solution generously over the scraps of paper as you position them in place where you want them.
4. Continue adding layers of tissue paper until the lampshade is covered to your satisfaction. Fewer layers will make the light shine through more brightly, and thicker layers will block more light.

5. When the paste dries after one full day, you can apply a surface sealant that is available at most art supply stores.

6. Place your colored light bulb or shade in a room in which you wish to change the color energy.

7. Note what differences you feel in the room once the light is changed. ⊚

Gemstone Color Therapy

Color experts say that when people purchase gemstone jewelry, they usually choose colors that reflect their personality. When you use gemstones to bring more of certain colors into your life, be sure to select ones that truly make you feel good. Color consultant Cynthia Cornell cites marketing studies that indicate that people choose things based on color 60 to 70 percent of the time. "Color is about feelings, what you feel good in. Color can never be separated in purchasing a gemstone. There's an immediate emotional connection to metal and jewels . . . we celebrate marriages, engagements, births (with them). So you have a product that in my estimation is one of the most powerful color experiences in peoples' lives."[25]

For thousands of years, people around the world have believed that gemstones can convey powerful benefits to their wearers. Gems have been called "the flowers of the mineral kingdom" and are said to "bear the imprint of lighter and more colorful planes of existence such as we experience in visionary dreams and trances."[26] Since 500 B.C., opals were considered to be a preventive for blindness, emeralds were thought to protect people from having epileptic fits, and garnets were considered by many to prevent "bad blood." Many survivors of the European outbreak of bubonic plague thanked the jewels they wore (such as opals, rubies, and sapphires) for saving them from disease and death.[27] There are gemstones for every color of the rainbow, and you may have already noticed that you have an affinity for a particular kind of gemstone. The following table lists gemstones for each color of the visible spectrum, along with some of the commonly associated attributes.

Gemstone Color Therapy

Color	Gemstone	Attributes
Red	Ruby	Courage, passion, beauty, love, enthusiasm, energy
Orange	Citrine	Creativity, happiness, prosperity, confidence
Yellow	Amber	Purification, wisdom, clearing, healing
Green	Emerald	Love, abundance, well-being, cleansing
Blue	Sapphire	Hope, faith, wisdom, intuition
Indigo	Azurite	Prophecy, truth, awareness, understanding
Violet	Amethyst	Spirituality, peacefulness, insight, protection

People who love gemstones have sometimes found that they receive many beneficial effects from wearing their favorite stones, and anecdotal stories abound about how certain stones were associated with improvements in health and fortune. While lists of common attributes provide a good general guideline, you will do well to allow your own intuition to guide you to choose a gemstone to help bring a certain kind of color energy into your life and aura. Keep in mind that gemstones affect different people in very different ways, and that each stone (like you) is an individual.

Exercise in Gemstone Color Therapy

1. If you have a good assortment of gemstones, select three different kinds of stones that you enjoy wearing, and prepare to try a colored gemstone experiment.

2. Select one of these stones to wear the first day, one for the second day, and the last one for the third day. Before you wear them, guess how each of them will make you feel, and why.

3. In a journal or notebook, make note of how you felt at the end of each of the three days. Did you feel or see a change in your energy field while you wore each stone? Was your guess correct about how each stone would make you feel? ⓞ

Color Therapy Meditations

Color therapy meditations can be very useful, especially when they are regularly practiced over a long period of time. This method is best for people who are self-disciplined and will diligently continue the color meditations for as long as it takes to notice a positive effect. Color meditations focus your mind on the colors you wish to bring into your life, either by visualizing the color, staring at the actual color placed in front of you, or imagining that you are inhaling the color. While meditation requires the least number of props (although you might wish to get a fabric swatch or paint chip to refer to), its practitioners boast of some pretty amazing success stories.

In *The Ancient Art of Color Therapy,* Linda Clark describes the remarkable story of a woman named Yvonne who used color meditation to reverse aging in her body. Linda confirms that Yvonne grew younger looking as the years went by, looking more like she was twenty-five years old at the age of fifty! Yvonne had a waking vision that instructed her to visualize inhaling the color pink every day. Yvonne practiced this meditation daily for months, when she awoke and again each day when she went to bed, and eventually, after eight months, she finally began to see some of the effects of her efforts. The brown age spots on her hands had disappeared, as had her sagging chin and the deep lines on the sides of her mouth. Yvonne's method for reversing effects of aging on her body was to work on one small area of her body at a time for each meditation when she imagined breathing pink. She might smooth out one wrinkle on her cheek, for example, to see how her face looked without the wrinkle. She would then breathe a light warm "baby" pink with a touch of lavender, and hold her breath, while visualizing that area as being smooth and unwrinkled, before slowly exhaling. Each small area to be treated was thus given three repetitions of color breathing. Yvonne reported that in addition to noting amazing improvements in her physical appearance, she also noticed a personality change. She became more loving, radiant, and happy after all the pink breathing meditations. Yvonne worked as a color therapist who taught people this method for breathing colors, and received many letters from people who practiced breathing pink and found themselves losing weight and looking young again. Yvonne advised people to visualize breathing green if they wished to attract others for meaningful relationships, imagining that they are swathed in green. Yvonne claimed that the green breathing meditation helped her find her husband, "a darling man."[28]

You can try breathing pink for youthful health, or green for attracting friends or romance, or one of the colors you identified as being something you specifically need. Whatever you choose to meditate on, keep in mind that color therapy meditations are a discipline, and results might take months to appear. Yvonne also believed that prior experience with yoga breathing techniques helps people who are learning to do color meditations, because people who have had such training are already somewhat experienced with the discipline required for this kind of meditation.

Exercise in Color Therapy Meditation

1. Select a color you wish to bring into your life.
2. Every day when you wake up in the morning or when you go to bed at the end of your day, visualize the color and imagine it slowly flowing through your breath into every cell in your body.
3. If you wish to specify certain parts of your body that will receive the

color (such as the chakra that this color is associated with), you can imagine that you are breathing this color directly into that chakra or body part.

4. Repeat these deep, intentional breaths at least three times. ◎

Chapter 10 Questions for Review and Reflection

1. What color or colors do you find you need more of in your life? Do you notice a relative lack in your wardrobe and physical environments of this color?
2. How do you plan to introduce more of that color or those colors into your life?
3. Which method of color therapy do you think would be best for you?
4. Imagine eating an entire meal of foods that are all your favorite color. Is this something you'd like to try some day?
5. Do you like the colors that are predominant in your home? Why or why not?
6. Which gem most appeals to you? Do you like this gem because it is one of your favorite colors?
7. If you could change the colors in your bedroom, which color would you like to add?
8. Have you ever noticed that you felt any healthier after you spent some time in the sunshine?
9. If you've ever spent any time in a room that was all one color, remember how that made you feel.
10. If you were going to give feng shui a try, which area of your life would you most like to improve?

Endnotes

Chapter 1 Notes

[1]Cayce, Edgar. *Auras: An Essay on the Meaning of Colors.* Virginia Beach, VA: A.R.E. Press, 1945, pp. 8.

[2]Cytowic, Richard E. "Synesthesia: Phenomenology and Neuropsychology. A Review of Current Knowledge" in *Psyche: An Interdisciplinary Journal of Research on Consciousness,* 2 (10), July 1995.

[3]Birren, Faber. *Color Psychology & Color Therapy.* Secaucus, NJ: The Citadel Press, 1960, pp. 163.

[4]Bruce, Robert. *Astral Dynamics: A New Approach to Out-of-Body Experience.* Charlottesville, VA: Hampton Roads Publishing Company, 1999, pp. 398–403.

[5]Tart, Charles T. "The Scientific Study of the Human Aura" in *Journal of the Society for Psychical Research,* 46:751, 1972.

[6]Sheldrake, Rupert. *Seven Experiments That Could Change the World.* New York: Riverhead Books, 1995, pp. 105–124.

[7]Braud, William G. "Human Interconnectedness: Research Indications," *Revision: A Journal of Consciousness and Transformation* 14, 1992, pp. 140–148.

[8]Schwarz, Jack. *Human Energy Systems,* New York: Dutton, 1980, pp. 42–66.

[9]Wolf, Fred Alan. *Mind into Matter.* Portsmouth, NH: Moment Point Press, 2001, pp. 13.

[10]Kokubo, Hideyuki, and Kasahara, Tosio. "Japanese Studies on Anomalous Phenomena in the 1990s," in *International Journal of Parapsychology,* vol. 11, no. 2, 2000, pp. 35–61.

[11]Bridgman, Percy Williams. *The Logic of Modern Physics.* New York: MacMillan, 1927, pp. 46.

[12]Pachter, Henry M. *Magic into Science: The Story of Paracelsus,* New York: Henry Schuman, 1951, pp. 212–215.

[13]Charleton, Walter. *Of the Magnetic Cure of Wounds*, London, 1650, pp. 13.

[14]Von Reichenbach, Karl. *The Odic Force: Letters on Od & Magnetism.* London: Hutchison & Co., 1926, pp. 19–62.

[15]Kilner, Walter J. *The Human Aura.* New Hyde Park, New York: University Books, 1965.

[16]Blavatsky. "What Are the Theosophists," in *Theosophist*, October 1879.

[17]Day, Langston, and de la Warr, George. *Matter in the Making.* London: Vincent Stuart Ltd, 1966, pp. 1–161.

[18]White, John, and Krippner, Stanley. *Future Science.* Garden City, NY: Anchor Press, 1977, pp. 391.

[19]Mann, W. Edward. *Orgone, Reich & Eros: Wilhelm Reich's Theory of Life Energy.* New York: Simon & Schuster, 1973, pp. 21–25.

[20]Oschman, James L. *Energy Medicine: The Scientific Basis,* Edinburgh, UK: Churchill Livingstone, 2001, pp. 16–22.

[21]Klingbeil, John S., and Klingbeil, Bruce O. *The Spindrift Papers: Exploring Prayer & Healing Through the Experimental Test,* vol. 1 (1975–1993). Lansdale, PA: Spindrift Inc., 1993, pp. 1:1–1:51.

[22]Mitchell, Edgar, and Williams, Dwight. *The Way of the Explorer.* New York: GP Putnam's Sons, 1996, pp. 72.

[23]Hunt, Valerie J., et al. "A Study of Structural Integration from Neuromuscular, Energy Field and Emotional Approaches," in *Project Report*, Boulder, CO: Rolf Institute, 1977, pp. 139

[24]Dobrin, Richard; Conaway, Barbara (Brennan); and Pierrakos, John. "Instrumental Measurements of the Human Energy Field," New York Institute for the New Age, 1978. Presented at "Electro '78, IEEE Annual Conference," Boston: May 23–25, 1978.

[25]Oschman, James L. *Energy Medicine: The Scientific Basis,* Edinburgh, UK, Churchill Livingstone, 2001, pp. 76–79.

Chapter 2 Notes

[1] Miller, Carolyn. *Creating Miracles: Understanding the Experience of Divine Intervention.* Tiberon, CA: HJ Kramer, 1995, pp. 276.

[2] Stout, C; Morrow, J.; Brandt, E. N. Jr.; et al. "Unusually Low Incidence of Death from Myocardial Infarction: Study of an Italian American Community in Pennsylvania" in *JAMA.* 1964; 188: 845–849.

[3] Bruhn, J. G.; Philips, B. U. Jr.; Wolf, S. "Lessons from Roseto 20 Years Later: A Community Study of Heart Diseases" in *Southern Medical Journal.* 1982; 75 (5): 575–580.

[4] O'Regan, Brendan; Hirshbert, Caryle; Lewis, Nola; McNeill, Barbara; Franklin, Winston; Poole, William; *The Heart of Healing,* Atlanta, Georgia: Turner Publishing, Inc., 1993, pp. 109–111.

[5] Brennan, Barbara Ann. *Hands of Light: A Guide to Healing Through the Human Energy Field.* New York: Bantam Books, 1987.

[6] Myss, Caroline. *Why People Don't Heal and How They Can.* New York: Three Rivers Press, 1997, pp. 1–263.

[7] Eden, Donna. *Energy Medicine.* New York: Jeremy P. Tarcher/ Putnam, 1999.

[8] Ritberger, Carol. *Your Personality and Your Health: Connecting Personality with the Human Energy System, Chakras and Wellness.* Carlsbad, CA: Hay House, 1998, pp. 171–197.

[9] Sui, Choa Kok. *Advanced Pranic Healing: Practical Handbook for Healing with Color Energies,* Institute for Inner Studies, Chino, California, 2000.

[10] Alijandra. *Healing with the Rainbow Rays: The Art of Color Energy Therapy.* San Jose, CA: Emerald Star Publishing, 1995.

[11] Stein, Diane. *Essential Reiki: A Complete Guide to an Ancient Healing Art.* Freedom, CA: The Crossing Press, Inc. 1995, pp. 2–5.

[12] Myss, Caroline. *Anatomy of the Spirit: The Seven Stages of Power & Healing.* New York: Three Rivers Press, 1996, pp. 41.

[13] Ramanathan, Lavanya. "Workers Grow Less Happy" in *Newsday,* August 22, 2002.

[14]"Survey Says Spirituality Is Alive and Well in Workplace," in *The Acorn* (NewsUSA), Aguara Hills, California, July 25, 2002.

[15]Leadbeater, C. W. *The Chakras.* Wheaton, IL: The Theosophical Publishing House, 1987, pp. 14–16.

[16]Besant, Annie, and Leadbeater, C. W. *Thought-Forms.* Adyar, India: The Theosophical Publishing House, 1925.

[17]Talbot, Michael. *The Holographic Universe.* New York: HarperCollins Publishers, 1991, pp. 183.

[18]Brunke, Dawn Baumann. *Animal Voices.* Rochester, VT: Bear & Co., 2002, pp. 35.

[19]Swami Prabhavananda and Christopher Isherwood, eds., in *How to Know God: The Yoga Aphorisms of Patanjali,* Hollywood, CA: Vedanta Press, 1983, pp. 173–201.

[20]Jahn, R. C. "The Persistent Paradox of Psychic Phenomena: An Enlightening Perspective," in *Proceedings of the IEEE*, vol. 70, no. 2, pp. 136–170.

[21]Katra, Jane, and Targ, Russell. *Miracles of Mind: Exploring Nonlocal Consciousness and Spiritual Healing.* Novato, CA: New World Library, 1998, pp. 36–82.

[22]Rauscher, Elizabeth A., and Targ, Russell. "The Speed of Thought: Investigation of a Complex Space-Time Metric to Describe Psychic Phenomena" in *The Journal of Scientific Exploration*, 2001, vol. 15, no. 3, pp. 331–354.

[23]Swedenborg, Emanuel (translation by JJG Wilkinson). *The Animal Kingdom,* W Londond: Newberry, 1843, part 1:19.

[24]Long, Max Freedom. *The Secret Science Behind Miracles: Unveiling the Huna Tradition of the Ancient Polynesians.* Marina del Rey, CA: DeVorss & Co., 1948, pp. 127.

[25]Sicher, Fred; Targ, Elisabeth; Moore, Dan; and Smith, Helene S. "A Randomized, Double-Blind Study of the Effect of Distant Healing in a Population with Advanced AIDS" in *Western Journal of Medicine*, vol. 169, no. 6, 1998, pp. 356–363.

[26]Harris, William S.; Gowda, Manohar; Kolb, Jerry; et al. "A Randomized, Controlled Trial of the Effects of Remote, Intercessory Prayer on Outcomes in Patients Admitted to the Coronary Care Unit" in *Archives of Internal Medicine*, vol. 159, no. 19, October 25, 1999, pp. 2273–2278.

[27]Dossey, Larry. *Reinventing Medicine*. San Francisco: Harper, 1999, pp. 9.

[28]Sheldrake, Rupert. *Dogs That Know When Their Owners Are Coming Home*. New York: Three Rivers Press, 1999, pp. 178–185.

[29]Long, Max Freedom. *The Secret Science Behind Miracles: Unveiling the Huna Tradition of the Ancient Polynesians*. Marina del Rey, CA: DeVorss & Co., 1948, pp. 127.

Chapter 3 Notes

[1]Smelser, Neil J. *The Social Importance of Self-Esteem*. Berkeley, CA: U.C. Press, 1989.

[2]Myss, Caroline. *Anatomy of the Spirit: The Seven Stages of Power and Healing*. New York: Three Rivers Press, 1996, pp. 50–57.

[3]Armstrong, Lance. *It's Not About the Bike: My Journey Back to Life*. New York: Putnam, 2000, pp. 38.

[4]Ruibal, Sal. "Cancer Survivor Armstrong Accepts New Role" in *USA Today*, May 22, 2002.

[5]Reeve, Christopher. *Nothing Is Impossible*, New York, Random House, 2002, pp. 104.

[6]Espinoza, Galina and Weinstein, Fannie. "Whisper of Hope" in *People Magazine*, vol. 58, September 23, 2002, pp. 78–82.

[7]Hawking, Stephen. *Black Holes and Baby Universes and Other Essays*. New York: Bantam Books, 1993, pp. 23.

[8]Besant, Annie, and Leadbeater, C. W. *Thought-Forms*. Adyar, India: The Theosophical Publishing House, 1925, pp. 16–17.

[9]Cayce, Edgar. *Auras: An Essay on the Meaning of Colors*. Virginia Beach, VA: A.R.E. Press, 1945, pp. 14.

[10]Smith, Mark T. *Auras: See Them in Only 60 Seconds*. St. Paul, MN: Llewellyn Publications, 1997, pp. 46–49.

[11]Jacobs, Henry. *The Seven Thunders of the Soul*. Ashland, MS: Trinity Research Center, 1994, pp. 8–15.

[12]Clark, Linda. *The Ancient Art of Color Therapy: Updated, including Gem Therapy, Auras and Amulets*. Old Greenwich, CT: Devon-Adair Company, 1975, pp. 118.

[13]Bowers, Barbara. *What Color Is Your Aura? Personality Spectrums for Understanding and Growth*. New York: Pocket Books, Simon & Schuster, 1989, pp. 18–24.

Chapter 4 Notes

[1]Miller, Hamish and Broadhurst, Paul. *The Sun and the Serpent*. Launceston, Cornwall: Pendragon Press, 1989, pp. 112–118.

[2]Cayce, Edgar. *Auras: An Essay on the Meaning of Colors*. Virginia Beach, VA: A.R.E. Press, 1945, pp. 5.

[3]Brennan, Barbara Ann. *Hands of Light: A Guide to Healing Through the Human Energy Field*. New York: Bantam Books, 1987, pp. 5.

[4]Karagulla, Shafica. *Breakthrough to Creativity*. Marina del Rey, CA: DeVorss & Company, 1967, pp. 78–79.

[5]Tompkins, Peter. *Secret Life of Plants*. New York: Harper & Row, 1973, pp. 3–6.

[6]Ibid, pp. 7.

[7]Mitchell, Edgar. *Psychic Exploration*. New York: G. P. Putnam's Sons, 1974, pp. 301.

[8]Radin, Dean. *The Conscious Universe: The Scientific Truth of Psychic Phenomenon*. San Francisco: HarperCollins, 1997, pp. 338–339.

[9]Blau, Evelyne. *Krishnamurti: 100 Years*. New York: Stewart, Tabori & Chang, 1995, pp. 243–244.

[10]Lindgren, C. E. *Capturing the Aura: Integrating Science, Technology, and Metaphysics*. Nevada City, CA: Blue Dolphin Publishing, 2000, pp. 316.

Chapter 5 Notes

[1]Leadbeater, C. W. *The Chakras*. Wheaton, IL: The Theosophical Publishing House, 1987, pp. 11–16.

[2]Hunt, Valerie V. *Infinite Mind: Science of the Human Vibrations of Consciousness*. Malibu, CA: Malibu Publishing, 1996, pp. 111.

[3]Koch, Howard. *Casablanca*. Woodstock, NY: Overlook Press, 1973, pp. 140.

[4]Moody, Raymond A., and Perry, Paul. *The Light Beyond*. New York: Bantam Doubleday Dell, 1988, pp. 50.

[5]*2002 "Sleep in America" Poll*, National Sleep Foundation, WB&A, Washington, DC, April 2, 2002.

[6]Maas, James. "Perchance to Sleep," *Cornell Magazine*, vol. 101, no. 4, January/February 1999.

[7]Schneider, Meir. *The Handbook of Self-Healing*. New York: Penguin Books, 1994, pp. 277.

[8]Tompkins, Peter, and Bird, Christopher. *The Secret Life of Plants*. New York: Harper & Row, 1973, pp. 3–19.

[9]Ibid, pp. 81–103.

[10]Grossman, Warren. *To Be Healed by the Earth*. New York: Seven Stories Press, 1998, pp. 12.

[11]Eden, Donna, and Feinsten, David. *Energy Medicine*. New York: Jeremy P Tarcher/Putnam, 1998, pp. 179–186.

[12]Feldenkrais, Moshe. *Awareness Through Movement: Easy-to-Do Health Exercises to Improve Your Posture, Vision, Imagination, and Personal Awareness*. New York: Harper & Row, 1977, pp. 38–39.

Chapter 6 Notes

[1]Hendrix, Harville. *Getting the Love You Want*. New York: Harper & Row, 1988, pp. 5–14.

[2]Larson, Cynthia Sue. "Reality Shifts" in *Magical Blend*, January 2000, #68, pp. 16–19.

[3]Gribbin, John. *Q Is for Quantum: An Encyclopedia of Particle Physics*. New York: Simon & Schuster Inc., 1998, pp. 109–113.

[4]Dossey, Larry. *Be Careful What You Pray For . . . You Just Might Get It.* San Francisco: Harper San Francisco, HarperCollins, 1997, pp. 18.

[5]Lipton, Bruce H. "Nature, Nurture and Human Development" in *Journal of Prenatal and Perinatal Psychology and Health*, vol. 16, 2001, pp. 167–180.

[6]Lipton, Bruce H. "Insight Into Cellular 'Consciousness'" in *Bridges, ISSEEM*, vol. 12 (1), 2001, pp. 5–8.

[7]Truog, Robert. "Is It Time to Abandon Brain Death?" in *Hastings Center Report*, vol. 27 (1), January–February 1997, pp. 29–31.

[8]Younger, Stuart, and O'Toole, Elizabeth. "Withdrawing Treatment in the Persistent Vegetative State" (letter) in the *New England Journal of Medicine*, November 17, 1994, pp. 1382.

[9]Shewman, Alan. "Recovery From 'Brain Death': A Neurologist's Apologia" in *Linacre Quarterly*, February 1997, pp. 68.

[10]Seeley, Monica. "Is Brain Dead Really Dead?" in *San Diego News Notes*, October 1997 pp. 3–4.

[11]Greene, Brian. *The Elegant Universe: Superstrings, Hidden Dimensions and the Quest for the Ultimate Theory.* New York: WW Norton & Company, 1999, pp. 188.

[12]Talbot, Michael. *The Holographic Universe.* New York: HarperCollins Publishers, 1991, pp. 211–212.

[13]Wolf, Fred Alan. *Mind Into Matter.* Portsmouth, NH: Moment Point Press, 2001, pp. 9.

[14]Cairns, John; Overbaugh, Julie; and Miller, Stephan. "The Origin of Mutants" in *Nature*, vol. 335 (6186), September 8, 1988, pp. 142–145.

[15]Wolf, Fred Alan. *Mind into Matter.* Portsmouth, NH: Moment Point Press, 2001, pp. 95.

[16]Dossey, Larry. *Reinventing Medicine.* San Francisco, CA: Harper San Francisco, HarperCollins, 1999, pp. 42.

[17]Morse, Melvin, and Perry, Paul. *Closer to the Light: Learning from the Near-Death Experiences of Children.* New York: Villard Books, Random House, 1990, pp. 24–26.

[18] Atwater, P. M. H. *Children of the New Millenium: Chldren's Near-Death Experiences & the Evolution of Humankind.* New York: Three Rivers Press, Random House, 1999, pp. 89.

[19] Radin, Dean. *The Conscious Universe: The Scientific Truth of Psychic Phenomenon,* San Francisco: Harper San Francisco, HarperCollins, 1997, pp. 121–122.

[20] Klingbeil, John S., and Klingbeil, Bruce O. *The Spindrift Papers: Exploring Prayer and Healing Through the Experimental Test, Volume One (1975–1993).* Lansdale, PA: Spindrift Inc., 1993, pp. 1:5–1:9.

[21] Perkins, John. *The World Is As You Dream It.* Rochester, Vermont: Destiny Books, Inner Traditions International, 1994, pp. 99.

[22] Mishlove, Jeffrey. *The Roots of Consciousness: The Classic Encyclopedia of Consciousness Studies.* Tulsa, OK: Council Oak Books, 1975, pp. 147.

[23] Larson, Cynthia Sue. "Top Ten Ways to Shift Reality" in *Well Being Journal,* Winter 2001, pp. 16–17.

[24] Larson, Cynthia Sue. "Comes True, Being Hoped For: The Hopi Understanding of How Things Change" in *Parabola: Myth, Tradition, and the Search for Meaning,* 25(1), Spring 2000, pp. 84–87.

[25] Bearison, D. J. and Zimiles, H. "Approaches to Developmental Research on Emotion-Cognition Relationships" in *Thought and Emotion* (C. Izardd, ed.). Hillsdale, NJ: Erlbaum, 1986, pp. 21–37.

[26] Luks, Allan. *The Healing Power of Doing Good: The Health and Spiritual Benefits of Helping Others.* New York: Fawcett Books, 1991, pp. 51–59.

[27] The Dalai Lama and Cutler, Howard C. *The Art of Happiness: A Handbook for Living,* New York: Riverhead Books, Penguin Putnam, 1998, pp. 308–309.

Chapter 7 Notes

[1] Miller, Carolyn. *Creating Miracles: Understanding the Experience of Divine Intervention.* Tiberon, CA: HJ Kramer, 1995, pp. 166–167.

[2]Barrett, Greg, and Redekopp, Christina. "A Direct Line with the Dead?" in *The Herald-Dispatch*, Huntington, West Virginia, June 24, 2001, pp. 1D.

[3]Day, Laura. *Practical Intuition: How to Harness the Power of Your Instinct and Make It Work for You.* New York: Broadway Books, 1996, pp. 83.

[4]Stone, Robert B. *The Secret Life of Your Cells.* Atglen, PA: Whitford Press, Schiffer Publishing, 1989, pp. 22–26.

[5]Ibid, pp. 68–76.

[6]Pickover, Clifford A. *Dreaming the Future: The Fantastic Story of Prediction.* Amherst, NY: Prometheus Books, 2001, pp. 150–192.

[7]Bruce, Robert. *Practical Psychic Self-Defense: Understanding and Surviving Unseen Influences.* Charlottesville, VA: Hampton Roads Publishing Company, 2002, pp. 83.

[8]Bruhn, J. G.; Philips, B. U., Jr.; and Wolf, S. "Lessons from Roseto 20 Years Later: A Community Study of Heart Diseases" in *Southern Medical Journal*, 1982; Vol. 75 (5), pp. 575–580.

[9]Bruce, Robert. *Practical Psychic Self-Defense: Understanding and Surviving Unseen Influences.* Charlottesville, VA: Hampton Roads Publishing Company, 2002, pp. 229–231.

[10]Reed, Anderson. Shouting at the Wolf: A Guide to Identifying and Warding off Evil in Everyday Life. New York: Citadel Press, 1990, pp. 292–293.

Chapter 8 Notes

[1]Krippner, Stanley. *Human Possibilities: Mind Exploration in the USSR and Eastern Europe.* Garden City, New York, Anchor Press/Doubleday, 1980, pp. 173–174.

[2]Pratt, S., and Schlemmer, J. "Electrography" in *Journal of the Biological Photographic Association*, vol. 7, 1939, pp. 145–148.

[3]Kilner, Walter J. *The Human Aura.* Secaucus, NJ: Citadel Press, 1965, pp. 262.

[4]Tompkins, Peter. *The Secret Life of Plants*. New York: Harper & Row, 1973, pp. 200–202.

[5]Ostrander, Sheila, and Schroeder, Lynn. *Psychic Discoveries Behind the Iron Curtain*. New York: Bantam Books, 1970, pp. 203–207.

[6]Ibid, pp. 217.

[7]Pehek, John O.; Kyler, Harry J.; and Faust, David L. "Image Modulation in Corona Discharge Photography" in *Science*, October 15, 1976, 194 (4262), pp. 263–270.

[8]Lee, Richard H. *Bioelectric Vitality: Exploring the Science of Human Energy*. San Clemente, CA: China Healthways Institute, 1997, pp. 12–14.

[9]Moss, Thelma. *The Body Electric: A Personal Journey Into the Mysteries of Parapsychology and Kirlian Photography*. Los Angeles, California, J. P. Tarcher, 1979, pp. 143–149.

[10]Moss, Thelma, and Johnson, Kendall. "Radiation Field Photography" in *Psychic*, vol. 3, 1972, pp. 50–54.

[11]Lindgren, C. E. *Capturing the Aura: Integrating Science, Technology, and Metaphysics*. Nevada City, CA: Blue Dolphin Publishing, 2000, pp. 27.

[12]Gadsby, J. Gordon. "Kirlian Photography: Critical Analysis" in *Complementary Medical Research,* vol. 5 (1), February 1991, pp. 523–528.

[13]Gadsby, J. Gordon. "Kirlian Photography Diagnosis—A Recent Study" in *Complementary Therapies in Medicine,* vol. 1 (4), 1993, pp. 179–184.

[14]Lindgren, C. E. *Capturing the Aura: Integrating Science, Technology, and Metaphysics*. Nevada City, CA: Blue Dolphin Publishing, 2000, pp. 23–26.

[15]Ostrander, Sheila, and Schroeder, Lynn. "The Schlieren System—An Aura Detector?" in *The Human Aura* (Nicholas M. Regush, ed.). New York: Berkeley Publishing Corp., 1974, pp. 191.

[16]Abate, Tom. "Penn State Chemist Seeks to Photograph the

Body's Elusive Aura: Inventor Says Process Can Detect Illness" in *San Francisco Chronicle*, August 7, 2000, pp. B1 and B3.

[17]Emoto, Masaru. *The Message from Water*. HADO Kyoikusha, Tokyo, Japan, 1999, pp. 135–138.

[18]Ibid, pp. 73–79.

[19]Ibid, pp. 100.

[20]Ibid, pp. 103–104.

[21]Krippner, Stanley, and Rubin, Daniel. *The Kirlian Aura: Photographing the Galaxies of Life*. Garden City, NY: Anchor Books, Anchor Press/Doubleday, 1974, pp. 30–31.

[22]Boswell, Harriet A. *Master Guide to Psychism*. New York: Lancer Books, 1969, pp. 214.

[23]Mishlove, Jeffrey. *The Roots of Consciousness: The Classic Encyclopedia of Consciousness Studies*. Tulsa, OK: Council Oak Books, 1975, pp. 203–205.

[24]Tiller, William A. *Science and Human Transformation: Subtle Energies, Intentionality and Consciousness*. Walnut Creek, CA: Pavior Publishing, 1997, pp. 18–22.

[25]Private communication with Elke Macartney, October 9, 2002.

Chapter 9 Notes

[1]Chopra, Deepak. *Ageless Body, Timeless Mind: The Quantum Alternative to Growing Old*. New York: Harmony Books, 1993, pp. 162–167

[2]Bleick, C. R., and Abrams, A. I. "The Transcendental Meditation Program and Criminal Recidivism in California" in *Journal of Criminal Justice*, Vol. 15, 1987, pp. 211–230.

Chapter 10 Notes

[1]Liberman, Jacob. *Light: Medicine of the Future*. Santa Fe, NM: Bear & Company, 1991, pp. 43–44.

[2]Paul, Pamela. "Color by Numbers" in *American Demographics*, vol. 24 (2), February 2002, pp. 30–35.

[3]Birren, Faber. *Color and Human Response*. New York: Van Nostrand Reinhold Company, 1978, pp. 107.

[4]Gimbel, Theo. *Healing with Color and Light: Improve Your Mental, Physical and Spiritual Health*. New York: Fireside Book, Simon & Schuster, 1994, pp. 24–25.

[5]Graham, Helen. *Discover Color Therapy*. Berkeley, CA: Ulysses Press, 1998, pp. 3–16.

[6]Clark, Linda. *The Ancient Art of Color Therapy: Updated, Including Gem Therapy, Auras & Amulets*. Old Greenwich, CT: Devon-Adair Company, 1975, pp. 45.

[7]Lucey, J. R. "Neonatal Jaundice and Phototherapy" in *Pediatric Clinics of North America,* vol. 19 (4), 1972, pp. 1–7.

[8]McDonald, S. F. "Effect of Visible Light Waves on Arthritis Pain: A Controlled Study" in *International Journal of Biosocial Research*, vol. 3 (2), 1982, pp. 49–54.

[9]Anderson, J. *Brain/Mind Bulletin*, vol. 15 (4), January 1990, pp. 1.

[10]Liberman, Jacob. *Light: Medicine of the Future*. Santa Fe, NM: Bear & Company, 1991, pp. 104–105.

[11]Gimbel, Theo. *Healing with Color and Light: Improve Your Mental, Physical and Spiritual Health*. New York: Fireside Book, Simon & Schuster, 1994, pp. 21.

[12]Ibid, pp. 97.

[13]Liberman, Jacob. *Light: Medicine of the Future*. Santa Fe, NM: Bear & Company, 1991, pp. 188–189.

[14]Morton, Jill. "Quirks of the Color Quest" in *Visual Arts Trends*, October 2000.

[15]Walker, Morton. *The Power of Color*. New York: Avery Publishing Group, 1991, pp. 50–52.

[16]Morgan, David Lee, Jr. "Zips Hoping to be in the Pink Against Hawkeyes" in *The Beacon Journal*, Akron, OH, August 27, 2002.

[17]Rossbach, Sarah. *Interior Design with Feng Shui*. New York: Arkana, Penguin Books, 1987, pp. 139.

[18]Emoto, Masaru. *The Message from Water.* HADO Kyoikusha, Tokyo, Japan, 1999, pp. 91–104.

[19]Grad, Bernard R. "Some Biological Effects of Laying-On of Hands: A Review of Experiments with Animals and Plants" in *Journal of the American Society for Psychical Research*, 59a, 1965, pp. 95–127.

[20]Ott, John N. *Health and Light,* Old Greenwich, CT: Devin-Adair Co., 1976, pp. 202–204.

[21]Ibid, pp. 119–120.

[22]Gimbel, Theo. *Healing with Color and Light: Improve Your Mental, Physical & Spiritual Health.* New York: Fireside Book, Simon & Schuster, 1994, pp. 108–109.

[23]Beckman, Howard. *Vibrational Healing with Gems.* New Delhi, India: Balaji Publisher, Gyan Publishing House, 2000, pp. 51–52.

[24]Kime, Zane R. *Sunlight.* Penryn, CA: World Health Publications, 1980, pp. 30.

[25]Wade, Suzanne. "Shades of Meaning: How Does a Gem's Color Emotionally Impact the Buyer?" in *Colored Stone*, vol. 14 (6). Devon, PA, November/December 2001, pp. 38–41.

[26]Beckman, Howard. *Vibrational Healing with Gems.* New Delhi, India: Balaji Publisher, Gyan Publishing House, 2000, pp. 10.

[27]Clark, Linda. *The Ancient Art of Color Therapy: Updated, Including Gem Therapy, Auras & Amulets.* Old Greenwich, CT: Devon-Adair Company, 1975, pp. 100.

[28]Ibid, pp. 128–140.

Index

A

American Medical Association (AMA), 23, 210
angels, 18, 71, 84–85, 115–116, 163–164, 179, 189, 195
animal communication, 41
attraction, theory of, 21, 129
aura, international words for, 16
aura functions
  accurately assess your environment, 31–33
  attract what you most desire, 127, 134–148
  communicate effectively, 40–44
  define your personal space, 9–13, 86
  find lost things, 49–51
  maintain a healthy physical body, 33–37
  make good choices, 44–46
  non-locally affect others, 46–48
  protect yourself, 30, 149–168
  sense your life purpose, 38–40, 100
aura photography
  dark areas in, 177
  high voltage electrical, 91, 170–173
  water crystals, 178–179
aura portraits, 183–186
auras
  children have smaller, 171
  collapse for invisibility, 43
  layers in, 13–15
  many children see, 4–5
  plants and, 24, 87, 89–92, 119, 120–121, 172, 219
  viewing, 5, 20–22, 42, 61–62, 84–103, 184
auraspecs, 22

auric cords
  animals navigate with, 49–50
  astral travel and, 9
  cording in along, 160–163, 168
  cutting, 9, 162
  grounding with, 50, 106–109, 138, 160–161, 204
  health benefits from, 162
  information carried on, 9
  practicing compassion enhances, 146–148
  sensing future danger through, 150
  healing others with, 46–48, 132–134
auric health
  aura guardians and, 163–165
  aura textures and, 200–201
  be playful for, 107
  best auric color and, 60
  breathing and, 17, 123–124, 190, 225–227
  dark patches correspond with disease, 177
  healthy aura self-assessment, 53–56
  Kirlian photography and, 172, 175
  meditation and, 60, 187–189
  natural spaces and, 120–122
  nutritious diet and, 118–120
  physical exercise and, 122–124
  sleep and, 106–107, 116–118, 188
auric horse stance, 166–167
auric love blast, 36–37
auric membrane, 11–12, 14, 115, 128, 130–132, 150, 200, 204

B

Backster, Cleve, 119, 153
bioenergetic healing, 34
brain death, 131–132
Brennan, Barbara Ann, 27, 34, 87

C

camay, 135
cancer, identifying and treating, 25,
    35–37, 57–59, 170–171, 175
Cayce, Edgar, 2, 24–25, 44, 60, 85–86
cell membranes, 131
Celtic weave, 122
ch'i. See also Qi.
chakra
    aligning a, 140–141, 193–194
    chakra check, 116, 140–141, 210
    crown, 8, 27, 37, 39–40, 100,
        109–112, 131, 140, 184, 191,
        194
    dowsing a, 111–112
    heart, 8, 13, 26–27, 33, 37, 39,
        50, 99, 110, 192, 146–148,
        182, 192, 195, 198
    musical notes for each, 98–100
    root, 8, 39, 46, 98, 106, 109–112,
        131, 138, 140, 193–194
    sacral, 8
    size of healthy, 111
    solar plexus, 8, 99, 192
    third eye, 8, 26, 90, 92–93,
        99–101, 192
    throat, 8, 26, 99, 110, 112, 182,
        192
choose the path that shines, 45–46
color personality characteristics,
    63–78
color practitioner, 210
color therapy
    clothing, 209, 213–214
    Egyptian healers and, 209
    eyewear, 60, 210, 214–215
    food and water, 210, 212, 218–219
    gemstone 223–225
    Greek and Roman, 209
    home decor, 215–216
    in school design, 209
    light, 219–223
    medical studies demonstrate
        value of, 209–210
    personal color assessment in,
        210–212
consciousness
    auric cords connect points of,
        133
    cellular, 133, 153
    expanded state of, 87
    mystical view of, 46–48, 92
    of brain-dead people, 131–132
    of food, 118–120
    of metals, 119
    perceiving, 204–205
    research, 25–26, 153
creating miracles, 20, 31, 58
curses, 130, 165–166

D

Dan Tien, 98, 193
death and the aura, 6–8, 131
depression, effects and treatment
    of, 22, 35, 63, 85, 130–131, 222
divination methods, 154
Dossey, Dr. Larry, 47, 130
dowsing, 82–84, 110–112
dreams, 38, 58, 117, 128, 135–137,
    141, 145–146, 197, 223

E

electrography, 170
Emoto, Masaru, 178–179, 219
energy blockages, 35–37, 122, 143
energy cords. *See* auric cords
energy intuitives, 34–37, 176
energy leaks, 53, 56
etheric double, 9, 14, 53, 173
expanded auric field, 8, 42, 83–84,
    91, 113–114, 124, 190
extra sensory perception (ESP), 150

F

Feldenkrais, 122–124
feng shui, 216–218, 227
fluorescent lights, 220

G, H

Gimbel, Theo, 220–221
gratitude prayer for welcoming
    food, 119–120
grounding a group, 109
hand viewing, 95–96
hara chakra, 98, 192–193
headache effects and treatment,
    115, 118, 210
healing power of the earth,
    120–122
healthy auras
    attributes of, 53–54, 85
    compared to unhealthy auras,
        171–172
helper's high, 147
higher sense perception (HSP), 88
    answering questions with,
        153–156
    avoiding danger with, 149–156
    children and, 4–5, 86–87, 134
    developing, 151
    doctors diagnose with, 25, 88,
        170–171, 175
human energy field
    children see the, 4–5
    coat hangers dowse the, 81–84
    drug abuse damages the,
        124–126
    electrical equipment is sensitive
        to the, 108
    everything links to the, 3
    history of the, 15–27
Hunt, Dr. Valerie, 26–27

I

inner skeptic, 142–143, 148
Institute of Noetic Sciences (IONS),
    26, 91
internal vision, 88
intuition, developing, 38–40, 150–156

K, L

Karagulla, Shafica, 88
kilnascrenes, 22
Kilner, Dr. Walter, 22, 170–171
Kirlian photography, 91, 170–176,
    178, 186
Krishnamurti, 94–95
kundalini, 26, 87, 98
ley lines, 81

M

mantra, 112, 187
martial arts, 9, 17, 124, 166
maya, 158, 166
medical intuitives, 34–37
medications, 125
meditations
    aura texture healing, 200–201
    benefits of, 187–189, 206
    best possible life, 190–193
    clearing tornado, 32–33
    color therapy, 225–227
    connection to cosmic source,
        198–199
    fast aura, 193–194
    fetal memories, 203–204
    good health and healing, 194–195
    integrated across all possible
        universes, 195–196
    nothingness, 205–206
    perceiving auric space, 189–190
    perceiving consciousness,
        204–205
    prosperity, 196–197
    summoning your true love,
        197–198
    tabula rasa, 201–202
    you-niversal energy body, 199–200
Miller, Carolyn, 31, 149
Mitchell, Edgar, 26
morphic fields, 49
Moss, Thelma, 173–174
muddy colors, 55–56, 63, 79, 212
Myss, Caroline, 34–35

N, O

near-death experiences (NDE), 87, 115
non-local healing, 46–48
out-of-body experience (OBE), 9, 181

P, Q

parallel realities, 133
petroglyphs, 104–105
prayer, 25, 60, 88, 119–120, 140, 152, 159, 188
psychic photographs, 179–183
psychic protection, 149–168
psychological effects of color, 208
Qi, 16–17, 45, 124, 173, 183, 216–218
QiGong, 15, 17, 88, 124

R

Radin, Dean, 91
Reiki, 34
reverse aging, 225–226
rogue thought-forms, 139, 141–144, 148, 163–164
Roseto effect, 33–34, 162

S

Schlieren photography, 177–178
scientism, 18
sealing the aura, 115–116
shadowgraphs, 169
Sheldrake, Rupert, 10, 49
skotographs, 180
spirit photography, 179–183
staring exercise, 10–12
superconducting quantum interference device (SQUID), 27
Swedenborg, Emanuel, 45
synesthesia, 5

T

Tai Chi, 17
Tart, Charles, 10
Tesla, Nikola, 170
Theosophical Society, 23, 95
thought-forms
    communicating via, 40–44
    expecting what you most desire with, 141–144
    grounding and releasing, 32–33, 44, 139
    plants respond to, 91–92, 119, 219
    seeing, 41, 61
Tiller, William, 181
tunâtyava, 142

W, Y

warning signs of weakened aura, 156–160
water responds to thoughts and feelings, 178–179
yin and yang, 16
yoga, 9, 17, 124, 226

About the Author

Bioenergy field researcher Cynthia Sue Larson helps people tap into the extraordinary powers that lie within them to make positive changes in their lives. Larson hosts a popular Web site, *www.realityshifters.com*, which provides visitors with information about auras and a forum to discuss their experiences. She participates in research at the Institute of Noetic Sciences, provides camera design advice for Aura Imaging Systems, teaches aura workshops, and speaks at numerous conferences. Her articles have appeared in magazines such as *Magical Blend*, *Parabola*, and *Well Being Journal*. Cynthia received a B.A. degree in physics from U.C. Berkeley and an M.B.A. degree from San Francisco State University. She lives in Berkeley, California, with her two daughters